Advance Praise

"As a member of the House of Representatives, Al Quie was a student of education and a consummate deal-maker with the Democratic majority such that he had as much influence in Congress as any elected official."

Robert C. Andringa
Former Senior Staff Member

"Of the many members of the House of Representatives and Senate with whom I served in my own 22 years in Congress, Al was one of the finest. Although he's a Republican and I'm a Democrat and we had our differences from time to time, I'm proud we were able to work together to produce significant legislation for the good of the country. Al is the very model of what a congressman should be."

John Brademas
President Emeritus
New York University

"Al Quie is a treasure, a role model for anyone who aspires to excel in his profession—in his case, politics—while being a thoroughly decent human being. The state and nation need his bipartisan graciousness now more than ever, and fortunately in his mid-'80s he's still going strong. Mitch Pearlstein has given us a memorable portrait of a great man."

John E. Brandl
Dean Emeritus
Hubert H. Humphrey Institute
of Public Affairs

"This book promises to be a multifaceted gem of a biography cum profile cum celebration of one of the most interesting and influential figures in American education policy (and much else) during the late 20th century, written by one of the subject's most perceptive and lucid observers."

Chester E. Finn Jr.
President
Thomas B. Fordham Foundation

"Al Quie is one of the most thoughtful public servants I have worked with. He focuses on people's problems without partisan bias and works to solve those problems. His approach to public affairs has been too-long absent from our state."

Don Fraser
Former Member of Congress

"For me, describing Al Quie is sort of a religious experience, as he's just that precious a person. He has a special way of engaging and bringing out the best in people, seeking to uplift them regardless of their walk in life. He is a wonderful example of servant leadership and I'm very pleased many more people will now have a chance to know all about him."

Reatha Clark King
Former President
Metropolitan State University

"Whether among farmers or foreign students, prisoners or politicos, the taproot of Al Quie's sacrificial friendship and statesmanship is his deeply Christian faith. There are few more rewarding stories in our era of political cynicism than his."

Robert Osburn
Executive Director
MacLaurin Institute

"Led by his faith, his honesty, and his principles, Al Quie is respected in Minnesota and around the world."

Tim Pawlenty
Governor of Minnesota

"I've always liked and respected Al Quie and have learned much from his example of leadership. In the way he has led both his public and private lives, he has much to teach us all."

Tim Penny
Former Member of Congress

"It's men like Al who model for men like me how to live a life of faith with integrity and commitment. I succeed today because he wanted inmates to have more than just time."

Dustin Shipley
Alumnus
InnerChange Freedom Initiative

Riding into the Sunrise

AL QUIE

Riding into the Sunrise

AL QUIE

A Life of Faith, Service & Civility

Mitch Pearlstein

Forewords by
Charles Colson and Roger D. Moe

ISBN: 978-1-880654-45-3 Hardcover
Library of Congress Control No. 2008932518

Front cover photograph and design by Dean Riggott

Interior photographic credits:
Roger D. Moe, xxii. Paula Keller, 249. All other photographs from the Quie family.

Pogo Press
An Imprint of Finney Company
8075 215th Street West
Lakeville, Minnesota 55044
www.finneyco.com
www.pogopress.com

Printed in the United States of America
1 3 5 7 9 10 8 6 4 2

Dedication

*To Gretchen and Diane
and the glories of marriage.*

AHQ
MBP

Table of Contents

Acknowledgments

Perhaps it paradoxically has something to do with having recently spent a lot of time with someone midway through his 80s, but I'm finding myself ever more alert to how generously I was taught and mentored when I was much younger. I cite this because if I'm getting up there myself at 60, my teachers—broadly defined and very much including Al Quie—have been advancing even steeper and it's important for them to know how thankful I am for their kindnesses, whether or not they're still corporally capable of reading all about it.

Their number was diminished this past year when my doctoral adviser of 30 years ago at the University of Minnesota, Prof. Samuel H. Popper died just as the governor and I were starting this project, having made it to age 90—"The Big Leagues," as Sam described the milestone. I'd rather not imagine how my life and career would be if it hadn't been for him and the others I'm privileged to salute.

The star of *Riding into the Sunrise*, a man I've long admired enormously, entrusted me with nothing short of getting his life right, not just his resumé. Suffice it to say I've appreciated the significance of the job, the confidence he invested, and the months of mornings we spent together, a small digital recorder humming silently between us.

The book opens with forewords by two of Al Quie's dearest friends, Chuck Colson and Roger Moe, and after you read their pieces, you'll understand the depth of their respect and affection for him. Be assured that the man I was first privileged to serve more than a quarter-century ago reciprocates every one of their sentiments totally. For me, I can only add how it's a personal highlight, a very tall one, to have my name in the vicinity of theirs.

I'm grateful for early conversations with Lori Sturdevant, a journalist who covered Quie when he was governor and who later worked with the late Minnesota governor Elmer L. Andersen on two books. A good friend in addition to being a top-flight reporter and writer, I was interested in any spare gubernatorial book-writing tips she might have hanging around. Capture Quie's voice and don't forget the more distant stories, she rightly urged, the latter admonition prompted by my original and over-heavy interest in his recent activities at the possible expense of older ones. She was on-target, of course, just as she was when I asked about transcribers and she effusively recommended Beverly Hermes, a woman she had worked with several times. To the extent people might ever think about the art and craft of transcription, I trust they don't fathom how hard it can be, especially if done well, and it's hard to believe there is anyone better at it than Beverly.

My longtime friend Kent Kaiser did an excellent, first-round job of editing the manuscript. So much so that when I sent it off to John and Molly Harris at Pogo Press all they and their colleagues had to do was take a quick look, say "looks good," and start the presses. That was my secret plan, anyway, and to the extent it didn't work out exactly that way, my apologies for the extra work. Needless to say, one of the most gratifying moments of the last year was when they and Al Krysan of Finney Company said they wanted to publish the yet-to-be named book. Also needless to say, I'm grateful for their enthusiasm, including that of editor Lindsey Cunneen, graphic designer Angela Wix, and marketing director Ann Prescott. And have I mentioned that Barry Casselman, whose second Pogo Press book was recently released, reportedly said favorable things to John and Molly about what I had in mind and that I'm much obliged he did?

I acknowledge that I've had barely anything to do with one of the most striking things about *Riding into the Sunrise*: its magnificent cover, which was both photographed and designed by Dean Riggott, a very talented photographer in Rochester, Minnesota. His shot of Quie with his horse Nugget in the background had been commissioned by Prison Fellowship Ministries in conjunction with a major award they recently bestowed on the former longtime member of Congress as well as longtime PFM leader. Thanks to the graciousness of all players, we've been able to admire and use the photo here, too.

Speaking of photos, my daughter Nicole somehow managed to take one of the few reasonably good ones of me ever. And for whatever it's worth the camera she used for the nearby mug shot was bought at a Holiday Station store for appreciably less than what Dean presumably paid for his.

I enjoy libraries for a number of reasons, one of which is that most librarians enjoy helping people track down information. This surely was the case at the Legislative Reference Library in St. Paul, where I was aided at one time or another by seemingly everyone on staff, but most frequently by Elizabeth Lincoln. (Note to young people and students of all ages: Googling on your own is great; miraculous, actually. But there's nothing like a live librarian to help you out and it's silly not to take advantage of them.)

My thanks to Dane Smith, years ago my colleague at the *St. Paul Pioneer Press* and now my first-rate counterpart at Growth & Justice, for tracking down an invaluable piece of research he did several years ago at the Minneapolis *Star Tribune* on various budget crises to hit Minnesota over the last generation.

Carol Pettitt worked with Quie on his similarly named 2003 book, *Riding the Divide*, about his nine summers trekking the Continental Divide from Canada to Mexico on horseback. It was most helpful in writing the concluding chapter, "Riding into the Sunset."

I have a very nice office at work and a very nice one at home, but often I just have to get out and about to read and write, and no place has been warmer and more accommodating than my favorite Caribou at 46th and Nicollet in South Minneapolis. Thanks, folks, for regularly asking about how the book was coming—and for any free muffin that free advertising like this might inspire.

A dozen people read one or more chapters, often saying pleasant things, but more importantly, pointing out mistakes and other inadequacies. Several of them served with Quie in Washington and/or St. Paul; some are currently working closely with him in ensuring judicial impartiality or expanding early childhood education; one was an American Experiment intern; and one was Quie's wife who, after 60 years of marriage, knows him pretty well. In alphabetical order, I extend large thanks to G. Barry Anderson, Bob Andringa, Christopher Beddor, Carl "Buzz" Cummins, Don Fraser, Beverly Hermes, Jean LeVander King, Bob Osburn, Todd Otis, Gretchen Quie, Art Rolnick, Chuck Slocum, and Rob Stevenson.

Everybody at American Experiment—officers, board members, staff members—has indulged me in my obsession, which my wife in particular will vouch this exercise has been. Representing the fiduciaries are Chairman Ron Schutz and Vice Chairman Tom Stauber. Representing everyone else is everyone else: Britt Drake, Devin Foley, Peter Nelson, Dwight Tostenson, and Peter Zeller. Please accept my thanks for your help, patience, and friendship in equal and substantial portions. This is in addition to my huge debt for your scores of contributions to the Center, along with those of many other men and women over the last nearly score of years.

I am grateful to the Sundet Foundation for its support in the early stages of the project.

Then there is Katherine Grace McGowan, our first grandchild, born right around Chapter Eleven or Twelve to Ashleigh and Brian in California. She wasn't a proofreader or anything like that, but this being her first mention in a book, maybe someday when she's asked about her favorite one, something will get lost in translation and she'll say *Riding into the Sunrise* instead of *Horton Hatches the Egg*.

And as for my beautiful wife, the Rev. Diane Darby McGowan, my adoration for you and our life together has always been boundless. Higher than the highest mountain, deeper than the deepest sea, the whole musical bit—though as I type madly away this evening, we're slow dancing to Louis Armstrong and "What a Wonderful World." Know and take joy that after spending a year of thinking and writing about love and devotion, it's impossible not to revere and give thanks for you even more.

Mitch Pearlstein
Minneapolis
July 2008

Foreword

Charles Colson

As Mitch Pearlstein reveals so compellingly in this wonderful book, Al Quie is one of those rare individuals who passes through this life leaving in his wake countless others transformed for the better. I am one of those. Al Quie changed my life forever. I have never known anyone quite like him and don't expect to meet anyone like him again.

The great devotional writers often repeat those comforting words from Psalm 46: "Be still and know that I am God." When we're tempted to despair, when we're empty and discouraged, when we feel utterly helpless, they tell us we are to lean on the shoulder of a strong, godly loved one as if we were leaning on the shoulder of God Himself. We often experience our Lord's presence.

Over the past 32 years of ministry, I have experienced some tough times: the usual personnel turmoil, donations not coming in well, resistance of some prison officials to our work, and frequent attacks in the press, some lingering from Watergate and many unfounded. I've also had two of my three children diagnosed with cancer at the same time. And where have I turned? On every occasion I have discovered God's comfort often by leaning on the shoulder of my friend, Al Quie.

When I was charged with crimes for my service in the White House at the height of the Watergate hysteria, Quie was in the courtroom. For a public official to befriend one of the leading villains of the Watergate scandal was to commit political suicide. But it made no difference to Al. He was there in the courtroom, very visible. He stood with me throughout, giving me that strong shoulder to lean on.

The day I was to be sentenced, the entire press corps was gathered in the Federal District Courthouse. The corridors and the steps outside were packed as marshals led me through. I had just been sentenced to one to three years in prison. I saw Quie standing there erect, strong, determined, and, above all, loving, as I addressed the throng of reporters on the courthouse steps.

As you will read in the following pages, when I was whisked away in a car and Al started to walk back towards the Capitol, a reporter from *Time* magazine stopped him to ask why he was there. Al explained that we were in a small prayer group together and that he needed to be there to give support to a friend in trouble. The reporter walked away shaking his head but only after saying to Quie, "Colson is a very lucky man." Imagine: I was sentenced to prison, and this reporter in a way envied me. Such is the human hunger for true friendship.

The way to measure good fortune in life is not by the accumulation of riches and material comforts. The good life is in the deeper things of life; knowing God, finding His peace, loving your family, and having a few true friends. Friendship is a great gift of God. Jesus told His disciples, "You are my friends" (John 15:15). It is not a term to be tossed about lightly, as we so frequently do.

I was with a very wise man recently, also a close friend, and in the middle of a conversation he looked at me wistfully and asked, "How many good friends do you really have?" As I was contemplating the answer, he said, "If you end up in life with two or three real friends, you're fortunate."

Well, that might be a slightly cynical view, but there's some truth in it. I've been in politics at the top: Special Counsel to the President of the United States with an office immediately adjacent to his. I had more "friends" than anyone could possibly imagine. I received letters from old college classmates, distant relatives, and people I had met in casual circumstances telling me how proud they were of me and how much, by the way, they'd like a special tour of the White House. When I fell from power I heard from none of these people. They were, as the old expression goes, fair-weather friends.

When I ended up in a prison cell, I took careful count of my "friends," that is, those who wrote me genuine letters. That included only one client from the days I practiced law, a couple of law partners, a few old family friends, and some new friends I made after becoming a Christian the year before going to prison. When I was released, I had a small file folder with maybe 50 letters that were worth saving. In times of trouble and distress, one's circle of friends tightens. But throughout all the turmoil of Watergate and prison, Al was not only writing me letters, he was visiting me. To the astonishment of the guards and prison officials, there was Quie at the gate, signing in to see one of the most reviled men in America. In human terms that made no sense. But if we understand what a true friend is, and particularly the Christian definition of friendship, it was for Quie, risk or no risk, simply the right thing to do.

Few men have made the impact on my life that Al Quie has made. In many respects he has shaped my Christian growth and my entire ministry. One of the reasons he's had such an impact is that he is a man who simply does the right thing. Frequently he has admonished me, when he sees me shading things a bit even to make them more palatable to people, "That's deceitfulness. You simply have to tell the truth and be totally honest with people." Such frankness is hardly politically correct these days, or sometimes even an appreciated quality. But Al Quie is a man who gives us the classic definition of the word "integrity." He is in private the same way he is in public. He does the right thing and always tells the truth.

He's also lived the most consistent life of anyone I've ever known. You will be hugely enriched reading these pages to see how this farmer's son of sturdy Norwegian stock learned the most fundamental truths in his own living room. They stuck. The idea of opening your house to beggars and setting your best table for people who had the least—as Jesus told us to do—became a way of life for Al Quie. It was simply the right thing to do. Mitch Pearlstein has done an extraordinary job in painting a vivid picture of this rock-solid, six-foot-two, part-time cowboy and great statesman. This is the kind of book you want to read and then read to your kids. This is a life well lived and worth emulating.

Al Quie has always heeded the call of duty. When his country was at war, he served as a Navy pilot. He went into politics not for personal gain (he may in fact have left office poorer than when he began) but because it was his duty. He was one of the most respected men in Congress. My boss, President Richard Nixon, when he would talk about Quie, would always draw back with a certain reverence. "He's a straight arrow," Nixon would say, "the one who is always drinking milk." That was Nixon's way of contrasting him with most of the members of Congress, who could be found at some bar most evenings and who often sipped whiskey in the cloakroom while they waited to vote.

Throughout his life, Al Quie has done his duty. And he continues to today. Though he is one of the busiest men I've known, much in demand to serve on boards, commissions, do church work and the like. But when his beloved wife of 60 years, Gretchen, contracted Parkinson's, Al drew back, resigned from a lot of activities, and took his post at Gretchen's side, caring for her.

In these pages you will read a story recounted with characteristic Quie humility, about the time that he, a sitting congressman, offered to serve my prison sentence. Al may consider it just one of the many good things he did or was willing to do in his life, but for me it was a turning point, and proved to be one of the most compelling witnesses of the reality of Jesus Christ that I have experienced. Let me take the privilege, since I'm writing this foreword, of telling the story from my perspective.

In January 1975, I had been in prison for seven months and a Christian for a year and a half. It was my Christian faith that sustained me while I was in prison, because contrary to the myth about converting to Christ and living happily ever after, from the time I went to prison, everything about my life deteriorated. A month after I went to prison, my dad, who was a heroic figure to me and my best friend, died. Since I was in the custody of U.S. marshals because of being called to testify at the Watergate trials, I was taken by armed guard to my dad's funeral. It was one of the low points in my life, as I wept over the open casket with two arms-bearing marshals beside me. The loss of a dad as wonderful as mine is a wound that takes a long time to heal. Soon thereafter, there was more bad news. Nixon was pardoned; and while there was speculation that President Ford might pardon the loyal Nixon lieutenants, he chose not to. Some efforts were made to ask the president to commute my sentence, which resulted in front-page stories and further rebuffs. Prison had its trying moments for me as well. One inmate threatened my life. (All former high government officials are in peril from those who blame them for their fate.)

But in January there was a series of even tougher blows. I was deeply worried about my mother, who was alone trying to care for herself through a very difficult grieving process. I was equally concerned about my wife, Patty, who never failed to visit me in prison, any time the doors opened. But after seven months of commuting back and forth, I knew she was exhausted. Though she concealed it well, she was worried that I might be in prison for another two and a half years if I were not paroled. Neither one of us had had any good news.

Then I was notified that I was disbarred in the state of Virginia, which is an automatic process for felons. (I was not disbarred in Massachusetts, where my license was instead suspended. At least I knew I could go back there to practice law.) But a few days after that painful news, I was called away from my prison work to take a phone call at the control office. I knew that meant some emergency, because inmates don't routinely receive phone calls. The news was like a hot knife to the gut: my second son, Chris, then a student at the University of South Carolina, had been arrested for possession of a minor amount of marijuana and was in the city jail in Columbia. When he was arrested I was told that he announced, "Now you've got both of us." My three kids, I realized, had suffered terribly through this process.

At the time, I was the last remaining Watergate figure still in prison. The other three who had been in prison with me, John Dean, Jeb Magruder, and Herb Kalmbach, had all been released by Judge Sirica, the man who sentenced them. But I had been sentenced by Judge Gerhard Gesell, who was known as a tough law-and-order, lock-'em-up judge, and who at the sentencing and the trial had shown little if any compassion. I remember thinking at one lonely moment, after the call about Chris, *how bad can things get before you hit bottom?* If I hadn't hit bottom, I was certainly close to it.

The very next day, Al Quie called me. "We've been meeting in your prayer group, your brothers and I," Al said, "and I think I've found some way that I might be able to take your place and serve your prison sentence so you can be with your family. I would like to do it; I'm going to be seeing President Ford soon, and I'm going to ask him if I can."

I could barely respond. I think I simply shouted, "No!" but I couldn't find adequate words to express what I felt at that moment. It was unimaginable that a senior U.S. congressman would truly be willing to take the place of one of the most infamous convicts in the American prison system. I knew Al well enough to know he meant exactly what he said.

I vividly recall going to my bunk that night, kneeling down to thank God that I was in prison, and that I now knew beyond a shadow of a doubt that the Christ to whom I had committed my life eighteen months earlier was real, alive with us at this moment, in our midst. Nothing more than the presence of the living God could cause a man like Quie to sacrifice everything for another brother who was hurting. Jesus' words rang through my mind, "Greater love has no one than this, that one lay down his life for his friends." I knew Christ was real, and I've known it every day since that moment that Al called. Needless to say, I also knew Al was real, perhaps the most authentic human being I've ever known.

Al never had to fulfill that promise, because two days later, Judge Gesell unexpectedly announced my release so I could be home with my family. As I was leaving the prison, one of the marshals, who was also a Christian and with whom I'd exchanged devotional literature, said to me, "Mr. Colson, I knew God was going to set you free." I turned to him and said, "Thank you. But He did it two days ago."

The Christian faith is under brutal assault today on all fronts, from radical Islamo-fascism on one extreme to aggressive atheism on the other. The Muslims tell us we're worshipping false gods in the Trinity. The atheists tell us it's irrational to believe in God, that life mysteriously came from some other planet, or that it arose out of the primordial soup. How could anyone look at the life of Al Quie and say there is no God? Never for a moment since Al offered to serve my prison sentence have I doubted the existence and reality of Christ. And though I've seen Jesus lived out in the lives of others, I have seen it in none more convincingly than the man whose biography you are about to read.

When I first heard this biography was going to be written, I thought it would be impossible to capture the real Al Quie. How does someone describe in words the intangible qualities of integrity and bearing and decency and kindness, of grace and intelligence, and plainspokenness, which are the characteristics of this Norwegian farmer's son? But I was wrong. Mitch Pearlstein has gotten him. He's gotten him because he has allowed Al to tell his own story. Much of what you will read in here will not only rivet you—the book is extremely well written—but it will give you an insight into one of the most remarkable men I've ever known.

Al Quie changed my life forever. I suspect that reading this book and meeting Al through these pages is going to change your life as well.

Al Quie with two of his best friends at his 80th birthday party (September 2003) in Bloomington, Minnesota. Chuck Colson is on the left and Roger Moe is on the right.

Foreword

Roger D. Moe

Complete disclosure. I am a left-of-center Democrat, raised in a family where my grandfather, a Norwegian Lutheran minister, was considered the "leading liberal" in the area and my parents thought Franklin and Eleanor Roosevelt were second only to God. What I heard in all those discussions and arguments had its impact, as I went on to serve in the Minnesota Senate for 32 years as a member of the Democratic-Farmer-Labor Party. So why would a guy like me write a foreword for a book about a Republican governor written by the president of a conservative think tank? Quite simply, I consider it a high honor to call both Al Quie and Mitch Pearlstein dear friends.

First a few words about author Pearlstein. We met on a very cold day in February 1975 on a flight to Crookston, Minnesota, which was in my state senate district and is closer to Winnipeg than to the Twin Cities. At the time Mitch was speechwriter for the president of the University of Minnesota, C. Peter Magrath. Mitch, Peter, and other university officials were in Crookston for the annual Red River Valley Winter Show and to visit the University of Minnesota–Crookston campus, and from that first meeting until today we have remained friends in spite of some very turbulent political times along the way. He has done a masterful job of putting into words the character and works of a great Minnesotan. Mitch has always had a way with both the spoken and written word, and in this book he blends sound research, firsthand observations, and Al Quie's narrative and many wonderful stories into a captivating read. He has accomplished something beyond capturing Quie's faith-centered philosophy; he has given readers a road map for their lives. Whether you're in politics, religion, business, or sports, *Riding into the Sunrise* is a compelling account of how one man has done it—and has done it extremely well in all parts of his life.

Al Quie was in Congress when I first heard of him. He had served in the same state senate chambers I did a dozen years before I got there. Since I lived in the opposite end of the state and he was not my congressman, I had little knowledge of him with one exception. My first job out of college was as a mathematics teacher in Ada, Minnesota. Teachers in the mid-'60s were becoming better organized, getting more politically involved, and pushing for higher salaries and bargaining power. Whenever faculty lounge discussions centered on Congress and federal involvement in education, Quie's name frequently was raised. He was highly regarded in both northwestern Minnesota and in Washington, where he was often referred to as "Mr. Education." Still, I didn't know at the time how the lives of so many people would be improved because of this man's lifelong commitment to learning.

I really got to know about Congressman Al Quie when he was the Republican candidate for governor in 1978. By then I had been in the senate for seven years and was chair of the Finance Committee. He had picked up on a tax theme; he wanted the personal income tax "indexed" (the concept is explained in Chapters Seven and Eight), and it struck a chord with voters. He even made an appearance before a legislative committee during the campaign and presented his reasons why the legislature ought to adopt his idea. In retrospect, that was a pretty gutsy move—a Republican candidate for governor appearing before a committee controlled by the DFL. I still remember his appearance and must admit I thought this guy should be easy to beat, as he was not exactly a candidate from *GQ*, with cowboy hat and western boots, a speaking style that's more soothing than exciting, and to top it off, a campaign centerpiece—income tax indexing—that wasn't exactly a gut grabber. Well, I was wrong, as the DFL took its worst election defeat in its history that year. Fortunately, the state senate was in mid-term or I'm sure we would have lost seats and perhaps the majority. The next four years would be both the most painful and most meaningful in both of our political careers.

Governor Quie (even today I always address him as "Governor") had a successful first legislative session in 1979–80. His tax indexing proposal passed but only as a trade-off with greater property tax relief. He got his proposal for "Initiative and Referendum" on the ballot and it, in fact, received a majority of votes in the 1980 general election, but because it needed a majority of everyone voting that November (not just those voting on the specific measure), it failed. He instituted an effective judicial selection process and continued his focus on education. I will address these last two issues in a moment.

The net effects of the tax changes proved to be problematic—and would have been so, I'd argue, even without a recession, which was on its way. Indexing the personal income tax slowed the growth of revenues and greater property tax relief meant greater obligations on the part of the state in assisting individual property owners and local governments. Bad economic news started hitting in August of 1980 and the next two years would see a series of special legislative sessions aimed at balancing an ever-sinking state budget. The span, as noted above, would prove to be the most painful part of my legislative career. But it was also a time when Governor Quie displayed great courage, a deep faith in the goodness of people strengthened by his personal faith, and the beginning of a close friendship between us that has grown each day since. Both the governor and I cite a particular event that marked a turning point in our personal relationship and that resulted in a bipartisan resolution to the state's budget crisis.

We had been invited to a winter event at Concordia College in Moorhead, Minnesota. Concordia has a strong Norwegian Lutheran influence so you can see how the two of us would be comfortable there. The governor was scheduled to give the main address followed by my giving the benediction. After the program we exchanged greetings and he invited me to stop by his office as soon as I got back to St. Paul. You will read about the event in Chapter Eight, but let me add something that happened just recently, which Mitch mentions.

A couple of months ago I was cleaning out some old boxes of papers from my senate days and found the handwritten prayer I gave that cold December night in 1981. I carried it with me for a month until I happened to be at an event with the governor and gave it to him. That night at Concordia College he had prepared to speak about our budget problems, but on the way to the podium he changed his mind and talked about how lucky we are to live in Minnesota. (He remembers his remarks in more religious terms.) His comments influenced my words, and that night the Holy Spirit got through to a couple of stubborn Norwegian Lutherans!

The rest, as you will read, is history. We worked together to balance the budget in the most wrenching ways possible: cutting budgets, raising taxes, and shifting payments. And then in a final act of selflessness, he announced he was not running for re-election and worked with the legislature, often against his own party, to prepare a solidly balanced budget for Minnesota's future. By the time Governor Quie left office, he had set the fiscal table for his successor (who also was his predecessor as governor), Rudy Perpich.

As I mentioned earlier, his first legislative session focused on education and judicial selection reform. When I was asked to speak at his retirement party in early 1983, I cited those two issues as areas where he would leave a legacy. He created a merit selection panel for judicial appointments that institutionalized Minnesota's habit of selecting good judges. But as you will read in Chapter Ten, recent federal court decisions have raised the possibility of partisan politics eventually damaging judicial impartiality in the state, and this has moved the governor to alert the public and encourage the legislature to take steps so that never happens.

Early childhood education is commonly supported today, but Congressman Quie was talking about such programs for pre-kindergarten boys and girls well before they were popular. And during his campaign for governor, he talked regularly about better preparing children for kindergarten as well as lowering class sizes in grades K-3. I'm convinced that had we not faced severe budget problems in 1981-82, he would have instituted educational reforms that would have led the nation. Even today as I write this, he's in Texas speaking to the Education Commission of the States. Not bad for a guy nearing 85 years old.

This book is about a truly remarkable man. Al Quie has committed his life to service—service to his family, service to his church, service to his community, and service to humanity. He has been an inspiration to my life, and every reader will be inspired by his faith-centered philosophy and how it can serve as a guide for all of us.

Introduction

The term in Latin for "one of a kind" is *sui generis*. In Norwegian-flavored Minnesota English, it's pronounced *Al Quie generous*. Yes, they do rhyme.

We are all God's children. We are all unique. But I've never known anyone like Al Quie, and I trust the same holds for just about everyone who has known him more than in passing during his 85 years. How and why is he an American original? Answering that question is the whole aim of *Riding into the Sunrise*, and if answers don't begin emerging clearly within pages, I will have failed an easy task.

I got to know Quie 27 years ago, in 1981, when I joined his staff slightly more than halfway through his four years as governor of Minnesota. That term followed his 21 years in Congress representing a mostly rural district in southeastern Minnesota, which came after his three years in the state senate in St. Paul, for a total of 28 years in elected office—not counting his stint as a school board member when he, in his early 20s, helped lead a district with five students. For someone whose name was eventually tossed around as a possible vice president or cabinet secretary, his public service kicked off extra modestly.

I first envisioned the book's peg and focus as the quarter century and counting since he left the governor's chair. We all know men and women who remain actively engaged late into life. For Quie, however, the list of civic enthusiasms is weightier than most, his passion for them is keener than most, and the difference he continues to make is more tangible than most—never mind his or anyone else's age—in areas ranging from educating young children, to ensuring an impartial judiciary, to ministering to the despised in prison. On more than one occasion in recent years, the most insightful and human thing spoken at meetings I've attended around town has been said by him. The classic example was when, at the end of a two-hour meeting on criminal justice at which all the expected things were said by all the expected people, including me, he simply (or not so simply) noted that a large reason why men wind up reoffending and going back to prison is that they're lonely on the outside.

Quie's more recent endeavors, indeed, would constitute the book's distinctive attraction if only he would have refrained from telling so many compelling stories stretching over the length and depth of his life. Memories, for instance, going back to when he was two and how wonderful it felt when his father sat him on a horse, a Morgan named Nancy, for the first time. Or about how during the Great Depression hoboes were always invited to eat in the dining room—not the everyday kitchen—of the family farm. Or about an abolitionist grandfather who was chased away by a Norwegian immigrant mother in southern Minnesota when he tried to recruit her son to fight in the Civil War and who himself was wounded at Antietam. Or about his grandfather's oldest daughter who lived to be 97 and from whom Quie learned about historical turning points like the Dred Scott Decision. Or about how, as a state senator, he voted for a fair employment practices bill even though there wasn't a single minority person in his district (or so he assumed).

Or, continuing the lifetime litany, how he came close to being the only member of the House of Representatives to vote against the Gulf of Tonkin Resolution, the main legislative action that led to American immersion in Vietnam, because he didn't trust President Johnson to tell the truth. Or how he was in prayer with Gerald Ford when his old friend from Michigan was informed that he was going to be president of the United States. Or how, 25 years before the I-35W bridge disaster in Minneapolis, he led a public forum on bridges and roads titled "Chicken Little Was Wrong: Everything *but* the Sky is Falling." Or how, as governor in contending with the worst economic crisis since the Depression and battered almost equally by fellow Republicans and opposing Democrats, he feared he had let God down. Or how, once he decided not to seek re-election, he was "resurrected," the governorship "became a joy," and he left his successor with a half-billion dollars in the till.

Before going on, I readily acknowledge that a prime and legitimate question is exactly how hard I challenged Quie during our more than 40 hours of conversations for the book. Since it's clear I like and admire the guy, with what kind of frankness do I report and analyze in the pages that follow? Do I ever rip into him? Of course not, for no other reason than I have zero interest in writing such a book about anyone. But you should know and take assurance in the fact that I don't know anyone who invites people to test him more eagerly than he does. He lives for a number of things, "congenial disputation" being one of them. (He claims to have invented the term.) To be on a big family vacation, for example, and get into vigorous but civil "exchanges of views" with sons, daughters-in-law, or grandchildren over political or theological questions absolutely makes his day and evening.

Over and above, I'm a reasonably assertive contrarian by nature who also, one might safely say, comes from a different world from Quie's—unless I missed something along the way and he, too, grew up on the largely Jewish sidewalks of a middle-class Queens neighborhood and not the Lutheran, dairy-farming hills of Dennison and Northfield. One of the reasons we have hit it off so well over the years is that while our political and wider cultural and social beliefs are akin in many ways, our histories are radically different. He frequently and graciously has said how I've gotten him thinking in different ways, just as he has reshaped me.

Does hindsight suggest I could have been more combative in some of our discussions, following up more pointedly on occasion? Sure. But I also assume not too many other interlocutors have ever questioned whether his legendary work in federal education policy— he was known as "Mr. Education" in Congress—really has made the kind of difference many observers assume. I was similarly direct when it came to his current efforts to expand early childhood education programs, as he's more confident than I am about what they can accomplish. And from another angle, I gather I was the first person ever to adequately convince him just how fortunate he was to come of age the way he did, when in our very first session I asked, "Do you ever think about how special your parents were?" I had been struck by how uncommonly nurturing (and properly demanding) they were, intellectually and theologically, and I've always believed kids growing up on farms have terrific advantages to begin with. Throw in other impressive family members, including three siblings who also wound up doing great things in life, and the best words I have to describe the Quie household in the 1920s and '30s are exceptional and stunning. But how *could* it have been special, the future governor first said, given that it had to do with *him*?

This is neither a copious biography nor a comprehensive history. For reasons of a long and jammed-packed life alone, don't expect retrospectives on every consequential thing he's ever done, and in no way expect any gossip, as that's as foreign to him as old-time Midwestern manners are to supermarket tabloids. Though having allowed this, the book does, in fact, delve deeply. As for precisely where, it's not overblown to say it's into his soul by way of his heart, with Quie drawing on a lifetime of inward exploration. He seems to entertain very little downtime when it comes to thinking hard about serious matters.

Yes, there are plenty of stories about politics, policies, events, and people, as the man has done much, with many different folks, in many different arenas. Yet more than anything else, I would describe the book as a keenly introspective self-portrait. Its words and memories, very much on purpose, are overwhelmingly his and not those of family or friends, be they in adulation or criticism. Did many of them want to talk to me about Quie, and did they have legions of wonderful stories and insights to share? Of course they did. But a collection of salutes was not the kind of book by which he wanted to be remembered, because it was not the kind of contribution he wanted to make. Early on, for instance, he emphasized the importance of my explicitly showing how his faith in Jesus Christ sculpted and infused every strand of his life. He was determined to have the whole book reflect it, not just a lone summary chapter along the way. He's not above having people praise him; as with everyone else I know, he enjoys it. But much more than taking pleasure in being eulogized while he's still around, he was most interested in teaching how people—all different kinds of people—might live together more respectfully and peacefully. Ask him what he wants most to do with his life, other than fantasize about making one final ride on horseback along the Continental Divide, and chances are he'll say he wants to make a *difference*, especially by helping people to understand how extraordinarily important human relationships are and then by helping them to build more fruitful ones. In laser sum, I saw my job as capturing as faithfully as possible his singular voice, rather than those of choruses of fans, as illuminating and joyful as their songs would have been.

For readers who are interested in a sampling of the many nice things people might have said about Quie if I only had asked, take a look at a special 2003 issue of *American Experiment Quarterly*, as it's keynoted by three distinguished American scholars on the major themes of Quie's life, both professional and personal: faith, family, and education. It also contains shorter pieces by people who have worked closely with him over the decades. (www.americanexperiment.org/uploaded/files/ aeqv6n3various.pdf)

——◦——

How did *Riding into the Sunrise* come to be? It's a title, I might add, that captures perfectly Quie's good-morning take on the world. I was approached early in 2007 by my friend Bob Osburn, who said someone ought to write a book about Al Quie, and since the governor was not inclined to do it, I should be the one. Bob, who is the executive director of the MacLaurin Institute, a center for Christian study that serves the University of Minnesota community, said he represented a small group that included another wonderful friend, economist John Brandl of the University of Minnesota's Humphrey Institute, and the distinguished writer Os Guinness. While Bob obviously was interested in the religious aspects of a possible book, he grounded much of his pitch on the civility with which Quie has conducted the whole of his life, not just the political part, and how other people both in and out of public life needed to learn from it. Who was I to say no to such a request by such an ensemble? Nevertheless, I didn't commit until the summer for reasons having nothing to do with the project's appeal.

That commitment process, so to speak, went like this.

Quie and I met in early July at one of his two favorite places for business meetings, a Perkins restaurant in Minneapolis. (His other favorite spot is a Perkins in Golden Valley.)

"You know I think the world of you," I said.

He nodded.

"Do you want to do a book?" I asked.

"Yes," he said.

"Do you want me to write it?"

"Yes," he said once more, though adding something this time about doing it while he still has his "marbles."

And we were off.

The main grist for the book, I correctly assumed, would be between 40 and 50 hours of recorded conversations he and I would hold over the coming months. The final number, as it turned out, wound up being about 40 hours, derived from 19 longer sessions (sometimes referred to as "regular sessions" in the text) and two shorter ones later on to fill in gaps. We met most Friday mornings from the end of July through the end of December 2007 at his church, Minnetonka Lutheran Church. He had suggested starting at 7:00 a.m., but I talked him into 7:30, and not just because I had a longer drive from south Minneapolis. As it turned out, however, I almost always got to a nearby coffee shop before 7:00 to prepare, and then for sporting reasons I would strive to drive into the church parking lot before he did. I was aided by the fact that he arrived with military and milking precision at virtually the same moment—right at 7:30—every morning.

We used a small digital recorder, the electronic contents of which my American Experiment colleague Peter Nelson turned into CDs and mailed to Beverly Hermes in Apple Valley, inarguably the world's best transcriber. She, in turn, turned the 21 disks into approximately 1,400 double-spaced pages of transcripts. My doctoral dissertation of almost 30 years ago was grounded in about 875 pages of transcripts, based on interviews with 52 respondents, so I was familiar—if a bit out of practice—in working with voluminous stores of stories. Next steps over the subsequent months included reading, re-reading, and then re-reading the documents again; coding parts of them first with blue highlighters, then green ones, and then orange (or some other multicolor combination), while scribbling hundreds of notes in margins and between lines. For scholars and buffs, all 21 marked-up transcripts eventually should be archived at the Minnesota Historical Society.

If a chapter dealt more with a policy or political matter than a personal or family one, I would reinforce Quie's recollections with library and Internet visits. For instance, in writing the two chapters about Quie's four years as governor plus the campaign leading up to his victory in 1978, I reviewed every news clip about him from 1977 through 1982 in the Legislative Reference Library at the Capitol in St. Paul. Likewise, I looked up all of the clips about his continuing work on early childhood education as well as on retention elections for judges housed in that terrific resource.

Beyond what Quie said in the conversations and what I read, I started off in the favored position of knowing him well, our friendship and professional relationship dating back to the early 1980s. That's not to say I didn't gain large new insights about him in the exercise. If I were to pick just one, it was that I had never understood how ambitious and driven he has been and very much remains—at least the driven part. I found it fascinating, for instance, that he considered himself a failure at age 30 because he hadn't yet been elected to anything sufficiently significant by his standards. His smiling countenance continues to belie his thirst.

I started the actual writing in October and finished a first draft somewhat more than eight months later in June, and while I sometimes had to immerse myself in quite a few transcripts in order to complete a single chapter, on other occasions, almost everything I needed was more manageably contained in one or two of them. For example, almost everything in the final chapter on Quie's life with horses and the next stages of his life originates in the final two full transcripts, numbers eighteen and nineteen. In contrast, his reflections about education, and certainly about faith, weave their way extensively throughout.

I truly didn't know what the pages would look like—what my line of attack should be—until I sat down to write the first one. But it quickly became clear that the best way of getting his words to sound like his idiosyncratic own would be to stay mostly with a dialogue between the two of us. I would frame and probe and he would hold forth. And then I'd jump in again with new questions and he would come back with further answers and clarifications, and so on.

Insofar as Quie's speech, like almost everyone's, doesn't always translate well to the written word, most of what he had to say was smoothened but always with the aim of retaining his flavor, meter, and the like. Some of his longer quotations in particular are amalgams, drawn from two or more different conversations. But given that he reviewed and corrected everything at least three times, what follows is exquisitely him. Similarly, a fair number of my questions have been massaged for clarity and fluidity (never to make me sound smarter or more erudite than I really am).

———◁○▷———

To paraphrase what the Speaker of the U.S. House of Representatives gets to say at least once a year, it has been high honor and distinct privilege to write this book. From the very start, I've been alert to the large trust that was placed in me to get it right, as Al Quie has been a very important servant for a very long time. But if my wife Diane is right when she claims that I metaphysically lived more in Quie-land than at home for a year, I guess I did live up to the trust, at least as measured by preoccupation.

I mentioned above Quie joked that we needed to get moving on the book while he still had his "marbles." Please know I was constantly taken by the power and vividness of his memory. To be real blunt, I might have been a tad skeptical if just about anyone else— including people a lot younger than he is—claimed to remember how it felt to be on a horse at age two. But since Al Quie is incapable of concocting tales or being purposely misleading, one can only marvel at the reach of his recall.

That's not to say, however, that I didn't check and double check whenever feasible. "Trust, but verify," as Ronald Reagan was fond of telling Mikhail Gorbachev. Clearly, there was no viable way of confirming what went on around the supper table when he was a boy, or what was going through his mind when he saw his future wife Gretchen for the first time on the steps of Ytterboe Hall at St. Olaf College, not that anything of such an investigatory sort was ever the point of the project. But when, for example, it came to Quie's recollections of his pivotal congressional work on what are now called Pell Grants, or of his decisions as governor during the tortuous depths of the budget crisis in 1981-82, I invited several of his former colleagues to critique pertinent chapters, and I added a fair amount of research myself. I also solicited outside comments about the later chapters that address some of his current activities. In another instance, Quie showed a couple of draft pages to his son Fred, as they told a story about him. Fred recalled the incident in question somewhat differently than his dad did, but their two conceptions were not decidedly different—never mind how it would have been close to miraculous if they had been identical. Gretchen provided further backup by reviewing germane chapters.

Quie and I had a grand old time, a fact that was both result and further encouragement of his openness. We laughed a lot more often than noted in the text, but he also broke down in sobs one morning when talking in quick succession about abortion, slavery, and genocide. It's hard to imagine he held very much back either intellectually or emotionally.

He certainly was never hesitant or remote when talking about his faith in God and Jesus Christ. Begged in many quarters by this last sentence, I'm rather certain, are questions and wonderment about how a Jewish fellow could possibly write such a personal book about such a serious Christian—or "follower of Jesus Christ," as Quie prefers to call himself. It would be fun, though on the cusp of sacrilegious, to say "Hell if I know," but I do know. First, I've been writing professionally for more than 35 years, and I would like to think I have some ability at this stage for writing outside of any expertise I may have or outside of any comfort zone. But hardly anything about this project has been wholly news to me, and nothing has caused discomfort. One reason is my wife, the Rev. Diane Darby McGowan. Let's just say I've spent a fair amount of time in Episcopal and other churches since we've been married. Another reason is Quie himself, from whom I've learned an enormous amount over the years, not just about Christianity but also about what I might describe as "Christian America," as un-felicitous as that term can sound. Even though Minnesota has been my home for almost 35 years, he has extended a valued and appreciated education for someone of my background, geographic and otherwise.

Rounding off this introduction requires one more marble reference. Fearing that Quie would lose track of a few wasn't the reason we worked without pause. Rather, it was a matter of how 2008 marks half a dozen perfectly rounded milestones: His 85th birthday; his 60th wedding anniversary with Gretchen; the 50th anniversary of his election to Congress; the 30th anniversary of his election as governor; the 25th anniversary of "A Nation at Risk," the most influential report about American education published over the last generation, a document he helped write; and for good measure, 2008 is Minnesota's sesquicentennial, its 150th anniversary as a state. Only a cosmic spoilsport wouldn't race to take advantage of such alignment and signs.

Chapter One

Growing Up
Law and Gospel

When Al Quie was a boy and broke bread with his parents, sisters, and brother on the family farm in southern Minnesota, they almost always did so in the kitchen, not the dining room. The dining room, rather, was reserved for sacred holidays and other special occasions, such as when their minister visited.

Or when hoboes came looking for food in the Depression years.

Towards the end of my first conversation with Quie recorded for this book, I asked him a question about his mother. Previously during the two-hour session, he had contrasted his parents by saying his father was "Law" and his mother was "Gospel." This time he added:

> When I look back now, I talk of a woman of grace, or as I said earlier, a woman of gospel, because she just reached out to everyone. They had hoboes in that time who would come off the train and they would know to come to our house and she would feed them in the dining room. We only ate there at Christmas and Thanksgiving and Easter, unless the pastor came, and then we would eat with him there. Otherwise, we ate in the kitchen. We also ate in the kitchen when neighbors and other people came over. But when hoboes came over, Dad and the kids ate with them in the dining room and Mother served us. I look back and wonder: How did those two do that? I think it was Mother's grace reaching out to them. Dad said, "That's the way I would want to be treated if I were a hobo." She had an influence of grace on him.

"People," he added not long later, "who have virtually nothing, need more than food for the body. What's important to their soul are

1

dignity and respect. Mother and Dad had the grace to understand and act."

Very shortly after Quie recalled this story, which followed several others hardly less glorious, I said, "I just wrote a note to myself two minutes ago. I wrote down something about special parents. Do you ever think about how special your parents were?"

Not really, was essentially his first and surprising answer, as he said, "I just figure that's the way parents ought to be or the way they can improve." Perhaps spurred by my unhidden amazement at his giant-sized confidence in other mothers and fathers, he quickly acknowledged how a person might well view his parents as extraordinary.

"They were totally committed to each other," he said.

"They also, it seems to me, were totally committed to the kids," I answered.

"But I never saw them hug each other," he allowed in a bit of a non sequitur. "That's interesting."

"I'll come back to that," I said, scribbling another quick note.

"They were committed to the kids, yes," he responded.

To which I added, "It seems to me they were theologically engaged, intellectually engaged, engaged fully with each other, invested fully and committed to the kids."

"Yes," he agreed again.

"I view all of that as special," I said.

"I guess it is, but because it was me," he contended with a self-mocking laugh, "how could it be special?"

"Let me put it this way," I tried one more time, "You and I have spent a lot of time over the years talking about, reading about, spending time with folks who have grown up in just terrible situations. It seems to me, to be real blunt about it, how blessed and fortunate you were growing up with the parents you did."

"Yes, yes," he agreed doubly and without any demurral this time, and told of how his father, a dairy farmer, "would take his family to the lake for a week."

"Who milked? The hired help?"

"He hired help, yes. It was just amazing."

"By my raising this issue the way I have," I asked, "are you sensing in a new way what a fortunate situation you grew up in?"

To which he said he guessed so, but that's what "every child should expect."

"That would be nice," was my sardonic reply.

———— •◆• ————

Several weeks later, Quie recounted another around-the-table memory of his family. The topic this time was civil rights, a subject not readily associated with dinner conversations in rural Minnesota three-quarters of a century ago.

We had been talking about how he was most likely the only resident of Rice County in the early 1950s to routinely read the *Congressional Record*, as he had a strong interest in a variety of both national and (especially) state issues, civil rights very much included. He was farming back then, causing copies, he conceded, to pile up at harvest time. "But I went after them," he made clear, "when the crop was in."

"How was it," I asked, "that a guy from rural Rice County at that time was interested in civil rights?"

"That's another thing that began in my childhood," he said, and went on to talk about his paternal grandfather, Halvor Quie, who had fought in the Civil War, and his oldest daughter, Ellen, who was born during the last year of the war, in 1865. While Halvor died in 1918, five years before Quie himself was born, Ellen, who never married, "lived to be in 97, so I got to know her and there was a lot of talk." What did they talk about? And just as importantly, what might he have overheard his aunt and other family members talking about while he played nearby on the floor, too young to participate in the conversations? He began taking part in them, he said, when he reached high school.

One of the things they talked about was the Dred Scott decision. Can you imagine that? When I went to school and heard about Dred Scott, I realized that's what my family was talking about. And my grandfather, I learned that he had read *Uncle Tom's Cabin* and that he had such a passion for civil rights, that in January 1862, as a 27-year-old man, he enlisted in the First Minnesota Sharpshooters and was wounded in September 1862 at Antietam. That put him out of commission. He was so opposed to slavery that he had gone around recruiting soldiers at other farms. They told the story of this one housewife who drove him away with a horsewhip because she didn't want her son to go into the war. So all that talk—including what my grandfather had said about how pretty southern women were—that's something I just heard all the time.

After reporting that another regular topic of conversation was the 1917 Russian Revolution, I asked how many adults participated in such substantial discussions.

It would have been my dad's oldest sister, Ellen. She was twenty years older than my father. There was his next sister, Emma, who graduated from St. Olaf College in 1898, which is interesting, given how few people were college graduates at the time. Dad's sister Melina was a musician, but I don't remember her ever engaging much in those kinds of conversations. Dad's brother Henry was a farmer next door, and I don't remember him participating in in-depth discussions either. But then there was Caroline, who was Dad's next sibling above him and a nurse at the Mayo Clinic, who later was head nurse at Children's Hospital in Seattle. She'd come back for vacations in the summer time and stay on the farm with us. Dad was the youngest child in the family.

Then, on my mother's side, we'd go visit her parents because they lived just a half mile away. We would engage with my maternal grandfather, Adolph Jacobson, and Mother's two sisters, who were school teachers, one in Colorado, Elizabeth, and one in Wyoming, Alma. They all thought about political issues, especially Elizabeth.

"That's a substantial number," I said.
"Yes, and all of them talked about religious issues, too," adding

that they were an exceptionally "attractive" group in terms of their talents and accomplishments, to be held in "awe and respect."

"I recognize, by the way," I said, "that your strongest memories seem to be from when you were a little kid."

"Yes, yes. They are."

What other very old memories might he recall? In the first minute of our first conversation for the book, I asked, "Governor, what's the first thing that occurs to you when I say, 'Tell me about growing up'?"

"The furthest memory I have is as a toddler."

"You mean about two years old or so?"

"Something like that. I know I was doing more things with horses when I was three years old."

"You were already doing things with horses at three?"

"I was, already. But first I'll tell you about when I was two years old."

I had gone down to the barn. Get a picture of it. Here's a large barn that was built about 1870. My dad had come out with a team of horses. This is so important for me that for some reason I can *see* it. One horse was a little ahead of the other. The one that was a little behind, I later found out, was the first horse his father had given him, a Morgan named Nancy. My dad picked me up and sat me on that horse. I can still feel the warmth of her body as I was sitting on her. I reached forward and put my chubby hands on the hames to hold myself there. The hames, I should say, are parts of a harness. Then my dad let me sit there for a while before picking me up and setting me down. It's just like a photo going off, a flash going off. I can see that beautiful brown Morgan mare with Dad standing between the horse and me, and then the other one in front of her. That was the beginning, and horses have been a big part of my life ever since.

Not bad when a two-year-old secures not just the hames, but a lifetime epiphany. But then he grew even older and wiser.

"When I was three, our hired man one day drove a team of horses from the field and let them stand there during what was probably a silo-filling time. A short time later, my dad's oldest sister, Ellen, stormed out of the house, angry with him. 'Why are you letting your little boy, three years old, do that?' she wanted to know.

"I had gone over to that team of horses standing there, evidently knowing they shouldn't be left there unattended, and I actually unhooked them from the wagon and put them in the barn."

"*How* old were you?" I needed confirmation.

"Three years of age."

"How do you interpret the fact that, at the age of three, you did what you did? And 'unhooking.' Is that the terminology?"

"Yes," he began to explain, as an instinctive teacher, "the team is hitched to a wagon, so the tugs are hooked onto what they call the whiffletree. You unhook those and move the horses forward just a little. I wasn't big enough or strong enough to unhook the neck yoke still holding up the pole, so undoubtedly I just had them step forward so that that ring would slide off the pole, and then I could reach up and unhook the neck yoke from the harness of each horse."

Quie is laughing at this point.

"So you see," he continued, "I look back at that and think it implies some things I've done over the rest of my life."

"Such as?"

And here Quie suggested a couple of traits, among others, that will circulate throughout his story, often surprisingly.

"Sometimes," he allowed, "I'm just oblivious to what's going on. But sometimes I observe what's going on."

I would amend this by saying that in addition to describing himself as occasionally oblivious and absent-minded (his term), Quie correctly recognizes that he's an acute observer—albeit not one who merely watches well, but rather, someone who is then driven to improve and lift up much of what he sees, be they institutions or individuals. "When I look back, I realize that wherever I am, I look at how an operation can improve in effectiveness and with integrity. That's just the way I am. It charges my batteries."

Here's another memory Quie recounted right after speaking of Nancy and the other horses. This one is about how young Al Quie definitely found God at age six.

He spent his first three grades in a four-room school house in Nerstrand, four miles from the farm. (He later attended a one-room school house, which we'll get to shortly.) As soon as the snows began every year, nearby roads would become impassable for cars, so his father would take him, along with his older sisters Alice and Marjorie, and brother Paul, to school every morning, driving through fields by sleigh, returning to the farm, and then picking them up and returning home again in the afternoon the same way.

His father jury-rigged a covered sleigh, with a windshield, and a bench seat for the kids. In order to stay warm, Quie and his sisters (Paul was too young for school for this story) pulled robes over themselves and kept their feet on flat irons their mother had heated and then wrapped in newspapers. The future congressman and governor took it from here.

"One day, when I was six, I knew I had gotten into the sleigh without putting my mittens on. For forty years, I never told this to anyone, because it's so blamed silly. I needed to make sure those mittens were on when I got off, because Dad would spot me and ask sternly, 'Why don't you have your mittens on?'"

More accurately, he never revealed this story to anyone until he confided it to his wife of 60 years, Gretchen.

Now, my parents had taught me to pray, but with rote and memorized prayers. We didn't do ad lib prayers. But as I sat there, in the dark in that sleigh with my pudgy hands under my robe, I prayed to God that I could get my mittens on. My mother had attached the mittens to the inside of my coat with elastic, so I reached over with my right hand and got my mitten for my left hand, and slipped my hand into it. Now, the problem was I couldn't see my hands under the robe, and with mittens it's difficult to get your thumb into the thumb hole. But as I slipped my left hand into that mitten, my thumb went *automatically* into the thumb hole.

At this point in our conversation, Quie just about whispers, "I was surprised," as he thought he would have to fumble around to find the hole. "So now I came to the more difficult task. With my left mitten on, I had to get the other one on. I got it pulled down from my sleeve, and my right hand went right into that mitten, *and my thumb went right into the thumb hole*. At that moment, it was just like a flash. 'There is a God!' This was the moment God became real to me."

"You were six years old?" I asked.

"Yes, six years old."

"And you had a religious experience at six?"

"Yes."

"Two of the most important moments in your life—sitting on Nancy and getting your mittens on—were when you were two and then six?"

"Yes, and they're still with me. The scene is still visible to me."

Later in life, he said, two not-unrelated thoughts occurred. The first had to do with what he described as "God's creation," as in: "If you have a tremendous love for a part of God's creation, you can then grow to love the rest of His creation. I think I immediately came to see horses as a unique and beautiful part of God's creation." And at some moment in one's life, he continued, "God becomes real to you, which is the beginning of your trust and belief in God. I think that's what it is."

————— • ◆ • —————

Albert Harold Quie was born near Dennison and Nerstrand, in Wheeling Township, in Rice County, Minnesota, on September 18, 1923. Save for those who call him "Dad" or "Grandpa" or something akin, everyone in his family has always called him "Albert" rather than "Al." As when his mother, who, after asking, "Albert, do you have your long underwear on?" would poke her hand down his shirt to check for herself, regardless of what he said. Or when Gretchen made it clear, not long after they had been married in 1948: "Albert, it's my job to make the breakfast." (Or, if she's upset because of something he's done, "*Albeerrt*," elongated for effect.) Quie had been making his own breakfast starting when he was fourteen, because, he says, "I just liked what I cooked up myself." No more, said his new wife.

Quie's father and mother married relatively late in life, especially given the times: his father, Albert Knute Quie, at 35, and his mother, Nettie Marie Jacobson, at 34. The year was 1920. They had put their personal lives on hold to care for aging parents (in his father's case) and to help raise younger siblings (in his mother's case). Despite their late start, they had four children: Alice, Marjorie, Albert, and Paul, in that order. "She had them pretty close, and I don't know if she ever had any miscarriages."

Alice, who was a teacher and a missionary in Africa, is the only one who has died. Majorie was an aeronautical engineer until she married one and is retired in North Carolina. Paul, a retired pediatrician, was a Regents Professor of Medicine at the University of Minnesota, the highest honor the institution bestows on its faculty. And Albert, too, has done pretty well for himself.

Their father attended St. Olaf College in Northfield, in southern Minnesota, for "a year or two." Their mother's education ended at the eighth grade "plus she got one quarter up at the farm school in St. Paul." Quie's grandparents were "100 percent Norwegian," something that has been known to make him smile (although Grandpa Jacobson, he less frequently has acknowledged, was born not in the old country but shortly after his parents arrived in Wisconsin.). All four of Quie's grandparents, in fact, came to Minnesota after first settling in Wisconsin. As for St. Olaf, more than a few members of the family have gone there, including Al and Gretchen, who met on campus in 1946.

"My parents believed in discipline," Quie said early in our conversations, "they were together and I never saw them divided in their relationship with the children. They expected us to toe the line. We were kind of a closed community, because there weren't any neighbors close by."

"How close was the nearest farm?"

"Two farms were a quarter of a mile away, but nobody our age lived there. The others were a mile away and more."

Linked as his parents were, Quie recalled, "We weren't a hugging family, but we weren't afraid of touching, like holding a hand or putting a hand on a shoulder. I was so anti-hugging that when my hugging relatives came to the farm, I would hide behind the davenport."

The family always ate together for all three meals: breakfast in the morning, dinner at noon, and then supper in the evening before milking. They were joined by the hired man and the hired "girl."

In addition to eating, supper was for reports on the day and serious conversations. "It didn't matter if the hired hands ever thought about it beforehand. They were going to be thinking about some theological and political question."

Quie describes his father as a man who was deeply interested in ideas and immersed in his church and who taught by telling stories. He was direct, and unlike many modern fathers, not terribly concerned about perpetually bolstering his children's self-esteem. "Dad never laid a hand on me, but I had more fear of him than of my mother, because his words were more painful than anything he could have done if he had laid a hand on me. He probed into the depth of my weakness and wrongdoing."

This was one of many times Quie would talk about what he saw as his shortcomings.

Yet his father was very much a modernist when it came to farming, as he owned a combine long before anyone else in the area did, as well as practiced contour farming before anyone else. (He also was the first to own a car.) Quie, in fact, says his father was a "conservation evangelist," a forerunner of today's environmentalists.

Direct as his father was, and as "sharp and quick" as his temper was, when he got mad at any of the kids, by the next meal, "my dad would welcome us back." It hurt to be chastised and to feel rejected, Quie said. "But Dad would just forget about what had happened and tried to engage everyone in the family in conversation."

His father was a teetotaler. Nevertheless, when Quie was just starting high school, his father said a time would come when he and his brother Paul would want to smoke and drink. "I want to tell you right now," his father said, "I want you to do it in front of me."

I asked Quie (whom I've never seen smoke or drink anything stronger than whole milk) what happened.

"Later, when it was time, the three of us lit up cigars."

"Why not cigarettes?"

"Because I figured I was so absent-minded, I'd probably smoke a cigarette while I was gassing the tractor and blow the whole thing up."

"You saw yourself as absent-minded?"

"Yes, I always forgot things. I'd turn on the faucets for the water tank and that stuff would run through the yard."

Quie laughed frequently when telling some of these stories. But his voice turned low and sober when I asked him about the day in

1940 when his father, who was 55 at the time, lost his dominant arm in a farming accident.

> Dad was combining, for a neighbor, alfalfa for the seed. He was in a hurry because he wanted to get to a football game at St. Olaf. The alfalfa stems get stuck into the racks that shake the straw and then the grains drop to the bottom of the combine. Every once in a while, he'd have to go in there and pull that stuff out that was stuck so that it would keep shaking. This time, he just stopped, put the tractor in neutral, and let the combine—powered by the power takeoff from the tractor's engine—keep running, in order to speed up things. He figured he could do that, but he couldn't.

> He reached in with his left hand—he was left-handed—to grab that alfalfa and pull it out. He had an old jacket on that had a frayed sleeve which got caught and it sucked him right into the cylinder and mangled everything. About the only parts of his arm that were still good were his index finger and thumb, as it went through a space that started off being about a quarter of an inch wide. It killed the engine, which stopped the combine cylinder. With what had to be superhuman strength, he reached around with his right hand and grabbed that cylinder and brought it backwards, and with the whole compression of the engine of the tractor and everything against him, he pulled his arm out of there.

When his father freed his arm, he saw that an artery had been severed and he was "just shooting blood." So he "took the end of the artery and pulled it back and made it twist around his finger and pressed it. He did a loop and pressed it, and he walked a half mile to the house of a neighbor. Mrs. Shasky was there. I forget her first name. He stood at the door sideways so she wouldn't faint. 'Be calm,' he said. 'I want you to drive me.'"

She drove him two or three miles to Nerstrand, but because she had just started learning how to drive a week earlier, he suggested that she run into the hardware store and ask one of the owners, Lester Larson, to continue driving him fast to the hospital in Faribault, another fourteen miles away. "The doctor there said he had five minutes-worth of blood left in him, so that was how close it was."

Quie, then a high school sophomore, was in school at the time, in Northfield, when the call came that his father had been hurt. Since they drove their own car to school, he and his brother Paul, a freshman, drove "like everything for Faribault."

"I went in to see him, and he had all those tubes in him and he was just lying there, not conscious. Some way or another, my mother had gotten there, so here we were together, with him, but there was not much we could do. The whole farm was waiting, so we drove home and just did chores and everything. We had cows to milk."

A day or two later, a family friend said "with a kind of chuckle" in his voice: "Well, I guess that's the end of education for you. You have to run the farm now."

"As he drove away, I just said to myself: 'I'm going to farm *and* finish high school.' How I was going to do it, I didn't know. But a hired man quit his job with a neighbor and came by and said, 'I'm going to work for you.' So that enabled me to continue in school." He graduated in 1942.

Physicians decided right away to amputate. I asked how his father dealt with losing an arm.

He was an amazing guy. A man from an artificial limb company in Minneapolis came down to see him. My dad didn't think he could use an artificial arm because the amputation was so high. Now, the first snow had come, and the guy from the prosthesis company (neither of whose names I can recall) got stuck. So he got out of his car and walked up to the house . . . on two artificial legs. When he showed Dad his legs, Dad decided right there, "If he can walk, I can use an artificial arm."

Quie's father's prosthesis "didn't help much." Still,

he could eat with it and even tie his shoes. It was best when he needed to carry two pails of milk. More amazing was that he learned to do most everything with his right hand. In time he was able to put milk machines on the cows with one hand.

Can you imagine that? He learned to work with shovels, spades, and pitchforks. He could shoot a shotgun. And he could handle all vehicles and machinery—all without his artificial arm, so he put it away.

Albert Knute Quie lived for another 38 years, dying at 93, two days after his oldest son was elected governor of Minnesota in 1978.

———— ◆ ————

Prompted by Quie's comment (which he offered more than once) that his "father was Law and his mother was Gospel," I tried a little theological interpretation of my own and asked, "Would it be fair, in some crude sense, to say your father was Old Testament and your mother was New Testament?"

Seemingly stopped short by the question, he offered a contemplative, as opposed to a dismissive, "Phhhooo."

I jumped back in. "Would that work at all?"

"No, that wasn't it exactly. I think it would be more like a combination." Speaking of his mother, he added, "She was very gracious. But she did take a switch to me once."

"How old were you?"

"I was somewhere between five and seven."

"What had you done?"

"I had done something out in the garden that wasn't right."

After a quick pause and then a laugh, more came back to him.

"No! I know what it was. I didn't own up to whatever I did or didn't do in the garden. The infraction has not stayed in my memory. It was deceptiveness. They were very watchful of that."

Quie remembers frequent visits to his mother's relatives on Sundays. "It seemed to me the Jacobson family was tighter than my father's side. Most were farmers." His maternal grandparents lived in a Luxembourgian community in Wisconsin, near Port Washington, north of Milwaukee, before moving west. "So they knew Norwegian cuisine, but also sauerkraut and sausages and all that."

"As in stories of Jesus," Quie said, "my mother met people where they were. She would try to find out, right away, where they were. For example, as soon as she found out that hired hands were Catholic, we had fish every Friday. She said, 'We like fish. Why do they have to get a special dispensation?' In her acceptance of people, she had such love for them that she wanted them to know her Savior the way she knew Him. That's really what it was."

Still, he continued, her qualities could be hard to capture or explain.

When I was in college after the Navy, for instance, there was a guy by the name of Grant Williams, also at St. Olaf, whose dad was a rubber worker in Eau Claire, Wisconsin. Grant had been a chief in the Navy in World War II, but he didn't have a job, so I talked to Dad and he hired him for the summer to work on the farm. He was not a believer at all, but afterwards, I heard that he had told a religion professor at St. Olaf, "There's something about that woman"—meaning my mother—"that's different from any woman I've ever met before." He talked about Christ *in* her.

Williams, according to Quie, had been a struggling student before his summer on the farm. But then something happened to him, and "theology and Greek and all that stuff started coming easy to him. It was just amazing."

For those keeping count, this was at least the third time (and it would seem fitting) that Quie has used the word "amazing." Nettie Marie Quie died in 1960. She was 74 years old.

———————— • ◆ • ————————

Quie was intent on continuing in high school following his father's accident despite the fact (or perhaps because), "I didn't think I really had a brain." It wasn't until he was in the Navy and beginning training as a fighter pilot that he did much better academically than he thought he would. He had been sick and hospitalized several times and his battalion commander urged him to stay back a class. He refused and wound up scoring the second highest grade in the group. "Right there I said, 'I do have a brain!'"

He was 19 at the time. And no matter what his self-doubts were back then—and exaggerated self-effacements since—he was not without academic victories earlier on, as in learning how to read bilingually. "I knew reading was important. My father's statement that he read well because he had read to his own father when his eyesight was failing caused me to look for opportunities to read out loud so I could improve. My mother had charts up in the kitchen and was training us to read in both English and Norwegian." And then, and as an example of his frequently demonstrated tenacity (more, often high-endurance examples to come), there was the time he taught his teacher how to teach math.

While Quie and his siblings all started their formal education by attending a four-room school, when he was preparing for fourth grade they persuaded their parents to send them to a nearer one-room school, as they had enjoyed going to summer Bible schools there. But in the sixth grade, during what was supposed to be math, "the teacher threw up her hands." She was a substitute who, according to Quie, "didn't know sixth grade math" and who said, "Well, you can learn your math next year." This provoked him to take the book home, read it, and work on it "till I could figure it out." Then he "showed her the principles in the book" and taught sixth-grade math "both to her and my one sixth-grade classmate." Quie admits to "really getting enjoyment out of that."

He and Paul were still at the one-room schoolhouse two years later (Alice and Marjorie had gone off to high school) when he and his brother and the other approximately eighteen students had another "lousy teacher." An eighth-grade classmate led what Quie described as a "rebellion" by, among other things, throwing erasers at her when she was working at the blackboard and her back was to the class. He and Paul, however, refused to participate in the harassment, leading all the other students to turn on them.

"I'll tell you," Quie recounted 70 years later, "while my brother walked with me, it was the most horrible thing to be lonely, friendless, the whole kit and caboodle." And in a foreshadowing of his now-decades of work with Prison Fellowship, he added, "In the years since then, I've come to resonate with people who are in prison, who are totally alone and have no friends or anything like that."

His father pulled him out of the one-room school and re-enrolled him in the four-room school in Nerstrand, four miles from the farm, where he again had to pay out-of-district tuition. The one-room school was only a mile away. By this stage, Quie recalls "I'd gotten so that it was just impossible for me to make friends, I was so down on myself." He also was of the mind that none of the other kids were making it easy for him. "How do you make friends when no one reaches out to you?" And to top it off, he remembers being behind in his work.

But this time he had a "marvelous teacher," Miss Bradley. And on about his third day at his new/old school, she said, "Albert, if you will stay in over the noon hour with me, I will tutor you so you can catch up to the other students." The only reason he agreed was that, "I didn't know any of the kids well, I was so bashful and, I think, hurt psychologically by what had happened in the early part of the year at the other school."

With a chuckle, Quie continued:

Because I was feeling so bad, I told Miss Bradley yes, as it was something to do. That marvelous teacher helped me catch up with the others. At the end of the eighth grade back then, you'd take a state exam, and I was just sure I was going to fail it. But I did well, though it still didn't get through to me that I might be smart. I look back with great admiration for this woman who could see inside me, give herself to me for that time during the lunch hour and help me catch up.

Caught up academically though he might have been, he still wanted to drop out of school at the end of the eighth grade. (Keep in mind that this was before his father lost his arm and before the young Quie determined that he would continue with his education one way or another.) Quitting school early was more the rule than the exception in the community at the time, with Quie, in fact, recalling no boys from the one-room school continuing on to high school. Instead, they went off to farm with their fathers.

"Dad said, 'Okay, that's all right with me, if you make me one promise: that you'll go to high school the year after.' I agreed, as I wanted to ride horseback a lot and, in the wintertime, ski and skate. I had no intention of leaving school forever, anyway." His father further stipulated that his son could ride, ski, and skate, but that he'd still have to work half days on the farm. Quie agreed again and they had a deal.

I asked if the future ranking member of the House Education and Labor Committee really did drop out of school after the eighth grade, when he was thirteen or fourteen.

"Yes, I took the year off, but what a miserable . . . ," his voice trailed off at the bad memory. Yes, he rode horseback, but "there was no snow that winter," making skiing problematic.

"I talked to Dad about it, and he said, 'You know, Albert, disappointments make character.' I'll never forget that, 'disappointments make character.'"

While Quie dated during high school, his lack of confidence didn't make doing so especially easy for him, as "I was too bashful to ask girls out a second time." He also had a hard time looking at any parts of them other than their shoes.

Again, if readers are keeping count of certain words in these early pages, here are a few of the less-than-self-congratulatory ways Quie has described himself so far, as well as during other times in our many hours of conversation. Some, he said, applied only to when he was much younger; others, he said, remain germane: absent-minded, lacking in confidence, missing a brain, bashful, lonely, deceptive, devious, and duplicitous. Or if he doesn't see himself as deceptive, devious, and duplicitous as such, he admits to a sometimes questionable "nature." (A congressional colleague once described him more accurately as "deceptive as one of his cows.")

Clearly, Quie really has felt these ways, although he also has viewed himself as a confident person ever since his Navy stint. Not incidentally, this was followed by his graduating from St. Olaf in the equivalent of less than four years—while also farming full time. Likewise, a part of Quie surely does think of himself as having a shadowed nature—although it's a plausible evaluation only as judged by the infinitely demanding gauge he sets for himself as a believer. In sunnier moments he also talks frequently about "integrity," his own included.

In much the way I asked earlier in our conversations about whether he felt blessed given the parents he had, I also asked if he ever "felt sorry for kids, and not just kids, who haven't grown up on farms, in rural circumstances, with demanding parents."

He didn't say he felt sorry for anyone, but after referring again to his father's hideous accident and how "adversity brings strength," he started talking about how farm life is marked by responsibility and self-sufficiency.

"When I was just starting third grade, I didn't have to get up in the morning to milk cows before I went to school. So I talked to my dad about it and I said, 'My classmates have to get up and milk cows in the morning, and I want to also.' So he said, 'Okay, you get up and milk cows in the morning, too.'"

"What time did you have to get up to milk?"

"Five o'clock. It wasn't that my parents *made* us do chores. You were moving towards manhood. You were moving towards independence, towards responsibility. If somebody else was assuming responsibility ahead of you, *you* wanted to assume responsibility."

A week after Quie spoke about his eagerness to wake up at five o'clock every day, he talked about how, as governor, while participating in a prayer group, he was asked to think back to when he was "totally at ease and in comfort." To think about the physical location in which "you were just at home with yourself." He said he couldn't find anything in his memory, until "I came to when I was a young person on the farm."

"How old were you?"

"Oh, when I was real little, continuing probably right up to the time I left for the Navy."

There is a hill that overlooked the creek in the pasture. It was a place where I'd sit and meditate when I was alone. Many times when I'd go out to bring the cattle back, I would just take a few minutes there. Other times, I'd be out there and just sit. I think back to how many times I was moved to prayer while there. Whether there was something troubling in my life, or whether things were just peaceful and good. I came to realize later in life that I learned two things on the hill. One is that I've made it a habit to get up early every morning. And when I do, I just sit there a while and pray and think.

Scores of years ago, on the hill above the creek that ran through the pasture, might Quie have prayed for a beloved wife like Gretchen and a stunning family of their own?

Chapter Two

Gretchen and the Kids
"The absolute cutest female I've ever seen"

Remember a few pages ago when we learned how Al Quie as a teenager was not entirely comfortable—certainly not forward—around girls and young women? Fueled by a malted milk, things are about to change, as he's about to meet Gretchen.

After two years as a Navy pilot at the end of World War II, during which time Quie is quick to point out he never saw combat, he entered St. Olaf College in Northfield, Minnesota, as a 22-year-old freshman. It was January 1946, and veterans back then dined in Mohn Hall while other freshmen ate in Ytterboe Hall, which not incidentally had malted milks that were "terrific." The malts also were free, albeit for Ytterboe students only.

"A friend of mine, Ove Peterson, one day suggested we go over there, saying they wouldn't know we didn't live in Ytterboe." Ove's point being, they could finagle free malts. "But I said, 'No, I'm not going to do that because we should pay for them.'" The extra-rich moral dilemma continued to eat away at him when they arrived at the dorm.

"As we walked up a flight of stairs, two girls also were coming up, but from another direction." Of one of them, Quie thought to himself, "She's absolutely the cutest female I've ever seen." Feeling as emboldened as a Navy pilot deserved to feel barely months after World War II, Quie informed Ove, "I feel like giving her a nickel so she can give me a call when she's old enough."

"Little did you realize," he confided to me proudly through laughs more than 60 years later, "what a character I was."

Good as the line was, nothing was actually said by either Gretchen or Al Quie to each other. Worse, there's no reason to believe that Gretchen even noticed him, and despite the school's modest

19

Navy pilot Al Quie in Minot, North Dakota, in 1944.

enrollment, it would not be until the following fall that he would see her again. This time Quie was talking to Dick Waldo, a classmate he had known from before college.

"So here I am in Dick's room, and he's just lovesick. 'Oh, there's this wonderful girl in my art class, and I don't know how to meet her,' he moaned. Well, I'm a big, old Navy guy and all, and I say, 'Hey, just tell me who she is and I'll introduce you.'"

Dick tried to explain and describe who she was, but Quie couldn't figure it out, so he asked his friend if he had a yearbook from the previous year, which included freshmen photos. Dick did, *"and he showed me Gretchen's picture! That's the girl I saw last January!"* So instead of introducing Gretchen Hansen to Dick Waldo, "I asked her for a date myself."

Dick later bewailed, probably even in more pain, "You stole my girlfriend!"

"You hadn't even met her yet," Quie rebutted.

To which I noted, "Evidently you picked up some courage with women along the way."

Yes, he acknowledged through another round of laughter, he had gotten braver, but for naught. His invitation had been for a homecoming dance at Northfield High School, but because Gretchen had taken a pledge at St. Olaf not to dance, she "turned me down." According to Quie, Gretchen "loved to dance" and had done plenty in high school. But it was her "great integrity" that led her to honor her pledge, both on and off the campus while at St. Olaf.

What to do?

I figured, I'm not going to let this go, and I studied where she would be on campus. I hope it wouldn't now be called stalking. I figured she probably would be coming out of the art building, the "Art Barn." I also thought she'd be heading to chapel, because everybody went to chapel. The plan was that I'd look for her, and then when I'd finally see her, I'd "accidentally" run into her. It worked. "Gretchen," I was finally able to say, "I'm Al Quie. I was the one who invited you to the dance." And we just walked together like that.

"You originally asked her out by phone?"

"I had called her, yes."

"So she hadn't previously seen you face to face?"

"No. But we talked so she would know who I was."

Not long later, she started inquiring about this six-foot-two-inch, farm-strong young man and realized he was the guy who drove a black club coupe to school every day despite St. Olaf's rule prohibiting students from having cars. What she didn't know at the time was he had received special dispensation to have a car on campus, as he got up every morning at 4:30 to drive home and milk the cows before driving back for a 7:50 class. His brother Paul, with whom he shared a dorm room, reversed the route for the evening milking.

"The car and flight jacket and all," Quie said, "didn't make me look like too safe a guy to date. But I asked her out again and she talked to her roommate, Marian Grandrud, about me. Luckily, Marian was a second or third cousin of mine, not that Gretchen knew it then. Marian said, 'Oh, that's my cousin.' So now Gretchen figured I was safe enough to go to a movie with."

"Do you remember the first movie you saw together?"

"No, I don't, but I remember that I learned about her love of classical music, and on our second date, we went to a concert by the Minneapolis Symphony at the University of Minnesota."

Without in any way suggesting that someone from Quie's rural background wouldn't or shouldn't be interested in such an evening un-coerced, the aesthetic fact was that he had not appreciated classical music until he made a concerted effort to do so during his previous Navy years. As if he just knew that someone like Gretchen would be in his life before long, he recalled: "When I was transferred to a base, before I started flying, I would go to the library, and with records I trained myself to enjoy classical music. So now, it wasn't, 'Oh, why does anyone want to listen to that stuff?'"

This was most fortunate, because he quickly learned that Gretchen "loved opera, orchestras, classical music, and all that," and that he "wanted to impress her that I wasn't just some hayseed from the farm. That was the beginning of our relationship. I was aware she was leery of me at first."

They continued to date through the rest of 1946 and into 1947. After the spring semester, Gretchen went off to Michigan to attend Cranbrook, an art school, for the summer. Quie takes it from there.

We wrote back and forth. When she came back just before school started, I picked her up for a date. We were driving along, but she didn't know I was going to ask her to marry me. There was a bridge across the Cannon River between Northfield and Faribault, one of those old bridges. We had gone on a picnic there in the spring, and I always thought that spot was the most idyllic place. So I drove there and stopped on the bridge. She asked, "What are you stopping here for?" I took the ring out of my pocket and held it up like this.

To show me what he meant, he took off his own wedding ring and held it up to his right eye and repeated his proposal, "Dear Gretchen, through this ring I see you and you're the only one I'll ever see. Will you marry me?"

"Whoa!" I said. "What did Gretchen say?"

"She wanted to know, 'What was that?'"

Let the record show that Quie and I were laughing a lot again. I asked if he had been reasonably confident she would say yes.

"Oh, yes. Yes," he said.

"And she did say yes?"

"She did say yes."

"At that very moment?"

"At that very moment."

"Oh, good," I concluded with as much relief as joy for my friend.

The very newly engaged couple then drove back to Minneapolis, where she was living with her parents until school began again. But now they were late, causing her mother and father "to be really upset." But after their daughter showed them her ring, Quie said, "Their anger and upset were just gone. I look back and think about what her parents were thinking. They were both college educated and their daughter was marrying a farmer. And on top of that, she would be leaving school to help run the farm. But Gretchen says they really liked me, so that was good."

"How late was late, by the way, when you got back to Minneapolis after you proposed?"

"I suppose it was after eleven."

They had dated a little less than a year before getting engaged, and then got married a little less than a year after that, in June 1948, at Our Saviour's Lutheran Church in south Minneapolis—the very spot, in a nice connection, from which I picked up Diane for our first date in 1990. She ran a homeless program there and we had met at a meeting in my office about six weeks earlier. A very sad Our Saviour's connection came one night about five years later when the old church burned down. I called the Quies early the next morning to let them know that the stone church in which they were married was physically no more, but they already knew, having watched the fire on television. Not incidentally, they had been volunteering at the shelter when Diane and I met.

A 1959 aerial photo of the Quies' dairy farm in Dennison. The farm was in the family from 1856 until it was sold in 1989, a span of 133 years. Dennison is in southeastern Minnesota.

The newlyweds went on a four-week honeymoon, staying only one night at the St. Paul hotel and camping the rest of the time in Iowa, Nebraska, Colorado, Utah, Oregon, Washington, and then back across the northern tier. They had hoped also to get to Lake Louise and Banff in Alberta, but ran out of time. Highlights of the trip included setting up camp in problematic places, such as inadvertently in a lover's lane in Iowa (a cop came by and offered congratulations) and amidst a herd of cattle in Colorado (causing city-girl Gretchen to "whip right back" into their mountain tent).

———•◆•———

There was a living to be made, so they both dropped out of St. Olaf in 1948 to work on the farm. Quie's parents were getting ready to move to Northfield, but the four of them shared the house for about three months which, he says, was a "little difficult" for

As she waits for bread to rise, Gretchen shows oldest son Fred how to sketch pots. She had already started what came to be an extensive collection of pottery.

Gretchen, not that he realized it at the time. "Good thing we had four weeks of a honeymoon."

The house had little in the way of furniture after the senior Quies left, except for a large oak dining room table bought at the Salvation Army store in Minneapolis. "Gretchen and I would put all the leaves in and she would sit at one end and I would sit at the other. We were just like a couple of wealthy people, sitting at the far ends. We would scoot serving dishes, *zoop*, across to each other."

But it wasn't only sharing a home with her in-laws, albeit for a short time, that was hard for Gretchen in the early years. Not only had she grown up in the Twin Cities, she was also an artist, talented enough that her departmental chairman at St. Olaf hoped she would succeed him some day. But just as Gretchen hadn't aspired to be a farm wife, her new husband didn't want her to be a routine one.

"It was either for her birthday the first year we were married or for Christmas, probably Christmas, I bought her a real good easel. I put a note on it to the effect that, 'God made you an artist, and I don't want you to be a typical farmer's wife. I want you to follow what God wants you to be.'"

Yet while Gretchen did do some teaching at St. Olaf in the following years, and while she finally completed her degree in 1971, her days quickly came to be filled with the farm and its countless chores, especially as her husband's many civic activities expanded into perpetual political activities and obligations, resulting in his frequently being away from the 240-acre, mostly dairy, operation. "In the beginning," Quie said,

> Gretchen didn't feel accepted in the church and community, because many of the other women would say, "She's got college." It was a problem. Most college people in that part of Minnesota moved away back then. It took a while for her to adjust, she has since told me. I couldn't tell so much then. You're so busy with your own things and insensitive to that. After a while, when the kids came, she learned to love the farm very much. She stayed on the farm alone during my first year in Congress, 1958, with just the (then) four kids and the hired man.

As Minnesotans and many others know, Gretchen has led a life immersed in art in different genres and ways. In addition to her own creations, for example, in the mid-1980s she co-owned "Celebration Design" in St. Paul, a shop she described as a "Gallery of Christian Art." And her 1981 book, *In the Potter's Hand* (written with Karen M. Hess), was exceptionally well-received—as witness its amazon.com ratings.

Quie himself returned to St. Olaf after a year once he realized he wanted the degree to do what he sought to do. Going to school and farming both fulltime, he graduated with a degree in political science in 1950. He actually had wanted to double up his academic load and graduate a semester sooner. ("I was just going to cram through.") But he was talked out of it by his adviser, who said "you'd kill yourself doing all that." The comment was a foreshadowing of how he pushed himself injuriously hard when serving in the Minnesota Senate.

Fourteen months after getting married, "that wonderful little guy Fred came along."

Then we were so blessed by Jennie, to have a daughter. Then Dan came along, who looked like Gretchen's family but who has more of my nature than any of the others. Then Joel came along, who was unique from the other three. Gretchen and I had thought they'd come boy, girl, boy, girl, so when our fourth child left the hospital, he didn't have a name. We were going to name the new baby Martha, but it didn't work for him. And then, six years after Joel, Ben was born when we were in Congress. To see him loved by his siblings so enormously was just wonderful.

Saying that he got "a kick out of it," Quie also made certain to recount the afternoon he and Gretchen told his family they would have their first child. "At the dinner table—dinner was at noon on the farm—we had just told everyone that Gretchen was going to have a baby. A little while later, Dad, Paul, and I were walking out to do work again, with my father walking ahead of us. I glanced over at Paul, and Paul looked over at me, and he just said, 'Naughty!'"

In telling the story, Quie's laughter was particularly hearty. Recalling it is also probably the right time to note his unsolicited comment that, "Gretchen and I were virgins when we got married," a fact for which he gave greatest credit to her moral integrity.

———— • ◆ • ————

"Talk to me more about each of the kids," I asked. Quie remembered one scene soon after they moved to Silver Spring, Maryland, from the Minnesota farm. Moments after Gretchen opened a bag of dried cow manure to fertilize a backyard garden, the kids circled around and inhaled it, enjoying the nostalgic fragrance. Quie said it either brought back smells of the farm or of their father. He opened the family album by introducing Cinder, a Doberman pinscher "I really loved. We were as close as a man and dog can be."

So here comes Fred, and he gets to the age where he's toddling now. I would say, "Fred, come here," and Cinder, knowing that Fred was competing for affection, would take her rear end, and in her excitement bump against him and knock him down. We would chastise her, but we all thought it was funny, including Fred.

Note: Neither Fred nor Cinder was ever injured, not even a little. No doctors or vets were ever required. Back to Quie:

I would say to Cinder, "Corner," and she'd lie down in the corner. I'd say, "Couch," and she'd jump on the plastic-covered couch. If I said, "Basement," she'd zip down to the basement. Fred was taking all this in, and after a while, when I would say, "Corner," he would dive for the corner and beat her there. I'd say, "Couch," and he'd head for the couch. And when I'd say, "Basement," she would go whizzing by him. Fred couldn't have seen it as sibling rivalry, since he was an only child at the time, but it still was competition for somebody else's affection.

"What's Fred doing now?"

Fred is an industrial archeologist, working on Super Fund projects, especially with mining operations out west. He also writes and is doing a book on Rosie the Riveter and has written one on bridges. He loves architecture. When he and his wife Melinda lived in Butte, Montana, the city was well beyond its heyday. I would be walking with him out there and we'd go to some old house, a big house, and he'd say, "Come in here. I want you to see something." He'd show me the beauty of the banister of this big stairway that comes around. And he'd say, "Look at that stained glass." He could capture the artistic beauty plus, I think, the pathos of bygone days and what the people were like. It's an amazing ability he has.

Fred is very liberal, and I kid him that he's gotten more conservative so that he's a Democrat now.

"He had been to the left of that?"

Yes, to the left of that. But it's so marvelous to have a son and a daughter-in-law who are just so liberal, because we engage in conversation and I learn so many things from them that I wouldn't have known. I really wouldn't have known anyone that far left unless I'd intentionally connected with them, which I've done a few times. They live in Philadelphia and Melinda—the Rev. Melinda Quivik—teaches at the Lutheran seminary there.

Yet Quie didn't always see Fred's politics and associated activities as so marvelous, though the following story, he acknowledges, is more about him than his son.

When Fred was at St. Olaf and so liberal politically he also had a beard and it was a real struggle for me, especially since I went to Congress with a butch haircut. He asked me at Christmas during that first year about whether I had smoked cigarettes, I said no, but I suspected it wasn't tobacco he was talking about. Then his political views started moving further left, with the Vietnam War and so forth. I was supporting the president and you could tell it was really bothering him that he had a Republican for a father. I was in agony about him. I could lose myself in my work and I could lose myself at home with the family, but driving to and from the Capitol in D.C. was agony. I was just struggling, talking to God about this son of mine.

A friend who, according to Quie, had just come to Christ himself, urged him to read a book about an alcoholic for whom nothing helped until his family decided to "just praise God for him."

I read the book and I said, "Okay, that's what I'm going to do." So I praised God for Fred as I was driving to work and then when I drove home every day. When you're praising God, you don't just say, "Praise God. Praise God." Instead, you start thinking about these wonderful things about Him, and I thought about pictures that depict Jesus Christ with a beard and long hair and I said, "I've got to change my attitude." So that's what happened and about thirty days later, I got a letter from Fred that said, "Dad, I just want you to know that Jesus Christ has come into my life," or however a Lutheran would say it. He also said that he was never going to touch marijuana again. I had never said a word to him about this for those thirty days and it was a long time before I said anything to him afterwards, either. But I was just astounded by that.

Fred goes by the last name of "Quivik," which is a merging with his wife's maiden name of Kravik. "At first I was upset when he changed his name," the governor said. "Wasn't he proud of me? But then I realized I was the one who was different, as all of my ancestors had changed their last names." Notably, his father's family spelled their named "K-v-i" even after coming to the United States.
"What about Jennie?"

You had to talk to Fred if he did something wrong. With Jennie, you just had to scowl and she would react. I could see in a girl, and with her, a much more sensitive nature. Fred is as sensitive as can be, but in a different way. To have a lovely daughter like that is just delightful, watching her grow and develop.

Jennie is married to Dave Coffin, a pastor of the Presbyterian Church of America and they live in Fairfax, Virginia. They have three children, a boy and two girls, plus four grandchildren. And as opposed to Fred and Melinda, Jennie and Dave are very conservative. The four of them don't engage in debate with each other, but I do it with all of them. *I* really enjoy it.

Jennie is an outstanding artist. In fact, all five kids have inherited Gretchen's artistic ability to some extent, every one of them. Jennie teaches and is a potter now. Some of her works are in galleries, so you know she's pretty good. I was more concerned with Jennie growing up than I was with the boys. That really concerned me.

"Concerned you how?"

You're just more protective of your daughter. You figure your sons can take care of themselves. What kind of guy is she going to bring home? Here's something about Jennie. She came to me one day, probably at the beginning of her junior year in high school in Silver Spring, and said there were drugs being sold in school, and she wondered what she ought to do about it. "Now Jennie," I said, "you're going to have to make this decision yourself. You can't do something, in this instance, because that's what your father wants you to do. But if you want to turn this guy in, I will help you with the authorities." Jennie didn't turn him in, but her friends thought she had because I was in Congress and all that. They called her a "narc" and she lost all her friends. So here's our daughter in total loneliness. The only people who were still her friends were her own family—just like when I was in eighth grade and refused to take part in a rebellion against our teacher.

Now here's what happened next. Jennie was befriended by some Young Life kids at school, who probably had been too conservative for her. She came to a really active faith in Jesus Christ because of them, and she led her brother Dan, and he led his brother Joel, and they all became active in Young Life. So the drug episode had a significant impact.

Here's one more story about Quie's daughter before giving equal time for the next three boys:

Jennie became a Charismatic and was going to a Charismatic church in Norfolk, Virginia, where she was in college at Old Dominion. ["Charismatic" is an umbrella term that describes Christians who believe that the manifestations of the Holy Spirit seen in the first century, such as miracles, prophecy, and speaking in tongues, may be experienced and practiced today.] She became romantically involved with a member of the church who had been doing and selling drugs, and who had served time, but who had gone straight. So she was getting ready to come home with this guy who, in my view, was absolutely not someone I wanted for my daughter. But they planned on getting married. Gretchen and I discussed what we would do when they got there, and we decided we were going to be supportive, because if we were negative in any way, they would just move their own way. They arrived, and I talked to the young man and said, "I believe in forgiveness and rehabilitation, and I accept you." That loving acceptance just caught both of them off guard. As they were getting ready to go back to Norfolk, Gretchen went to Jennie and asked, "Are you sure this is the person you want to marry?" Jennie began to cry and said, "No, I've come to realize he isn't the one."

"We're up to Dan."

"Boy, his nature as a mountain man started right off the bat. Gretchen would try to keep eyes on him, and he'd just move and travel around the farmstead. Finally, we put up one of those wood-slat snow fences and made a yard that would hold him. It was the only way we could keep him out of trouble." Quie told the story of a 55-gallon barrel of oil and how Dan "just went up there and turned on the spigot and all the oil ran out all over the garage floor."

"How old was he at the time?"

"Oh, he was probably two and a half."

"You were preparing to unhitch a team of horses at that age."

No, Quie corrected me. "I was about three."

Then there was the time that Dan took the bayonet gauge for testing the oil for the tractor.

"I asked, 'Dan, where is it?' A little kid like that, he didn't remember, but I couldn't use the tractor without it. How was I going to find another? A while later I just happened to be down by the barn, which is quite a long ways away, and there, outside a barn window where you could see all the milking going on inside, was the bayonet gauge. So there were all those adventures with Dan."

Quie then told a story about when Dan was about four, in which it's impossible not to remember his own father's farm accident.

Quie demonstrating the finer points of milking to son Dan in 1958.

He was an inquisitive guy. I was gassing up the tractor and the three oldest kids were standing there. "Now you stand back," I said and they all went back by a tree. I was adjusting some parts and Dan came over and stuck his finger in to see if a part was sharp. It was and it cut through his thumb nail and part way back to the knuckle. The nail, bone, the whole thing was split into two sides.

Gretchen couldn't go with us to the doctor because Joel was too little and she had to take care of the other kids, too. So I headed off to the doctor with Dan who, even though he had been given a shot to deaden the pain on our arrival, struggled so the doctor couldn't finish sewing him up. I was holding Dan, but the doctor couldn't do it. "I guess," I said, "we'll just have to leave it that way."

From Quie's current description, the scar isn't as bad as it might
have been.

"What does he do now?"

Dan lives in Vadnais Heights and manages a number of gravel
operations. He started out in Montana, and he's the one who did all
things I dreamed of doing.

"Such as?"

In the summertime, when he was in high school, he began
working on ranches. He worked on a race horse farm in
Kentucky one summer. Then he went to work for the U.S.
Forest Service in Montana, first for a summer during college
and then full time. He worked on a trail crew with the horses
and ran a pack string, hauling in timber and supplies. He was
then put in charge, but he left the Forest Service because they
began integrating men and women in two-person teams. The
crew member they assigned him was a very pretty girl, so if
the two of them continued working together, they'd be out on
the trail for ten days alone. He said he wouldn't do that, as it
was just against his principles. His superiors said he had to, so
he left the Forest Service and went to work for an outfitter,
also in Montana. He wound up marrying the boss' daughter,
Penny Jo Hoeffner, and they ran elk hunting camps, so he
became an excellent elk hunter. He also would do marvelous
things such as herd and bring out 20 head of horses east of the
Rockies onto the prairie, 40 miles away, to spend the winter.
In the spring, he would go out and bring them back. I asked
him how he could ride a horse fast for 40 miles. He said he
roped a different horse at 20 miles to herd them the next 20.

"So of the five kids, he seems, by far, most in love with the outdoors?"

"Oh, he is, by far, yes. He really knows the outdoors. But Fred does,
too, with his political and environmental interest thrown in. We've done
a lot of things together out-of-doors. But when Dan and Penny Jo had
three kids of their own, he didn't want to be out in the mountains for
long periods away from them, so he quit outfitting and eventually went
to work for a gravel operation back here in Minnesota."

Dan and Penny Jo subsequently divorced—the only divorce among the five children—and his new wife, Luanne, according to her father-in-law, is a "wonderful woman." Quie also volunteered that, "When people say divorce is hell for the kids, I've seen it. It's so difficult."

"What about Joel?"

Joel has always had a great sense of humor and sees the funny side of life. Neither he nor Fred liked horses like Dan and I did. When we lived in Silver Spring, I'd get up early in the morning and rub my whip on the screen and say, "I'm all saddled up. You guys jump into your clothes, we're going riding." Joel was never very enthusiastic about doing that. But both Joel and Fred had a keen love of baseball. Fred picked it up from neighbors and Joel picked it up from Fred. They knew *all* the statistics of all the players and all the teams in the majors. They also played a kind of baseball, using a sack swing on what remained of a big locust tree I cut down.

"Joel is the minister, right?"

Yes, he's a Lutheran pastor, at Prairie Lutheran Church in Eden Prairie, Minnesota. He's the least direct of all the kids, and he meets people where they are. He doesn't say, "Here's where I stand and that's not where you are." That makes him an excellent pastor. He really wasn't turned on to school when he was young. After high school he went out to a place called Holden Village, a Lutheran study center on Lake Chelen, in the North Cascade Mountains of Washington State, for a whole year. That's where he met his wife, Sarah. There were twelve students and fifteen professors out there on sabbatical.

"Nice ratio," I said.

"That's where he learned Greek. He came back for Christmas vacation, and he was doing all that conjugating. When he went to Luther Seminary in St. Paul, instead of studying Greek, he tutored other people in it."

Talking about Joel's wife Sarah, Quie mentioned her own, lay ministry: "I told you the story of how Gretchen didn't go out with me the first time because she didn't dance when she was at St. Olaf. Well, Sarah teaches liturgical dance, and she's just marvelous. It brings tears to my eyes when I see her portraying sermons and liturgy through dance."

Joel and Sarah (who have three children) had done a short stretch of graduate work in Graz, Austria. According to Quie, Joel had been concerned about learning German fast enough, but in the six weeks he was there, he became surprisingly proficient in the language. In addition to German and Greek, he also learned to speak French and Aramaic.

At this point, I asked Quie if he took particular satisfaction that one of his children—in addition to a son-in-law and a daughter-in-law—is ordained. The exchange that followed was reminiscent of one, a week earlier, when I asked if he had ever thought how special his parents were and how favored his home life had been. His first answer then was not really, although it changed a few minutes later upon additional consideration.

"I take satisfaction in all those kids," he said this time around.

"I know *that*," I said.

"I'm trying to think about that. No, I don't view Joel's ordination as anything special compared to what the others have done. Now, why is that? I don't know."

"I wasn't juxtaposing Joel against the other kids, but I was focusing on the idea that you have a child who's ordained. I remember when my wife was ordained. It was very special. Have I asked a question that you really haven't considered?"

"No," he said, "I haven't considered that. But I'm trying to think now how that's so."

After a short pause, Quie went on:

"As I think back to when Joel was ordained, when they laid hands on him, I remember my feeling about how that was a more thrilling experience than when I was sworn in as governor. So I guess that's right. I do take a special kind of satisfaction in his being ordained. I hadn't thought back on that."

This new insight led to a lovely and loving soliloquy.

When I think about this, I think about Fred and how he's so excellent in what he does as an industrial archeologist. He's so good. When you look at Jennie—you can hear the pride in my voice—she has some of her pottery in art galleries. It's so good. When you think of Dan, he did what I wanted to do. When we're together, we don't even have to talk because we're so in sync with each other. Look at Joel and his capacity for languages that I've never had and his ability to proclaim the Word of God in his sermons. He uses drama and everything. The truth of the Word comes through. And then when you look at Ben, who's a home remodeler, his quality of work is such that people wait up to two years to get him.

Five kids, and you see in them all the things that are not in me. I realize, "Man! How blessed I am. How God has blessed me." Then I see so much in them that I see in Gretchen as well as in her relatives. So much comes from Gretchen. What a blessing it was that we walked up from two sides in Ytterboe Hall and I saw her on that landing.

Ben, the youngest of the five, is the one Quie child I've known halfway well, but that was 25 years ago when he was barely out of high school during his father's time as governor. When I was informed that one of Ben and his wife Virginia's four kids was about to be married, I realized I hadn't kept up. "Tell me more about Ben," I asked. He and Virginia live in St. Anthony Park, a St. Paul neighborhood.

"Ben came six years after Joel, and what I noticed first was there's no such thing as too much love, as he prospered in the love of his sister and brothers." (All of the other four children were born two years apart.)

"But I recall he had problems along the way," I was compelled to note.

"Yes, he did have problems, but they weren't from too much love. One of the other things I noticed was his mechanical ability. I had been in Japan and bought an electric shaver there. After a while, it didn't work well anymore. It was just too weak. So since Ben loved to take things apart, I told him, if he wanted to take it apart to see how it worked, he could. So he went up to his room and he came back a short time later and it was working much better, even better than when I bought it new."

"How old was he at the time?"

Oh, maybe he was nine or ten, if that. He wasn't a good student though. We worked and pushed him, because we found that if we didn't push him, he would fail. But he'd get only a "D" even when we did push him. In the ninth grade we decided to get him tested, and the school psychologist said, "First I want to say that you and Gretchen are to be commended because of the strong character your son has. But here's what we've found: When we were with him, he read at the twelfth grade level. But when there was no one in the room, he read at the sixth grade level."

"More than interesting," I said.

Yes, it was fascinating. So Gretchen and I asked, "What do you suggest?" The psychologist said there weren't any good public school options in the Silver Spring district and urged us to put him in a private school. But this went against all my principles, because up until that time, I was a *total* believer in public schools and racially integrated schools, and the latter was one of the reasons we picked a school in Montgomery County, Maryland, in the first place. We would have gone to Virginia, but they were closing public schools in order not to integrate when Gretchen and the family came there to live at the end of 1958. So I just had to bite that bullet, and we sent him to Harker Preparatory School in Potomac, Maryland. They ran from eight to twelve students in a class, and by the end of that first school year, Ben was in the National Honor Society.

"That was a nice jump," I understated.

One of the things Ben did after high school was study to be a nurse's assistant, and because his academic skills and confidence had improved and because the subject matter was important to him, he was better equipped to study, retain, and perform well.

"Then I saw another thing had happened to him," Quie said. "He was learning to understand patients and he would tell warm and funny stories about them. There was this woman (I'll call her 'Katie') who was very small and who was supposed to get up and exercise, but she didn't want to. So Ben got her out of bed and held her up by her armpits. Now, Ben was about six-foot-two.

"'Katie, you've got to walk,' Ben said.

"'But I can't,' she objected.

"'You've got to try,' Ben implored.

"'But I can't,' she insisted again.

"'Why not?'

"'Because my feet aren't touching the floor.'"

Stories like that, Quie said, witnessed a combination of understanding and persistence on the part of his son, of which he was proud. They also highlighted the importance of truly listening, another theme we will return to over and over.

Quie went on to talk about how Ben's experience at Harker reinforced his preference for small classes. But he also talked about how his decision to send his son to a private school further displeased the National Education Association, which was never enamored with him at the time.

"I had always wanted to have the support of the NEA, and I had some friends there. But they didn't like some of the things I believed in, and our sending Ben to Harker ended whatever good relationship we had." In later years, Quie was to become an increasingly strong advocate for educational freedom, including the right of parents, especially low-income ones, to send their children to the schools of their choice, public or private, religious or secular.

———•◆•———

Not long after we talked about Quie's adult children and their spouses, along with his grandchildren and great-grandchildren, he and Gretchen vacationed with 21 of them on Minnesota's North Shore, on Lake Superior.

The whole family at their home in Silver Spring, Maryland, in 1965.
Starting with Quie and moving clockwise: Fred, Jennie, Gretchen, Ben,
Dan, and Joel. Nonni is front and center.

"Would you say the week went well?"

"Oh, yes!" was his exclamation of an answer, not just because of
the scenery from atop Lookout Mountain, but also because it afforded
him an extended opportunity for serious but always mannerly
conversations with generations of loved ones about very tough
subjects, not the least of which was the war in Iraq. Quie's term of art
for such exchanges is "congenial disputation."

All told, Al and Gretchen have fourteen grandchildren and six
great-grandchildren.

For a host of reasons, starting with the deep and capacious love
that radiates for his children through each of these five portraits, it's
not a leap to assume that Al Quie was a wonderful father. But also

clear, particularly as revealed in the first chapter, is the high standard to which he holds himself. I think about the several times he criticized himself in our early sessions for not spending enough time with his family during his days in elected office, especially early on. There was a period, for instance, as a young congressman when he got back from his district in Minnesota, but for two weeks none of the kids knew he had returned to Maryland, since he left for appointments and meetings at the Capitol early in the morning before they woke up and then returned home at night after they had gone to sleep. "That was bad fathering," he told me, striking the table for emphasis (just about the only time I remember him doing that).

This segues to saying that Gretchen has been a magnificent mother to five children, raised and nurtured under often unusually demanding circumstances. The kind of hard routes, without question, routinely faced by many, perhaps most, wives of major political leaders. But hard routes in her case were made even tougher, especially during their first decade of their marriage, by the dawn-to-dusk calls of farm life.

What kinds of lessons might she have taught her children? By dint of sacrifice, how might she have driven home essential rules about honesty in particular? Somehow, and at the risk of ruining the mood, it's time for another story about the *Congressional Record.*

I want to tell you something about Gretchen's integrity. We were on a vacation out in Colorado and we realized we hadn't packed some things, like winter jackets, so I called someone on my staff to send them to us. The big package arrived, but there was no postage on it. I wondered how in the world it came that way. We opened it up, and there, lying on top of the clothes, was a single *Congressional Record.* The rule in Congress is that they're sent for free.

Well, Gretchen was really upset. "Never let that happen ever again," she declared. She also declared that I would indeed be talking to the staffer who did it. To me, the rule-bending was surprising, and he shouldn't have done it. But to Gretchen, it was entirely contrary to her ethical standards. I mention this

because when you know your spouse lives by such standards,
it enriches the whole relationship.

Quie did not seek re-election as governor in 1982, and in 1983 he
and Gretchen moved back to Rice County, not far from the family
farm. A number of months later I got in touch to set a day to visit them
for a Sunday brunch. Quie wasn't around when I called, and in talking
with Gretchen, I said something about how she must enjoy being back
in the country. "No," she said matter-of-factly, "I like the city."

Not long after that, they returned to the Cities, as Minnesotans call
the Minneapolis–St. Paul area. But in what's easy to interpret as a
continuation of lives in concert, I can't begin to describe the
beautifully rustic home and neighborhood they found.

Chapter Three

Religious Roots and Branches
"More like rivers gushing"

"How come," I asked Quie not long into our conversations, "you never sought ordination?"

"The short answer," he said, "was that I was ticked off at God."

Even by the standard of to-the-point answers, this was a rather crisp one. I followed up by asking when and why he was so displeased with a God he loved so much. He went on to talk about the time, shortly after he left the Navy following World War II, when others with whom he had served were entering "pre-sem" programs, but when he just "didn't sense any calling to go into the ministry."

"Did you want to have the call?"

"Oh, yes," he said, although he wasn't nearly as enthused by the same idea as a child, when some of his aunts would say, "Albert, you're going to be a minister someday." That had "shocked" him back then, although he had taken comfort that being a minister wasn't as bad as being a missionary in a distant country, like those that members of his extended family were then supporting. "I sure didn't want to be a missionary to China."

"Why not?"

"Go live in China or Africa? Good land! That wasn't anything I wanted to do."

That was around the same time when Quie's father wanted to help him and his three siblings learn how to handle money, so he gave him an allowance of 25 cents a month.

The first thing I did was save two months of allowance and with that I bought a jackknife, which led to quite a discussion with my dad about whether that was the right thing to do, because he was teaching us tithing at the same time. So here I am, I'm going to have to tithe now. How do you find ten percent of 25 cents? Do you round down, which I wanted to do, to two cents? In my mind, I thought God must be this irascible God. So I figured, well, I'm not taking any chances here, so I put three cents aside for Him.

I continued saving my allowance until I was probably twelve years old and Dad asked me where I wanted the money to go. "I want to send it to the China mission," I said, thinking if I did so, God would send someone else there. So Dad—and this shows how wise he was in driving home the lesson about tithing—he took me to Minneapolis, which took a long while in those days, to the office of the Evangelical Lutheran Church, so I could hand the money to Dr. Henry Shurson, the head of foreign missions.

"Do you remember how much money it was?"

"No, I don't know, but I can still see Dr. Shurson in his three-piece suit and that chain across his vest. I hadn't seen anyone at that point who was rotund with a chain across his vest that way. I was intrigued by that, but I sat there saying nothing, as Dr. Shurson and Dad discussed missions and all."

When Quie had been married for a year, still wondering why no call to ministry had come from God, he attended a series of classes in Northfield taught by two professors, Carlyle Holte and Howard Hong, on the doctrine of vocation.

As I sat there, they quoted Martin Luther when he said that a farmer pitching manure and a maid scrubbing a floor are doing work in the sight of God as great as a monk on his knees praying in a monastery. Well, Gretchen was scrubbing floors, and I surely was pitching manure on our farm, because we didn't have an automatic barn cleaner yet. And it was just like, "Hey, you can be in politics and serve God." That just came to me, and I decided I was going to finish St. Olaf but switch from majoring in chemistry to being a political science major. That's when I realized that God had gifted me in this whole area of politics.

Quie had already served on the local (very small) school board and had been involved in Republican politics at St. Olaf as chairman of the Republican Club, among other political activities. "In effect," he later would say, "I was ordained for politics."

I noted at this juncture that on a couple of occasions, Quie had spoken of moments when he had similar revelations about larger matters in his life. After we agreed that "epiphanies" was a better description, he asked with a laugh, "Doesn't everybody have them?"

Before picking chemistry as a major as a St. Olaf freshman, he had hoped to attend Cornell University in Ithaca, New York, where he could major in soil science, but various complications at home—including his father's injury, his brother's education, and then getting married himself—kept him in Minnesota. His choice of chemistry as a major was inspired in large part by his father's vivid interest in soil conservation and conservation issues generally. The fact that his dad had majored in chemistry for the short period he was at St. Olaf himself possibly contributed to his decision, too.

"I was moved," Quie said, "by what my dad had helped me understand about the whole question of soil conservation and stewardship of the soil. I was really turned on by that. I figured that if I was going to do something for God, the best thing would be to learn to be a soil scientist so we could learn how to produce enough food so there wouldn't be any hunger in the world."

But referring again to the Holte and Hong lectures in 1949 and factoring in how he was better comprehending his talent and interest in politics, "I came to realize that when you accept a call to Jesus Christ, you are called in whatever your occupation is and however God has gifted you. I had previously thought, how could you go into politics and do what it says in the Scriptures—care for the widows and children and keep yourself unstained from the world? Politics didn't seem like it was very much unstained from the world." This observation was followed by a chuckle. But as with the insight above, "It just came to me: Hey, this is okay. Politics is okay. So I became a political science major in my senior year."

———•◆•———

These episodes describe the spiritual underpinnings of Quie's early thoughts about a life in politics; a pursuit that obviously we'll focus much more on in coming chapters, starting with the next one, when we dig into the philosophical bases of his political views. Clear and continuing throughout will be an intimate and concrete melding of his faith with all other aspects of his life.

Some readers, I take for granted, will view as disconcerting, even threatening, the phrase just above: "an intimate and concrete melding of his faith with all other aspects of his life." They will read infusions of his religious commitments into his political activities as problematic, even dangerous, seeing the mix as inviting assaults on the wall separating church and state, leading possibly, even inescapably, to incivility and much worse. Let me do away with such fears, pronto, wherever and with whomever they might exist.

One of the remarkable things about Al Quie is that it's impossible to spend any time with him without experiencing his ecumenical arms embracing all. Skeptics of various sorts often assume an inverse relationship between a person's strength of denominational belief and his or her tolerance and love for "others." It's a fallacious and intolerant assumption far more often than not. In Quie's case, it's absurdly so.

During his Navy stint, for instance, in order to understand better the beliefs of a Mormon buddy, he read the Book of Mormon. His mother might not have been entirely happy about it, but Quie found profit. In more recent years, in order to understand Muslims better, he read the Koran—twice. Again, he was pleased that he reached out for a variety of reasons, one of which, he says, is that reading both the Book of Mormon and the Koran deepened his own faith in Jesus Christ.

"How," he asked during one of our conversations, "do you live in grace with one another?" Answering his own question, he said, "It's by respecting people for the way the idea of the transcendent comes to them." Quie does so as completely as anyone I've ever known.

Of similar cloth, a little more than two months into our conversations, I started a morning session by asking if he wanted to fill in any gaps from previous weeks. No, he said, but he did want to make certain that the book's early chapters (the ones I was then writing) would "carry the threads connecting what I do and that form my principles: my faith in God and my relationships with people." I said it would be impossible *not* to accentuate two streams so strong—more like rivers gushing—and that the book would return to them repeatedly. And as attested by our dozens of hours of conversations during the project, as well as everything I've ever known about him, when Quie speaks of his "relationships with people," I'm here to report he means everyone.

Nevertheless, a few weeks later, in a conversation about why he describes himself as a "follower of Jesus Christ" rather than as a "Christian," he said, "When you follow Christ, you tend to want to be around other people who do so as well," as a person "can get joy out of that." He also said, seemingly in direct opposition to what I grandly claimed just above about his enveloping arms and love: "I read once that a person who comes to be a believer, in a couple of years, they have all new friends."

To which I said, "There's no question that your range of friends and contacts is very broad. But if a person changes all his friends because he's a believer, how do you make certain that you maintain a wide variety of friends?"

After a short pause, Quie said, "I think that comes from having a comfort in the way God made you. Have I told you about the first black man I ever saw?"

He hadn't, and proceeded to recall his first visit to the Minnesota State Fair, in St. Paul, around 1929 or 1930, when he was almost six or seven years old.

When I was a little kid, my dad and mother, along with the wife of a cousin of his, took their two families up to the State Fair. Olaus Finseth was the cousin's name. Selma and Olaus' kids were about the ages of my brother, sisters, and me, so we'd get together real often on weekends. To make it possible for families to spend a couple of days at the Fair, there was sort of a tent city, and for a kid, staying in one of them was a fun thing to do.

With all these tents around, my parents pointed out to me where the latrine was, in a green building. Well, I woke up the next morning and had to go to the bathroom bad, and I took off from our tent and ran to that place. But just as I came to the door, it opened, and a black man came out. I had never seen a black man before in my life. When I saw him, I was so shocked that I turned around and ran back to the tent, forgetting all about relieving myself.

When I look back on that, it's a child running to his comfort zone. I think that's what people do. When they're insecure, they run to their comfort zone. There's a security in being around people of similar faith. That's one of the reasons people belong to churches or synagogues or mosques. It's where they can belong.

Quie paraphrased here the famous Robert Frost line, "Home is the place where, when you have to go there, they have to take you in." But then, in getting to the nub of the concern I raised about people of passionate faith cloistering amongst their own, he spoke of reaching out as one becomes more secure. "You reach out to people, hoping they'll know the truth as you do." But in doing so, he acknowledged with pleasure, "you might find that they know some truth that you didn't."

God is a just God. God is a loving God. Christians came to believe in this man Jesus Christ. We believe He is the Son of God. That He was crucified to take away the sins of the world. And that He rose again and gives us hope for the future. In Him I find truth. We come out of the whole Hebrew and Jewish past, so the Old Testament and your heritage, Mitch, are part of this. Then you look at the Muslim faith, and that grew out of it, too. Each of us has our way of believing and coming to conclusions.

If we insist that everybody believe like we do, then we're forcing other people outside. God put us all here together on this earth and we try to make this American experiment work. How can we live in grace with each other and at the same time have different beliefs and all look for truth?

Yet as powerful as his beliefs are ("I don't remember my spiritual birth, and I don't remember my physical birth, but I'm sure of both of them"), Quie then allowed, "You always have to have that question in the back of your mind: What if I'm wrong? So you have to be open to listening. There has to be intentionality about it. My faith in Jesus Christ is paramount. But we haven't got a corner on belief. We can learn from other people, too."

Later in the same conversation, we were talking about how, growing up in rural Minnesota, two things "kept me from being narrow." One, as discussed in the first chapter, was his family's remarkably substantial conversations around the supper table every day, especially about politics and religion. But now he also noted the "global" interests and commitments of his family's local church, Grace Lutheran. The congregation was explicit in believing that "God loved all the people in the world and that we have a responsibility to people everywhere, in China, in Africa. It just gave me a different concept and made a big impression on me."

———— • ◆ • ————

While he talked frequently about how often he prayed, it finally occurred to me that I should ask the obvious: "Governor, exactly what do you pray about?"

My first thing in the morning is that I open myself to God, meeting Him first thing. The fresher I am, the better I think I'm listening to Him. I start out just praying to God that I will love Him, serve Him, be obedient to Him in everything I do, and have faith all the days of my life. Then I move out to people. First in the family, I pray for everybody beginning with Gretchen. I think about them and pray for all of them. Then I move to people who have illnesses, and people who have been in prison or who are still in prison. Then I move to leadership and pray for them. That's where my prayers run.

Then I pick up my copy of *My Utmost for His Highest* by Oswald Chambers, and I read the daily devotion there. I've been reading it now since 1977. Each page begins with a Bible passage, and I have a Bible by me. I think about the passage, which is frequently very familiar now after 30 years. If a new thought comes to me and I want to check back, I open my Bible and meditate on what it means both for me and my relationships with other people. Then I listen and just let the thoughts come to me. Out of that, sometimes I take a pad and write down notes. I didn't used to do that because I could remember everything I thought about. But now, sometimes [he's laughing here] I come to the end and I think, "What was that again?"

I write down things that are important to me, like my relationship with Gretchen. I also write about my involvement with organizations and programs such as Prison Fellowship Ministries and the InnerChange Freedom Initiative at Lino Lakes Correctional Institution. I was chair of InnerChange for a long time. I think about all of that, and what comes through is what I would describe as the importance I put in congruity and integrity. Running through all of this is my conviction that what I believe, what I say, and what I do all have to be in harmony with each other. And when it isn't, I tackle the inconsistency.

Quie went on to talk about how this conception applies to issues as diverse as protecting the impartiality of the judiciary, expanding early childhood education, and improving the governance of organizations more generally. "I am convinced that if there is not similar congruity in an organization, it corrupts its soul," he said.

Quie's shift over the last several paragraphs, from the personally sublime to the organizationally fundamental, is anything but subtle. But it's sublimely and fundamentally him. Often in our sessions he spoke about how he's compelled to figure out how organizations and groups of all kinds, sacred and secular equally, can be improved. How their governance can be more responsive. How their aims can be more just and riveted on pursuing truth. How their performance can be made more effective and helpful—especially for people without power.

A few weeks earlier I had noted that there was no part of him—or no more than a very small part—that says, "I'm 84. I've made my contributions. I'm just going to sit back, relax, and spend more time smelling roses." But rather, I remarked to him, "You still have a drive to make just about everything you come into contact with better."

"Yes."

"You have to fiddle with it all."

"Yes, fiddle with it all." And laughing at the thought, he said, "If you don't do that, you'll die."

"Call it a compulsion? Call it your instinct? Call it your temperament? What would you call it?"

"To me, it's giftedness. I think everybody has a gift. People need to do what they're gifted at."

Returning to details about his prayer life, he continued, "All this is part of it. But a lot of it is listening and letting those thoughts come over my life. How does a person know where those thoughts are coming from? It could be the devil. It could be other things. It could be you. I've learned to have confidence in listening to God. That's it."

On another occasion, he said he liked Mother Teresa's response when she was asked what she said to God.

"I don't say anything," she said, "I just listen."

"And what does He say to you?"

"He doesn't say anything. He just listens."

Quie completed the thought by citing something he had read long ago about how a settler had once met a group of Native Americans in a general store. They told him, "We had a most wonderful visit with you." But the settler, recalling no such visit, asked incredulously, "Visit with me?"

The Native Americans, the governor said, "had come and sat with their backs to his cabin and they communed with him that way, just to be in his presence." Quie said he viewed this "as a spiritual presence."

Also on another occasion, he talked about how farming—which he views as a stewardship—likewise had a "tremendous impact" on his prayer life. "You know, when you're plowing or disking or anything like that, you go to one end and then back to the other end, time after time. You would think that would be enormously monotonous, but that's when I asked myself: 'What are you going to do? Who are you going to talk to? Who are you going to listen to?' I began talking and listening to God."

Reverting to the pedestrian on my part, given that Quie touches so many bases in his prayers when he rises, I asked how long it takes to complete them.

"Well it depends on what else I have to do in the morning. They run about a half-hour if I'm in a hurry and about an hour-and-a-half if I'm not in a hurry."

"That's a lot of time," I said, even more mundanely. "Do you ever view your morning prayers as a chore? Or are they always a great joy?"

"The half-hour ones are a chore."

"They're a chore, the shorter ones?"

"The shorter ones are harder, because I don't have much time and there are all those I want to remember before God."

He then leaned back, and with arms extended and a bigger smile than usual, said, "But the hour-and-a-half of prayers, there I'm listening to God, and it's a *joy*. I have time alone with Him. It's like sitting on a hill, just totally alone, and the sun is shining and the stream is flowing, and you feel you have the purity of God's creation all around you."

Another metaphor came to him. "It's like being with a good friend you haven't talked to in a while. You can be in their presence and not even talk, but there's a joy in the relationship."

Or, for that matter, the joy of his longer morning prayers, which, he said, are "also like being together with somebody, in synch, solving a problem. It's really neat."

———— •◆• ————

How else does his love for Christ sculpt the granite of his life and repair its fractures? Here's a story about forgiveness a quarter-century in the making.

We had been talking about what Quie calls "congenial disputation" when he said, "confession is just an amazing thing," and "boy, does it ever help the soul when you forgive." This led him to ask, "Have I ever mentioned the telegram Bill Morris sent me at the end of my term as governor?"

No, as with the State Fair story, he hadn't, but now he did. For background, in 1982, Morris was chairman of Minnesota's Republican Party, officially known then as the "Independent-Republican Party of Minnesota." (The word "Independent" was added right after Watergate, as a labeling salve, but later deleted.) As will be discussed in Chapter Eight, the second half of Quie's four-year term (he was elected in 1978) was racked by severe revenue shortfalls caused by the deepest economic downturn nationally since the Great Depression. The legislature wound up being called into special session repeatedly, compelled by the state constitution to keep the budget in perpetual balance, and it did so with a combination of tough spending cuts and contentious tax increases. I was Quie's speechwriter then and can attest to just how painful a time it was. I can also attest that never in my lifetime have I witnessed leadership that was more self-sacrificial than his, as he led Minnesota out of a financial chasm.

Back to the story, picked up by Quie:

When I came to the end of my term, we were able to leave Rudy Perpich [his Democratic-Farmer-Labor Party successor] a $500 million surplus, which eventually turned into a $1 billion surplus when the economy turned around. We increased taxes to do it, and even increased income taxes temporarily, which the legislature later repealed, proving that death and taxes really *aren't* always permanent. Death is, but taxes weren't in that instance. But because we were forced to raise taxes, Bill Morris sent a statement to the media saying I wasn't a real Republican. He also sent me a telegram saying the same thing, but I received it after I read it in the papers.

I didn't always do exactly what the Republican platform said, as I was elected to serve both Republicans and Democrats, and my responsibility was not to be subservient to anyone but to use the best judgment I could. But his statement really hurt me; it just hurt me terribly. I stuff things, and I remember that when I was doing an interview after my term, there was a lot of bitterness in me, and I told myself that I needed to deal with it. The way I deal with things like that is through prayer, with the first thing being to forgive. I thought I had, but just a year ago something happened, and I realized I hadn't.

He went on to talk about a friend, Todd Otis, with whom he works closely on early childhood education activities, in a program called Ready 4 K, and who recently had been baptized. Quie suggested that the two ride together to a speech in western Minnesota so that they could "talk about Jesus." On the way back to the Twin Cities, Otis (who is a former DFL state party chairman) asked him to participate in a bipartisan news conference regarding a public opinion survey about early childhood education—one that had been co-conducted by Bill Morris. Once Quie heard who the pollster was,

> I *immediately* knew I was going to be busy that day, as I realized I really hadn't forgotten or forgiven. But as we rode along, I was just quiet for a while, and then I said, "Todd, you know, something just happened. I think God wants me to do that news conference." I needed the reconciliation in me.

> At the news conference, those of us in Ready 4 K said our spiel and then Bill started coming up on stage but then he just stopped. There was this look on his face. It was the first time we'd seen each other, or talked to each other, in all those years. I held out my hand and said, "Hey, Bill." After he made his presentation, he was alone in the corridor, so I walked over there and just talked with him. I didn't refer to what happened back in 1982, but I just talked with him so we would be in communication with each other.

I asked if Morris was uncomfortable, knowing that Quie was not pleased with him, or whether he thought that Morris had perhaps forgotten the episode.

"No, he hadn't forgotten it. You could tell. He knew exactly."

But Quie, at least, was at peace, having finally forgiven what he viewed as a former Republican leader's uncommonly unfair insult more than two decades earlier. We'll delve next chapter into his often distinctive conception of Republican principles and policies.

———•◆•———

A few weeks before telling this story, Quie, in reviewing the third and most draining year of his governorship, spoke of how he would meet every Tuesday morning during his term in Bible study and prayer with an accountability group of about half a dozen male friends. One morning, instead of meeting in a restaurant, they met in the master bedroom of the governor's residence when he blurted out, "I feel like I've let God down."

Dick Bragg, who has since passed away, said to me, "Albert! You can't let God down. You just can't do that. You just seek His will." Dick really hit me right between the eyes about who God really is. We all prayed fervently, and when they left, I sat there on the edge of my bed, continuing to pray, and Psalm 51 came within me: "Create in me a clean heart, O God, and renew a right spirit within me." The presence of Jesus Christ was palpable and in my joy of His presence, I wept, I just wept, and I felt the presence of Jesus Christ right there beside me like I never had before. It cleared my head and I was renewed.

I asked if this was the case—the rest of his term being a "joy"—even during the particularly tough times.

"Yes, even during the tough times."

"Why?"

"It goes like this. If you do God's will, you'll be blessed. And if you don't do God's will, He'll teach a lesson, so you can't miss either way."

I don't know what Quie enjoyed more, the ultimate no-lose situation or his turn of phrase, but he laughed zestfully at this point and said, "That's what came to me."

"It's the opposite," I noted, in my own exegesis, "of damned if you do and damned if you don't. In this instance, it's blessed if you do and blessed if you don't."

"Yes," he finished off the exchange, "God will create a clean heart and renew a right spirit within you, which He did. I didn't realize it until then."

Quie's first experience with prayer groups as an elected official began virtually on the day he was sworn into Congress in March 1958, following his victory in a special election a month earlier.

"Right after I was sworn in by Speaker Sam Rayburn, Rep. Cliff McIntyre of Maine came up to me and said, 'I'm going to give you an invitation and pay for your breakfast. There's a prayer breakfast here in the House every Thursday morning. Be my guest.' Well, I was out there by myself, since my family hadn't come to Washington yet. If they had been out there, I would have said sorry, but I'm going to have breakfast with my kids."

Instead, he joined the group.

About 25 to 30 House members would meet every Thursday morning in a room next to the House dining room in the Capitol to talk about their faith and relationship with Christ. There were Democrats and Republicans, and I got to share with them and know them differently than the partisan ways you see on the floor. I became the chair of the group in about 1961.

I had noticed there was a group of conservative Republicans who would come early, and before their Democratic colleagues got there, they would belittle and degrade liberals. I told those Republicans, "Even though there aren't any Democrats around when you get here early, it sets a bad tone with each other, an attitude. How can you do that and then come together as people of different views?" The liberal Democrats evidently sensed this because they didn't show up at all. It was only more conservative southern Democrats who attended.

After I became chair, I went out to talk to liberal Democrats because they have faith as well. I spoke to Jerry Cohelan, who had been a leader of the Teamsters before he was elected to Congress from California, as I'd noticed something about him, and thought maybe he was a believer and he'd want to do that. He said he'd be glad to. I told him there were pretty conservative people in the group, and I asked him to look for some other liberal friends to join him. He did and that opened things up.

Enter at this stage Doug Coe, a man who became one of Quie's closest friends for life.

Doug had come to Washington to assist in an organization called International Christian Leadership. For some reason, he picked me as the first member of Congress he wanted to talk to. He walked back and forth in front of my door for five days, he tells me, before he got the nerve to come in. When he finally did come in, he told me what he was there for and what his dream was, and I said, "Well, let's pray together."

He started coming to the prayer group, and after a while, he said, "You ought to go deeper," by which he meant smaller groups. There's a much different chemistry in groups of 25 or 30 compared to those of a few people. Doug was driven by an understanding of John Wesley, who had built the Methodist Church on the concept of five to ten people in a group.

I couldn't figure out how to put such smaller groups together, but Doug was involved with one, so I asked if I could come down and be with them. Just being there with those men as they met on Friday mornings, I got the concept of what they were doing. In many ways, they were at odds with each other, coming as they did from different parts of government and churches.

This is turning into quite a story, but I guess we have time.

"That's why we're here," I assured him.

I figured what I needed to do first is pick the best politician in the whole House to do this with. I wasn't about to go over to the Democratic side, as I didn't feel *that* kind of comfort at all. I thought Mel Laird of Wisconsin was the best politician as I watched him operate. So I decided to ask him—though I never got around to doing so.

One day, I was sitting in the front of the Chamber, since I wanted to pay attention to the person who was speaking and see the charts he was using. Laird just came down and sat next to me. I thought to myself: "Oh, oh, now God wants me to talk to him." I turned to him but nothing would come out.

I turned back again and composed myself with the words, "Mel, we ought to get together and pray together and invite some of our friends to join with us." But when I turned to say that to Mel, I lost my nerve. I couldn't do it. So now I'm feeling terrible, and I silently prayed to God, "God, I can't do it. I can't do it. You've got to get somebody else to do it, because I can't." And then Mel just turned to me right there and said, "Al, we've got to get together and pray together."

I asked why he was so uncomfortable, so frightened about asking Laird.

It was something in my background, I wasn't courageous enough. Who knows why I was unable, but I was. Mel and I started talking, ignoring the person who was addressing the House, and we went instead to the Speaker's lobby. It isn't too uncommon to ignore what somebody is saying in Congress.

Mel said he was going to ask Gerry Ford to join us, and I said I'd ask Charlie Goodell. So I went to talk to Charlie, who was from Jamestown in western New York. This is also interesting. I'd never talked about Christ or faith or anything like that with him, even though we were close friends working on education legislation. So I asked if he would join and he said, "Yes." So I said, "Why don't we pray together right now?" This is so funny.

Charlie got up and locked the door to the outer office, as he evidently didn't want to be caught praying and he didn't want to be interrupted. He locked what I call the "escape door," the door that goes out to the corridor. If there was someone you did want to see, you'd buzz out there. He locked that door, and then he went over and locked the door to the bathroom, too. Charlie and I prayed together and he broke down in tears when the prayer was over.

"Do you know why?"

"No, I don't know why. I never asked him why. This has happened to other people when we pray like that. Some, including prisoners, have just sobbed, their bodies shaking."

The reference to prisoners pertains to Quie's longtime work with Prison Fellowship and other prison ministries, a subject we'll address at length in Chapter Ten. Shortly after Goodell agreed to join with Quie and Laird; Ford came aboard as well.

It was Charles Goodell, by the way, who was picked by Gov. Nelson Rockefeller to complete Bobby Kennedy's Senate term after the second Kennedy brother was assassinated in 1968. After Goodell lost the seat in 1970, he was replaced in the group by Rep. John Rhodes of Arizona, who would eventually succeed Ford as House Minority Leader. The group did not meet often after Ford became president in 1974.

But immediately before that, Vice President Ford, Quie, Laird, and Rhodes were praying in Rhodes' office one August day in 1974 when a secretary came in and said, "Mr. Rhodes, I know you told me never to interrupt this meeting, but under the circumstances I think I should. There's a call from the White House for Mr. Ford, saying that he should come down there, because he's going to be the president."

Right then, my concern was for Gerry. Somehow, we didn't pray right after we heard, since he had to get up and go. But I said, "Gerry, I know you don't wear your faith on your sleeve." Nobody knew he was involved with our small group. We kept that totally secret all the time. "What if," I asked, "at your press conference they ask where you were when you heard you'd be president? Who were you with? What were you doing?"

"Ah," he said, "no one will ask me that." Well, he went through the whole press conference and he said, "I'll take one more question and then I have to leave." Well a reporter for the *New*

York Times asked exactly that, and Ford, a totally honest man, was *outed*.

"Why," I asked, "do you think it might have been a problem for him to say where he was?"

"To so many people," Quie said, "a person's faith is completely private. That's the way you grow up. That's the way I started out, totally private. Much of the public likes it that way."

What about the media's reaction on hearing that Ford was with Quie, Rhodes, and Laird when he learned Richard Nixon was resigning? Quie reported it was "amazing how the press descended on me, as if they thought Christians like us were now going to take over the world."

The Bible study and prayer group with Ford, Laird, Goodell, and Rhodes was not the only one in which Quie was involved with congressional colleagues at one time or another; there were three other small ones, plus the original larger one. And there was what has come to be known as the National Prayer Breakfast. "Yes," he said, "I was involved with that. We made a big change in it. When I was chair, we wouldn't allow any clergy to be on the program."

"Just about every time," I said, "I want to go someplace else, you say something really interesting. Expand on that if you would."

It used to be called the Presidential Prayer Breakfast, since a committee that was behind it thought we could draw more people by using the president's name that way. But I said, "Someday, we're going to have a president who won't come, so we can't call it the *Presidential* Prayer Breakfast. It's more honest if we call it the *National* Prayer Breakfast. Also, the House and Senate, for integrity's sake, took responsibility for it away from the committee, which had comprised all non-legislators. And no rich person paid for the breakfast anymore, meaning guests had to pay their own way from then on.

Almost a half a century later, no president has declined to attend. But when Quie became governor, he changed the name of the

The dais at the National Prayer Breakfast in Washington in 1970. From left to right: Rep. Mel Laird of Wisconsin, First Lady Pat Nixon, President Richard Nixon, Gretchen Quie, Al Quie, Sen. Frank Carlson of Kansas, and Judy Agnew, wife of Vice President Spiro Agnew. Others in the picture are unidentified.

Governor's Prayer Breakfast to the Minnesota Prayer Breakfast, which proved prescient and useful, as Jesse Ventura, elected governor of Minnesota in 1998, was not a fan of such events.

Back to the ban on clergy in the Washington program.

People involved with the breakfast tended to get clergy so at least some of the prayers would go right. But I said, "If a lay person speaks, it moves people more than anyone else. When a politician talks openly and is vulnerable about his faith and his walk with God, or a general or somebody in the cabinet does it, it's powerful." So we had no clergy. Billy Graham didn't know how to handle that, so he became "busy" for two years before he could figure it out. My colleagues said: "What are you going to do with Billy Graham? He's always been part of this." I said, "He can sit at a table like everybody else." And he later did.

Our conversation then turned to Jews and Catholics and their participation in programs like these.

> Arthur Burns, who was Jewish and just a fantastic person, was on the Federal Reserve Board and then became Ambassador to West Germany. A friend from the White House asked, "Why don't we have Burns speak at the National Prayer Breakfast?" Several of the more conservative Protestants wondered, "A Jewish person speaking at the National Prayer Breakfast?" I said I'd talk to him, and a couple of others joined me. This is the way I've always been. You just lay everything out for people to see it all. So I laid it out to him and told him what kind of people we were and that we'd like to have him come and speak, and he said he would. I said we were people with faith in Jesus Christ, trying to make sure that he understood exactly who he would be talking to. Burns talked about Jesus as a great prophet, and I think that finally broke the ice in opening things up. Anyone who truly has faith in Jesus Christ can benefit from being challenged.

I asked if Catholics also were involved in his various Bible study and prayer groups, and Quie said yes, though not as much as Protestants. In groups of "very conservative Protestants," he sought to bring Catholics along with "intentionality," making sure their faith was respected and they felt comfortable.

Years later, Quie was asked to chair a 1996 Billy Graham Crusade at the Hubert H. Humphrey Metrodome in Minneapolis. "I'll do it on only one condition: Instead of planning all this and then inviting Catholics in, they're going to be part of planning everything. Everyone agreed, so the first thing we did was to go over and talk to Archbishop Harry Flynn."

A last word needs to be added about the aforementioned weekly Bible study and prayer group during his time as governor:

> The first thing I expected the men in the group to do was assume the responsibility of challenging me. And they had to

call me "Al," not "Governor," so we'd all be on equal footing. We'd go around, and everybody would say a prayer, so we listened to each other pray. We'd talk about Scripture, and then we'd go around again, and people would talk about what was going on in their lives. And then I'd make sure they looked at what I was doing as governor, and what state government was doing, to make certain it was all congruent with what I believed in.

The group was pivotally helpful during times of crisis. This did not mean, however, he was quick to make clear, that it was pivotal in "figuring out how to solve the thing."

"They couldn't make any money?"

"No, they couldn't make any money," he confirmed.

This exchange paralleled another one Quie had at the time with a major Republican player. According to the donor, the governor had said that "God will provide." To which the donor replied, "Let's hope He has a big checkbook."

———— • ————

Let's bring this chapter about Quie's most personal devotions to a close in ways that are once again miles removed from budgets and politics. Instead, join him, as we did in the last chapter, at Cascade Lodge on Lake Superior's North Shore, where he and Gretchen took a week-long summer vacation in the middle of our conversations, along with just about all of the kids, their spouses, grandchildren, and great-grandchildren—23 folks in all. Once again his answer was, "Oh, yes," when I asked if the week went well, and he proceeded to talk about a couple of times he spent alone, or not quite.

You can sure tell you're older, because I didn't even try to hike with everybody in the family, but I did hike myself. I just love the waterfalls. There had been rain, so the water was coming down even harder. I hiked up Lookout Mountain twice, taking in that magnificent scene.

When I started out the first day at the falls, I waited for a photographer to take some pictures and then I stepped up to a good spot, all alone. Two women then came up, one from one side and the second woman from the other side, along with three children. I figured they weren't together, so I just said "Hello. Isn't that a beautiful falls?" The woman to my left who was alone said, "You're Al Quie." I said I was, and she said we had never met but that she recognized my voice. Now, isn't that remarkable, somebody can recognize you by your voice?

We came into conversation, and I said, looking over the scene, something about how amazing God's creation is, and we started talking about our faith. To me, I just thrill when conversations move in that way.

I was thinking about that as I was coming back down the mountain on the way back to the lodge when six young women walked by. They were knock-outs, slim and athletic. But now I'm embarrassed. I mean, I'm 83 years old, and it was like I was a bashful boy again. So I cast my eyes down and walked by them. I just asked if they were going swimming. They said, "Yup," and they giggled as they went by.

I walked some more, and there came three more girls, and I could tell they must have been from the same group. It turned out to be the Bethel University running team. Again I cast my eyes down, but as I did, I noticed one was wearing a T-shirt that said "Raider" and then when she turned towards me, I could see the "Northfield." I'm a graduate of Northfield High School, as she was. Now we had something in common, so we engaged in a conversation.

I told her the story that Mark Hanson, who runs the North Shore Folk School, tells about his late dad, Pastor Phil Hanson, who ran for the U.S. Senate a long time ago. Phil would talk about how "God is in people" so that when the telephone rang he would say, "That's God calling." I was thinking about the woman who had come up by the falls and how God had come alongside me through her. I said the same thing about the Bethel students, and you could just see their faces light up as they recognized what I was saying.

"Did they know who you were?"

"Yes, I introduced myself right away. I said I used to live around Northfield."

"But in terms of being governor?"

"Yes."

"They were all born after you left office."

"Yes, they were all born after I left office; quite a bit after I left office."

Quie and I were both laughing again, just as we were when he was telling of how uncomfortable he was when he first encountered the young women from Bethel, a Baptist university in Arden Hills, just north of St. Paul. It recalled a previous conversation when he talked about how he has "always had problems with temptations" and how he has benefitted in mostly silence from a rare and largely unknown affliction he calls a "Joseph Syndrome." It's easy to have fun here, but despite the laughs, it's a real issue for him. He named the reaction after the biblical Joseph, who "ran away, losing his robe and everything," he said, "when Potiphar's wife tried to seduce him." More clinically, he defines the compulsion as a need to run in the opposite direction whenever he's in a situation that might viewed—by him or anyone else, plausibly or not—as sexually compromising. It's the reason, for example, that he has hardly ever been in a car alone with a woman other than Gretchen or his daughter or another relative.

The last story Quie wanted to recount about his vacation up north prompted no digressions, of this sort or any anything close to it. "I don't know if you want any of this in the book," he said, "because it sounds so foolish, but you get an idea of who I am."

My great-granddaughter Lizza, who's four, slipped off the trail a bit and dislodged some yellow jackets, which stung her, stung her sister, stung her mother, and stung her father. They stung him three times. The family couldn't get away from there quick enough. So the next day when I was up on

Lookout Mountain sitting there alone in a sort of Adirondack shelter that's up there on the top, here comes one of those yellow jackets and he's flying around my leg. I'm sitting there with my cap off, because I'm out of the sun. I'm holding it in my left hand and I'm just raising it, saying, "I'm going to nail you." But then I thought to myself, no, the bee hadn't done anything to me.

So I put my hand down and I figure I'm going to watch it. I laid my right hand out and held it there to see what it would do. It flew around, came up and flew around my head, and then it buzzed on the tops of the hairs on the back of my hand, just buzzed around on there, and then flew off. That was really neat. About two minutes later, it flew back, as if it were saying, "Hey, there's something I forgot to tell you." It swung around my head and I thought it was going to make a nest in my left ear. It buzzed there for a while and came and sat on my ear for a while longer. Then it flew off, and I never saw it again.

"I'm no Albert Schweitzer," Quie said, "but to me, that was the most marvelous experience with a blame bug that God had created. I love those little things that happen in nature."

Chapter Four

Political Groundings
"Was I ever going to get somewhere?"

Al Quie says he has a "natural propensity to be a lone wolf." Yet he continues to be a master coalition builder and seems comfortable, even joyous in crowds.

When asked to talk about their most cherished political values, most Republicans use words like liberty and freedom. Quie instinctively uses words like justice, love, and mercy.

His political principles are clear-cut, having been sculpted over a lifetime of serious thought and introspection. Also clear is his constant search and testing of new ideas, consistent with those principles.

He thinks something's wrong if politicians *don't* change their minds or at least "evolve."

Public servants routinely claim to have confidence in the good sense, even wisdom of everyday people. For Quie, there's not a fraction of doubt.

He grew up on a farm in the provincial Midwest of the 1920s and '30s. Yet he was an internationalist and civil rights partisan just about from the start.

He's uncommonly tolerant and kind to those with whom he disagrees. Yet during congressional debate of the 1964 Civil Rights Act, he told Republican colleagues that he considered anyone voting against the bill to be "un-American." And "not a Christian" either.

His high school classmates have said if there had been a yearbook category for the person least likely to go into politics, Quie would have been chosen. But he wound up serving three years in the Minnesota Senate, 21 years in Congress, and then four years as governor.

While he has been an architect of immense and complex public programs, he measures much of their success by how well they engender intimate ties in small groups.

And while his personal manner and equanimity have tended to leave a much different impression, the fact is, Al Quie has always been driven by ambition, albeit in the most public-spirited sense of the term.

———— • ◆ • ————

As introduced in Chapter One, Quie grew up in a home in which political, theological, and other conversations around the supper table were rich, routine, and often internationalist in subject and spirit. Several times in our conversations he mentioned reading a book called *Union Now: A Proposal for a Federal Union of the Democracies of the North Atlantic* by a former *New York Times* reporter named Clarence K. Streit and how it shaped his thinking as a teenager. He also spoke several times of meeting a young Jewish escapee from Hitler's Germany, a "lad whose parents had been killed by the Nazis," and how the story seared and has stayed with him ever since, in part, because the young man said, "What the world needs more than anything else is love."

Quie describes his immediate and extended family during his childhood years as anti-communists and anti-fascists; individualists, in crystalline sum. As such, they were uniformly opposed to Roosevelt, disliking New Deal programs "immensely." He clearly remembers a Herbert Hoover poster in the kitchen, first hung in 1928 and then put up again in 1932. Nevertheless, when he was in high school, as remains his wont, he sought to think matters through for himself by analyzing and conveying, in conversations with his father, the views of a liberal history teacher. In return, he also passed his father's views on to his teacher. This all led to Dad accusing his oldest son of being a dreaded New Dealer, though one gets the sense he did so more in needling than chastisement.

Quie rejects any notion that his intellectual and ideological explorations caused him to move left during his high school years. He says a similar consistency held during college at St. Olaf, following his stint as a Navy pilot in World War II, when in addition to wooing

Gretchen, he commenced his career in high offices by being elected president of the campus Republican Club. The fact that it was only fifteen minutes before the big meeting that he even knew he'd be attending it—much less knowing his friends would nominate him for the presidency—should not be allowed to underplay his brewing quest for a career in politics. For proof, it was about this time that he led the way in starting a campus-based chapter of Toastmasters, as he "understood how important it would be to prepare speeches and make cogent arguments so that people would hear and understand you." In fact, with no small amount of pride, Quie boasts (albeit without notarized proof) that his was the "first and last" student-run affiliate of Toastmasters ever sanctioned by the national organization.

Between being elected president of the St. Olaf Republican Club in 1946 and winning a special congressional election in 1958, Quie was elected to his local school board, elected to the board of the Rice County Soil and Water Conservation District, elected to the board of the Twin City Milk Producers Association, and elected president of the Rice County Farm Bureau. Nevertheless, as he approached 30, he was depressed. "I mean, a good chunk of my life had gone by, and what had I accomplished? I had purchased the farm, but was I ever going to *get* someplace? I wasn't fulfilling what I had been dreaming of politically. I had that political science major, and I knew which way I wanted to go." Berating himself, he just wasn't getting there.

I asked at one point if he thought he has been more ambitious than people have assumed. He agreed that their impressions may have been consistently wrong, though he couldn't say why. I would suggest that perpetually smiling, soft-spoken, religiously animated guys in cowboy boots have a leg up in conveying equanimity rather than burning fires.

———•◆•———

Containing only one classroom and with enrollment down to five kids, Quie's Oak Grove school district was not the biggest in the state; still it's not every twenty-something college student who's drafted to succeed his father in a respected community assignment. He says he wasn't intimidated, though he did learn he disliked being secretary, finding himself inadequately organized to keep records and insufficiently excited about taking notes. But in an early example of his need to fix and improve just about anything sitting or standing nearby, he pushed for a consolidation with the larger district that served nearby Nerstrand. (Its school building had not just one but four rooms.) He succeeded in persuading his four colleagues on the board to merge the districts, but the effort ultimately failed, when "everybody" in the district made it to the annual meeting despite lousy March weather and voted no. "This was *their* school district and had been since Moses," Quie came to understand. People were so upset at the prospect of change that his four counterparts on the board reversed their positions, leaving him the only "aye." Bloodied though he might have been, he persisted.

The following year, and still "believing in the principle," he talked to a few people "who were leaders," this time urging a consolidation plan that would assure that at least one person from their own end of the district would sit on the new board. "When we put it on the ballot, after these opinion leaders had talked to their neighbors and after we made phone calls to make sure we had a quorum, everyone was for it. So I learned something about politics: Just to have an idea is not enough. You have to sell other people on it."

Once again Quie succeeded his father, this time as a Soil and Water Conservation District commissioner. And despite his previous less-than-world-class performance as a school board secretary, he again was named scribe-in-chief. As discussed earlier, Quie revered his father for being an "evangelical for the environment" and sought to emulate his approach to farming. Service as his father's successor on the conservation board afforded him a chance to spread nature's word, or more precisely, word of how nature's requirements, and those of humans, could best be balanced.

The job also gave him a first, hands-on chance to view relations between and among different levels of government, as the board worked with federal, state, and local officials. Some people, he found to his disappointment, deferred too quickly to federal authorities, even when more proximate ones better understood the lay of local lands and had a better grasp of local problems. In attempting to correct what he viewed as an instance of such an upside-down policy, he again lost a skirmish. Afterwards, the head of the district, perhaps a bit paternalistically, asked, "Are you all right about that?"

"Listen," Quie recalls saying (not that he remembers the loss in question), "there's another day, and I'll just have to help other people understand," thus providing what he described as "another learning process" for when he was elected to the Minnesota Senate and afterwards. "Those two forces are always there: new days, and the need to help people understand what you're trying to do."

From soil and water he moved on to dairy, getting elected as a local representative to, and board member of, the Twin City Milk Producers Association, a cooperative. And from there, he was elected president of the Rice County chapter of the Farm Bureau in 1951, beating the incumbent and keeping the job until his election to the state senate in 1954. He stepped down from the Farm Bureau post at that point, as he saw a conflict of interest in holding the two jobs simultaneously. While still in his 20s, he had been elected to four different positions in four different organizations (not counting the august presidency of the St. Olaf Republicans). Putting aside his fear that he hadn't done anything and wasn't amounting to much, this was strong preparation—especially when combined with military experience, farm ownership, and a growing family—for more demanding political assignments on bigger stages, starting with the Minnesota Senate. But first, in 1952, there was an unanticipated and rushed write-in campaign, which ended unsuccessfully, for a state House seat that opened abruptly.

Two weeks before Election Day in November, Rep. Ralph Illsley died in a car accident. Several people urged Quie to run for the suddenly open job, but because legislative candidates in Minnesota back then were not identified by party, nor would they be for almost another twenty years, there was no place to go for an endorsement, be it quick or otherwise. This severely complicated matters.

"The *Northfield News* had the contract that year for printing the ballots," Quie recounted, "and Herman Roe, the paper's publisher, said he would hold up the printing so I could get enough people to sign petitions. We wound up with twice as many names as we needed, but the county attorney for some reason questioned the process, and he sent the case up to the attorney general, J.A.A. Burnquist, who said he would rule on the issue—but not until after the election, so that wasn't any good."

That dead end consumed a full week, leaving only one week to go. What to do?

So we decided, "Let's go for it." We'd do a write-in. Some people in the western part of Rice County decided that if they elected a dead man, they could have a special election after Election Day. It was fascinating how the vote turned out. About 1,800 voted for Illsley. I was credited with 4,456 votes, and another candidate, A. O. Sundet, the man I had defeated for the Farm Bureau presidency, got 400 votes more, 4,856, and won.

Quie's good Norwegian name may not have served him politically well here, as "we figured they threw out about another thousand ballots for me because voters spelled my name wrong." The family name earlier had been spelled "K-v-i," which, along with additional variations penciled in that day, were not accepted by the election officials.

"No hanging chads?" I asked.

"No hanging chads, but I guess they hadn't made the decision yet that a vote can count as long as you can figure out a person's intention." He didn't challenge the results, however, dissuaded by farm responsibilities and potential legal costs. He also didn't want to leave a sour and ungracious impression which might hurt him with voters in the future. So he accepted the defeat and figured "maybe someday the opportunity would arise again." It quickly did, as two years later, in 1954, Quie defeated a longtime state senator named Homer Covert. Like Sundet two years earlier, Covert was a "Conservative," which was nonpartisan talk back then for a "Republican." The two legislative races would not constitute the only occasions in his political career in which he would either challenge his own team or work with other insurgents (like Gerald Ford) to install new party leaders.

I asked what led most directly to his decision to run for the senate.

"I kept looking at how you can make things better in the state, and I also suppose it was my piety. I really admired Luther Youngdahl and his efforts to clean up gambling." A Republican who was sometimes mocked as the "Sunday School Governor," Youngdahl served in the job from 1947 to 1951.

> I'd hear stories of roadhouses where state liquor control inspectors would find gambling infractions and tell the local sheriff about them. But the story was that the sheriff would then signal the proprietors, and they'd get rid of all the evidence before anything happened. There were many stories about this happening around the state and that some Chicago people were involved. The Minnesota Council of Churches wanted the liquor control inspectors themselves to have the power of arrest, but Covert was opposed, so I used that as my issue and I defeated him.

Quie's father had been opposed to his son running for the senate, as "he'd watched people who had been farmers and legislators and how their farms had gone to pot because they got more interested in politics than farming." His father even offered to run in his place, but Quie said, "'Nope, Dad. Even if you run, I'm still going to run.' So he backed off that idea. I did not have his blessing to run, but I wanted to do it. I thought and prayed on it, and I figured that's where I'm going to go."

I asked Quie what his own reaction was right after he learned he had won, but he says he doesn't remember. "We didn't have a party or anything. I just listened to the results on the radio at the farm. I think we spent about $600 on the campaign."

Quie went off to St. Paul as a freshman senator a few months later, but shortly after introducing legislation that would, in fact, give new powers to state liquor control officials, he began having serious doubts, not just about the bill he authored, but about his very stance on the very issue that got him elected in the first place.

> I was at church back home during the legislative session when one of my fellow parishioners told me about driving early in the morning, before it got light, and passing a barn with the hay door open and seeing a farmer dressing out a deer. It wasn't deer season, so I asked, "Well, did you go to the game warden and turn

him in?" "Oh no," he said, "I wouldn't do that. That's the state's problem." Just like that: "That's the state's problem." When I ran for the senate in the previous fall, the incumbent sheriff was defeated, so I realized right then you can have law enforcement as good as you want without relying on state government. You just elect a new sheriff if you don't like the old one.

And all of a sudden it dawned on me: I had introduced legislation contrary to my philosophy of government. You shouldn't give the state that extra power. People at the local level should struggle with the issue and enforce the laws the way they believe they ought to. Now I was really stuck. What in the world was I going to do? I said to myself, "If I vote against my own bill, everybody in my district who had such confidence in me and my character would say, 'He sold out to the liquor interests as soon as he got up there.'" There wasn't any time to educate people about it, so I voted for it. It's the only way I could do it. I figured I could not let them down in that way. After that experience, I made sure to talk to the people in my district, and later, throughout the state, working with them to understand my views. I again realized that you have a responsibility to educate your people. There's nothing wrong with changing your mind, but you better educate your people. That's your responsibility.

I asked Quie if his bill passed. To his relief, it didn't. I also asked if roadhouse corruption in Rice County ended once a new sheriff was elected. Yes, it did, as the new man enforced the law, as Quie put it, "without fear or favor."

The senate committee on which he most wanted to serve but couldn't was the education committee, as seats on it were heavily sought by more senior members. But he was appointed to what was commonly known as the Legislative Commission on Exceptional Children, which turned out to be his singular learning experience during his three years in the senate. The official name of the group was a little wordier: the Minnesota Commission on the Problems of the Mentally Retarded, Handicapped, and Gifted Children.

The commission was chaired by future governor Elmer L. Andersen, with whom Quie had previously served on a Lutheran Welfare Society board and whose talents and skills he found extraordinarily impressive. Although Andersen was a Republican, Quie saw him as much more liberal than others in their caucus yet still able to maintain good relations with legislators well to his right. "I just watched how that was possible with him. To be on a commission with someone like *Elmer* . . . ." Quie's voice tailed off here in respect bordering on awe.

Elmer Andersen, who had a long "retirement" as misnamed as Quie's, went on to become a revered public figure before dying in 2004 at age 95.

Oh, man! The story that all of us remember most was when we were watching a group of very handicapped children in a gym. There was a boy, about fourteen years of age, who was skinny as a rail and extremely spastic. The teacher—a woman who was really a teacher and therapist combined—asked him to walk straight along one of the lines from the free throw line towards the basket. That's all he had to do, but he got only about a quarter of the way before he crumbled and fell. There was no cushioning on those bones. I *still* feel the pain in myself as he hit that hard floor. My immediate reaction was to help him up, but then I wondered if the teacher was going to do it. She wasn't, but she also put her arm in front of me so I couldn't. There we stood and watched him in the most excruciating way struggle to get up and fall back again and *finally* get to his feet. She then went over and put her arm around him and congratulated him. At that point, I knew the love she had for that boy, as she let him struggle to learn for himself.

I also remember sitting in a home—and it was so important that it was a home and not an institution—and here was a blind boy and his father, who also was blind. The father was so brilliant he would oversee the construction of new buildings for a company all over the United States. What he would do was sit and memorize every part of the blueprints and then he'd go, as a blind person, and supervise all the construction, a most amazing thing. His son wanted to be a musician. His father disagreed, because he knew of other blind people who wanted to be musicians but who were stereotyped and forced to tune pianos. He didn't want that happening to his son. "They're exactly like we are," I thought, "exactly the same way. They don't want their children stereotyped and limited either."

Loving someone with a serious handicap was nothing new to Quie, of course, given his father's loss of an arm years earlier. But experiences like these on the commission made unusually strong impressions on him and played a significant part in the passage of a path-breaking bill not long later: statewide legislation making it mandatory, according to Quie, that "every educable child in Minnesota be provided an adequate education in his school district, or the district would pay for such an education some place else."

Congress would not pass a similar bill, the Individuals with Disabilities Education Act (IDEA), until 1975, with Quie playing a key role in the enactment of that legislation, too.

There's one final state senate episode from the '50s that Quie had long forgotten and that I particularly enjoy. We had been talking one morning about the importance of politicians holding to principle, which we did often, and he recalled how Dick Fox, who had served as ambassador to Trinidad and Tobago during the Carter administration, reminded him many years later about a speech the young legislator had given about a civil rights bill in the Minnesota Legislature:

Dick told me he was up in the senate gallery, sitting with Cecil Newman, the publisher of the *Minneapolis Spokesman* and the *St. Paul Recorder*, which were well-read and important newspapers in the African-American community, as I was speaking on the floor shortly before the bill came up for a vote. The bill itself, which dealt with creating a Fair Employment Practices Commission for Minnesota, didn't have much chance of passing, or at least it was assumed, because most of the Conservatives in the chamber were opposed, although an amendment of mine had been accepted. Once Dick mentioned the incident, it came back to me.

I had said something like, "There's no reason why I should vote for this bill, because I don't know of any people of color in my senatorial district and it's not important for our economy. But I'm going to vote for it for only one reason: Because it's the right thing to do." I didn't realize it at the time, but Dick said right at that moment, my remarks "changed that body" and the bill passed. When I look back it wasn't my political savvy that caused me to win elections. I believe, instead, it was because there were enough people who respected that I tried to stand on principle, even when it meant getting political allies and friends mad at me.

The legislation had been opposed by most of my caucus as well as by my father-in-law. I needed to figure out the right thing to do. But I also realized that my caucus would have some impact on my legislative future. So the choice was between doing what was right and what was expedient. But doing the right thing in such situations gives you courage to the same thing the next time.

———•◆•———

As I was in the early stages of writing this chapter, a political scientist friend asked what kind of conservative Al Quie is. It was a perfectly fair question, and one of my first responses was to repeat what another member of the governor's staff told me in the early 1980s: Quie did not like referring to himself as a "conservative" and never did so, even though the term was then in a rebirth of acceptance and was perhaps more popular than ever before in this country because of Ronald Reagan's popularity and his reshaping of the political and ideological landscape. In fact, in terms of political designations, I don't think I've ever heard Quie describe himself as anything more complicated or exotic than the male equivalent of a cloth-coat Republican. And attempts to calculate or calibrate simply don't compute when it comes to determining whether he's a paleo-conservative or a neoconservative, an economic conservative or a social conservative, or whether he's affiliated with any other recognized genus at all. The word "unique" is routinely tossed around with nullifying abandon. But I have no hesitation in describing Al Quie as occupying a political category of his own.

How, exactly, is this the case? Let's start with what I've long viewed as the heart of his political soul: his respect for regular folks and his faith in their good sense.

We had been talking about Geoffrey Canada and his book, *Fist Stick Knife Gun: A Personal History of Violence in America*. Canada is the brilliant and brave educator who has performed scholastic and other wonders in Harlem, and Quie said that meeting him was "one of the great moments of my life." Their conversation had been on the White Earth Indian Reservation in northern Minnesota, with Quie asking what Canada considered the key principle in helping poor children succeed academically. Canada told him that "the most important principle is to listen." And that the only adequate way of listening is to "respect the person." To this Quie added, "You can tell my passion in talking about this, because so many people on my side have failed to respect people on the other side. They kowtow to them but then leave them as victims."

By "other side," I asked if he was talking about poor people.

"Poor people, people of color, even individuals who have totally different political and theological beliefs."

"There's a very short and direct connection," I followed up, "between what you just said and what I was going to ask next, which is why do you have such a deep confidence in the wisdom and talents of everyday people? It seems to me that if there's one theme that has characterized your public life, a very good argument can be made that that's it."

"Yes," was his unembellished reply.

Pushing him to add flesh to the bare bone he had just tossed back to me—and keeping in mind that Quie really does admire scholars, experts, and other successful people and the contributions they make—he continued by saying that one of his reasons for celebrating the good sense of average citizens is "the stupidity of the elite and powerful." Pride gets in their way, he said.

> Now, you look over at poor people. You spend time with them, and a moral strength and curiosity come out, and that's just amazing. They have an understanding of life that I had no comprehension of. You're likely to miss pearls and rubies if you aren't discerning. One of the greatest joys in life is when I have an "ah-ha" moment with someone different from me. I think, "Hey, I just gathered some wisdom from them."

> I'll give you an example. The neat thing about being on the House Education and Labor Committee was that I had the opportunity to do things I otherwise wouldn't. For example, I once ran with a street gang in New York, and I spent time in Watts after the riots in 1965. First we had a hearing, and then I walked around the neighborhood with the people. One person who talked to me was going to start a bar, and he was going to serve only red wine, to symbolize the blood that had been shed. I thought, what a weird thing to do. Then I thought to myself, there's something sacramental about that, so I decided to spend a little more time with him. Now, I represented the federal government, and he wondered, "Why are you funding the revolution?" Because that's what we were doing, he said, through Great Society programs. I had never thought of the Office of Economic Opportunity as funding the revolution, but I realized he was thinking politically, just as I was, and he was just amazed that we could be so stupid.

None of this, it needs emphasizing, is to suggest that Quie was not enthused about intimately involving poor people in governmental programs aimed at improving their lives. The opposite is true, especially as we'll see in the next chapter when he talks proudly of his role in structuring Community Action Programs so that they still survive around the country, more than 40 years since they came to be. Suffice it to say for now, Quie is of the mind that, "The whole part of government, the whole part of democracy is to give voice to people who don't have power and to protect people who don't have power." Not incidentally at this point in our conversation, he gave a high salute and low bow to *Les Misérables*.

Earlier that morning, though, he talked about power in terms more taxonomic than theatrical.

> There are really four groups of people, I think, when it comes to power. There are people without power, and they don't think they can ever get it, so they're in victimhood. Then there are people without power but who pretend to have it. They move falsely by trying to get other people to come along. Then there are people who have power but deny having it because they can better manipulate people that way. And then there are people who have power and who are honest about it, and they use it for the betterment of other people.

I asked how he was defining power.

"Power," he said, "means the ability to really influence people. People can use their personality. They can use their wealth or other economic resources they may have. Power can be exercised by pulling together in organizations. That's why, for example, single issue groups have power, by zeroing in on one thing, demonizing other people, and getting their own views through."

A week earlier, we had been talking about why he's a Republican and not a Democrat (more on this in a moment), and I was struck by certain words he did *not* use. "Republicans today," I said, "especially conservative ones, favor words like freedom and 'liberty.' It seems to me you were just implying the importance of 'justice' more than the other two ideas."

After taking a half-joking shot at libertarians, he acknowledged, "That's right. I realize the two words that come together with me are 'justice' and 'love,' or 'justice' and 'mercy.' Getting what is coming to you is justice. Forgiving is mercy. 'Forgiving seventy times seven' is love."

So why has he stayed a Republican?

I believe the South still wouldn't have changed without the civil rights movement and federal action. And I agree, for example, that the federal government has to be involved with the environment, because water and air move from state to state. But when you talk about justice and mercy, who can take money away from people easier than anyone else? It's the federal government. The land, as I look at it, is really God's and we're only stewards of it for periods of time. I think many people on the left don't see it that way but instead think the land belongs to the government, and therefore, the people. And then I see what happened when the left put people on the dole.

Why am I a Republican? It's because Republicans are what Democrats used to be. There's a new book about the history of Minnesota by Steven Keillor [*Shaping Minnesota's Identity: 150 Years of State History*], and he says that at the beginning of the state, Democrats were for local control. I'm going to be with Republicans, because they're the ones now at least trying to do local control.

Quie then talked about his preferences on taxes, a subject we'll deal with at length in the two chapters about his four years as governor. For the time being, imagine his views as Main Street Republican, with an unexpected trip down a side street. Here, he spoke of divisive social policies.

But most of the time, the difference really comes down to the social issues. I'm just prone to be over on the Republican side on them. To put it flatly, I have a hard time saying it should be legal for a person to kill their child in the womb because it isn't convenient for them. I can understand if it's a twelve-year old child impregnated by her father or a 56-year-old woman who is probably going to die if she has the baby. I can understand that. But the other part of it, I can't.

As for issues such as same-sex marriage and capital punishment, Quie is unsurprisingly opposed to the former, and given his ties and friendships with men in prison, he's been unsurprisingly conflicted on the latter. We'll return to both matters: same-sex marriage in the chapter on congenial disputation and capital punishment in the chapter on his prison ministry. In regards to my own political views, I gravitate to terms and ideas such as the much revered "ordered liberty" and the frequently reviled "compassionate conservatism." Rightly (and especially in regards to the latter term, *rigorously*) understood, the two conceptions of government might both be said to capture Quie's thinking.

———————•◆•———————

I suspect I had been working for Quie for a couple of months in 1981 when, in a car ride from one reception to another in Greater Minnesota, I noted that for a basically introverted guy, he seemed genuinely to enjoy meeting and talking to people at such events. His response has stayed with me. He had realized early on that interacting with lots of people was intrinsic to a political career—which, in his case, was a ministry—and since he was not naturally extroverted, he had taught himself to enjoy such occasions. In essence, a man who had been too shy to look girls in the eye when he was a boy had willed himself just shy of being the life of political parties as an elected official. While still considering himself a "lone wolf," he virtually boasted in one of our conversations that he derived much of his energy from other people (a classic definition of extroverts). "I've gotten enough courage to step forward and see, hey, there's joy there. I think it's the same thing that causes me to want to read. I want to learn. When I'm with other people, I'm trying to watch and learn from them."

While working on this chapter, I mentioned to a major political figure in Minnesota what I interpreted to be a more-than-surface change in Quie's personality over the years. I didn't describe it as a full-fledged transformation from extreme introversion to epitomized extroversion, but I did claim it to be an unusually substantial, perhaps even remarkable change nonetheless. The senior official suggested with some emphasis that I was over-interpreting matters. But the more I've thought about the exchange, the more I believe I'm right.

Coming out of the 1960s, people often spoke of how the "personal is the political," how personal disappointments were transformed into political grievances. For Quie, the dynamic is reversed: Political efforts are measured by how well they enable people to work successfully with each other face to face—and even better, heart to heart. Absent such human terms and figurative touch, he contends, governmental and other programs intended to help people can rarely work well enough. "Part of the process is figuring out how people can interact with each other in ways so they move together in fixing problems and finding a better system. I've noticed all through my career how important human relations are, and trying to better understand them has played a big part in the development of my political thinking."

We'll delve more deeply into Quie's interpersonal approach to policy-making and implementation when we consider his congressional career. But one story that he likes to tell from his time on the House Education and Labor Committee is both exquisitely and mundanely illustrative.

Republicans and Democrats on the committee were disagreeing and fighting with each other in the '60s more than Quie viewed as constructive or wise, and he thought it had something to do with how they sat during hearings and other meetings—in straight lines making it difficult to look one another in the eyes. He persuaded the chairman, Carl Perkins, a powerful Democrat from Kentucky, to hire carpenters to build a diamond-shaped table so that "when we marked up bills, we looked at each other." I suspect he agrees it wasn't the only reason, but Quie recalls the seating change as the "beginning of putting together education legislation that both Republicans and Democrats could support."

This is not to say his main challenge was always getting Democrats to agree with him, as throughout his career he also had disagreements with Republicans whom he might describe as overzealous. As a new state senator in the 1950s, for example, he was not in sync with the fervor with which various gubernatorial appointees were vetted for communist sympathies or sensibilities. Orville Freeman, a Democrat, was governor at the time, having been elected the same day as Quie in 1954. In Congress, a main challenge was getting Republicans to concur with his view (which had been difficult for him to accept) that competition with the Soviet Union required Washington to play a larger role in improving American education. One Republican colleague in particular confided to Quie that he would, in fact, keep following his lead on the issue but questioned whether the crew-cut Minnesotan really had to move so fast.

Yet he was only so much of a maverick, as he was a member of mainstream Republican caucuses in Congress such as the Acorn Group and the Chowder & Marching Society, the latter having included the likes of Richard Nixon, Gerald Ford, and Mel Laird. Quie did wonder at one point if the Wednesday Group, made up of mostly liberal Republicans from the Northeast might be a better fit, as "sometimes it was just hard to push my principles and ideas fast enough in the more conservative Republican groups." So he became a Wednesday member but lasted only three meetings before he realized, "They were way to the left of me."

In talking one day again about the young Jewish man whose parents were exterminated by the Nazis, he recalled the boy saying that what the world needed more than anything was love. "Yes, yes," Quie agreed upwards of 70 years later. In such moments, the former state senator, congressman, and governor is a romantic, an idealist. But decidedly over a long public life, he's been a pragmatist—a philosophically rooted one, to be sure, intent on working within principled frames, yet clearly someone who has been willing to be flexible, exploring different policies and approaches. And as such, he has not been of the mind that changing one's mind is a terrible or disqualifying thing for a politician occasionally to do. Exactly the opposite is the case. "There *should* be evolvement," he said, "in the thinking of politicians as they go along, as they look at the world around them and the conditions we live in." Or in another instance urging measure, "You can't alienate your base by taking too many unexpected positions. But there's nothing wrong with changing your mind." As long, that is (Quie repeated the requirement several times in our conversations), that politicians fully explain the reasons for their changed positions.

So I asked how often he had changed his mind during his decades in office. The list, frankly, wasn't as long as he might have implied. During his first year in the state legislature, as noted, he realized that the very first bill he introduced, giving state liquor control officials more authority at the expense of local officials, ran counter to his principles, though for reasons also noted, he felt compelled to vote for it anyway. Jumping all the way to his time as governor, and for reasons we'll discuss later, he was embarrassed, but realized he had no other choice but to veto an income tax bill he himself had proposed. He amended his views about higher education to include a more significant role for the federal government once he got to Congress and recognized the new global demands being made on the United States. Studying the Northwest Ordinance and the Land-Grant Act also played a large part in his change of thinking. And while he has spoken about the irreplaceable contributions of parents more passionately than any politician I know, he wasn't as convinced on the subject until he made an early trip to the Soviet Union and until he had a conversation with a Catholic nun at a White House conference on families just before that.

———— • ◆ • ————

Just two days before this book went to the publishers, Quie thought there was something about his views in regards to politics and governance—more precisely, something about how his views about politics, governance, and horses share common ground—that hadn't been addressed yet. For example, he said his political tenacity has been akin to his patience in training horses, as getting Congress to pass favorite amendments frequently took years. He also said, "I've been told there is a great commonality between my relationships with people and those with horses." Quie explained:

I enjoy analyzing and studying systematic ways of better developing and improving relationships, and I find there are two components for building the trust that's necessary so they work well. The first is consistency. If signals are constantly changed, trust is lost. The second is continuity, since good relationships usually never happen based on only experience in one location. These two ingredients are important parts of my fascination with governance. Governance occurs not just at all levels of government, but in families, businesses, nonprofits, churches, and other organizations, too. It also includes horses, though their governance style is more likely called a pecking order.

Most fascinating to me is when horses and I, through consistency and continuity, develop a partnership. I used to say I like horses so well because they don't talk back. Now that I've learned their language, I realize that human relationships and governance also depend on the language of the invisible. In research and disputation—both of which are absolutely essential—it's important that we learn to discern the language of the invisible in our relationships.

The weight Quie puts in consistency and continuity will be seen particularly clearly in Chapter Ten when he talks about the mentoring of prisoners.

———— • ◆ • ————

As readers may have noticed, Quie is not inclined to tell out-of-school tales about the many public figures with whom he served over the years. Perhaps ironically, given what a social leader he has been (in the best sense of the term), he talks much more instinctively and comfortably about ideas and issues rather than personalities. And with more of a sense of history than self-regard, he often talks with eye-opening vulnerability and openness personally. But I did ask him one morning about the "really interesting people" he had met. Who were they? Who had the most outsized personalities and presence? He gave me two: Alexander Solzhenitsyn (who died as this book was going to press) and Anwar Sadat.

I really appreciate the picture of Solzhenitsyn and me together taken at some speech or conference in the middle 1970s. I just went up to him and we engaged. Hearing him and the way he thought. How he moved from a communist and an atheist to a believer. The way he looked at his own country. And the way he saw not only our strengths but the weaknesses that were going to hurt us and pull us down. To be with a person who was the darling for a while and then people turned against him because of the harsh things he said about the United States. It's easy to point out the evil in someone else. But to see the evil that's within us—that's a tough thing to do. I so admire his clarity of thought and his courage when he was here to say that. That was really strong.

Quie's Sadat story is fascinating and leaves a person wondering why he didn't relay it at the time to a then-departing President Ford. History might have moved quicker if he had.

Another amazing experience for me was with Anwar Sadat in 1976. Through President Ford's office, I was on my way to a UNESCO conference in Nairobi, Kenya, but first stopped in Israel, since the Israelis were getting a lot of criticism for allegedly doing archeological digs where they shouldn't have been. They showed me some of the locations and the falsity of the claims, and then I went to Egypt, where it happened that Sadat was to give what we would call a State of the Union address. Somebody arranged it so that I could sit in the balcony and hear the speech, and then I could visit him at his home just an hour afterwards. I opened our conversation this way: "President Sadat, instead of talking about politics, here's a question I have for you. I just heard your speech and I've never heard a speech like that from a president of the United States. It was clear you had had a spiritual experience. Would you tell me about it? Then I'll talk about a spiritual experience of mine." And he did.

I asked what Sadat had said that Quie interpreted as a spiritual experience.

It was his reverence towards God. The way he spoke both at the beginning and the end of the speech; not just something like "God bless America" as we have here and those things. But a reverence to God that comes from within a person who not only has had an experience with Him, but a recent one. It just came out of him like that. I thought, am I reading him right? He said, "I've gone back to my five prayers a day." So we shared in that way. And then he just opened up. "If only that old woman was still there." He was referring to Golda Meir, who had been prime minister of Israel.

Sadat said, "They've got this coalition government, and nobody can make a decision." He talked about the 1973 Yom Kippur War by saying, "When I started the war . . . ." I had never heard anyone say anything like that: "When I started the war . . . ." Sadat went on to say something like, "I did not realize it at the time, but I do now, we could never defend our boundaries. We could never put up enough defenses for that. There's got to be *some* way for us to come together and talk." He wanted to meet with someone tough enough to lead Israel, and he also wanted to talk directly to the Israeli people. [The strong Menachem Begin would not be elected prime minister until the following year, 1977.] He wanted to talk to the Knesset. He wanted to do that. He had thought all this through. He also talked about how, if he could bring Egypt and Israel to peace, then he could go to Jordan. Then he went through each of the countries in the Middle East, but when he came to Libya, he said, "But I'll never be able to get that crazy man in Libya," meaning Muammer al-Gaddafi. "I'll never be able to bring him along."

He just analyzed the whole thing for me. I was talking just three or four years ago to the Israeli ambassador to the United States, and I told him the story, and he said he thought the idea for the meeting had come from Begin. He didn't know it had come from Sadat. He was just amazed.

"Was your conversation with Sadat before Ford lost to Jimmy Carter?"

"No, it was in November, after the elections. Ford was on his way out, so I didn't think it was something I could go and talk to him about, because he wasn't going to be around to do anything about it. I don't know if Sadat expected me to do that, but it was just an amazing thing to meet with a person like that."

Quie's next trip to Israel was in about 1983, after Sadat's 1981 assassination. People there "were just speaking about him in awe." But then Quie went to Egypt, "and people there just hated him for what he had done. Just talking to rank and file people in Egypt, they had no time for that man."

What does Quie now make of the reactions, especially the Egyptian one, particularly in terms of his own most basic political beliefs?

Sometimes when you do something necessary, you wind up abandoned. I'm talking about doing things that are good not only for your own people but for other people, too. When you work only from power, you want good things only for your own citizens. We should always move in our national interests, of course. But there are times you've got to look at the best interests of mankind. But how can you do that? That's a tough walk. If you think your own people are going to love you for it, it might not happen. You continue your life, and after a while, respect comes back to you. But you shouldn't worry about things like that, because mankind is more important than you, anyway.

Quie was chuckling at this point. "Why in the world worry about those things?"

Chapter Five

Congress (I)
Agriculture, Civil Rights, and Vietnam

As discussed in the last chapter, Al Quie lost a severely truncated write-in campaign for a state House seat in 1952 following the accidental death of the incumbent. At the risk of opening the Washington chapter of his political career on a macabre note, revealed here (maybe) for the first time is what immediately precipitated his decision to run for Congress a little more than five years later.

It was January of 1958, and Gretchen and I were sitting at home after lunch. My dad's cousin had died, and his widow was attempting to sell their farm, which was across the road from our farm. So Gretchen and I were sitting there, trying to decide if we should buy the other farm, which meant I would have to go into farming full-time and drop politics. Or go into politics full-time and not increase our farming operation.

So there we were on the couch trying to decide what to do when a news flash came on the radio announcing that the congressman for the First District, August Andresen, had just died of a heart attack. And just like that I said to Gretchen, "That's the decision. I'm going to run."

After saying something about the timing being remarkable, bordering on spooky, I asked if he saw it all as a sign.

"No, I don't think so. I just moved on it. It was way later in my life that I began to wonder if things are signs or not."

Right before this exchange, Quie had been talking about how, as a state senator, he had met with Andresen in Washington in regards to moving the Twin Cities international airport (then known as Wold Chamberlain Field) to another location. Quie was one of the few who had been opposed to moving the airport. Sometime later he heard from the congressman's administrative assistant (congressional talk for "chief of staff") that Andresen privately said of Quie, "He wants my job."

"Did you?"

"Oh, yes, sure did. That's where I wanted to go. When Gretchen and I were dating, she asked what I was going to do. I said, 'I'm going to be the congressman for the First District.' She looked both ways and said, 'Don't tell anyone or the men in the white jackets will come and get you.'"

Immediately after hearing about Andresen, I got up and called a professor of economics at St. Olaf College, Lionel Anderson, as we had been talking politics with each other. I said, "Andy, I just heard the news," and he said he had, too. He was very active in the Republican Party and I said, "I want you to help me get on the ballot as a candidate for Congress," because I had no ability in that sort of thing, the nuts and bolts of politics. I cast the vision, but there are people who are really skilled at organizing and running a campaign. A woman by the name of Louise Knauss was excellent at it, and she was great help when I was running for the Legislature. Andy also was the kind of person who could network in an organized way. He said, "Okay, we'll do it." He hung up and he quickly got another call, this time from Senator Ed Thye. They talked about who might get the endorsement and, according to Andy, Thye said, "There's one person we should make sure doesn't get it," and he was talking about me.

I asked why Thye had said that.

"Because I had been very vocal in opposing the farm policies of Eisenhower's secretary of agriculture, Ezra Taft Benson, and Thye supported them. This was a huge, by far the biggest, issue in the First District at the time. Andy didn't tell Thye he had just gotten off the phone with me and promised to help with my campaign." Edward J. Thye, a Republican, represented Minnesota in the U.S. Senate for a dozen years, from 1947 to 1959.

In reasonably non-technical, abbreviated terms, Quie described how the "Ever Normal Granary" program, which had worked well throughout the Depression, World War II, and the beginning of the 1950s, was hurting farmers by the late '50s. The program's aim and method were to store commodities in order to create shortages and, therefore, raise prices—the latter of which always fell at harvest time. Farmers would receive storage payments as a "loan," the deal being that when prices rose later in the crop year they would sell what they had and pay off the supposed loan. In order to avoid great surpluses, the Department of Agriculture controlled production in various ways, but this aggravated those farmers who wanted to earn more by producing more. For a variety of reasons, including the fruits of research at land-grant universities, production increased significantly anyway, as did commodities kept in storage, growing from one year to the next. In sum, surpluses grew, because in Quie's words, "government controls were no match for farmers' ingenuity." Such large surpluses acted as "huge clouds over the market," although many politicians, he acknowledged, liked them, as "they remembered the poor crops of the 1930s."

Quie's alternative was to go "completely to world market prices, guarantee farmers 90 percent of the average world price of the previous year, and if farmers sold their crops for less than that, Washington would make up the difference. There would be no government-held surpluses to hold prices down." An important part of Quie's plan was precluding any farmer from receiving more than the equivalent of a welfare payment for a family of four. Without such a low ceiling on payments, and given the fact of guaranteed prices, American agriculture, he assumed, was destined to grow much larger in scale, and "we eventually would have mostly huge farming operations." It took a decade before some of his ideas were enacted, though he lost on the key point of limiting payments—and farm operations have, in fact, grown immensely.

Returning to the brand new campaign, I asked how many other people announced their candidacies, too.

"Oh, quite a number of them did, but it boiled down to five at the endorsing convention. Everyone thought state Rep. John Hartle would get it, because he had been Speaker of the House and state chairman of the Republican Party and was well respected. There was another man with a great Norwegian name, someone named Lundquist. And Andresen's aide, Reynold T. "Barky" Berquist, the guy who had talked about my wanting his boss' job, also was in the race."

One is left to guess what Andresen might have thought about Berquist seeking his job, as according to Quie, "Every time he was re-elected, he would come back to his administrative assistant, whoever it might have been, and ask, 'Now, if something happened to me, would you run in my place?' If the guy said, 'Well, yes I would,' Andresen would fire him." (Since he was worried less about such things, Quie would shortly hire Berquist as his own administrative assistant, and "he served me well for eleven years.")

Quie said an early poll in the district, which covered southeastern Minnesota, had him receiving three percent of the vote. "I was telling people, if Marilyn Monroe was one of the candidates, she would have done better than I was doing at the time."

"So how did you win?"

"What I did was just build on the relationships I had with people through the Lutheran Welfare Society, the church, Farm Bureau, and other activities I had been involved with, and we got a person from each county who would support me. A farmer named Elton Redalen from Fillmore County asked if he could make the nominating speech at the Republican district endorsing convention, and I said, 'Of course.' He was a person who could speak with passion."

Redalen later served as a state legislator and as Minnesota commissioner of agriculture.

Came the convention, and Quie took advantage of a trick he had learned as a college student from the master, Hubert Humphrey.

Back when I was at St. Olaf, there was a fledgling United Nations committee in Northfield, and Hubert Humphrey was asked to speak at one of the meetings. The high school auditorium was virtually filled with people, it was getting late, but he still hadn't arrived, and Republicans in the room were beginning to say things like, "There he goes again. He doesn't think enough of us to come to the meeting." Finally, there was Hubert, but instead of just coming out on stage, he came in from the back, took his coat off, dropped it on a seat, and walked down the aisle, shaking hands, walking around up front, and mounted the stage. So I figured I was going to come in the same way when it was my turn to speak.

As with all the other candidates, Quie naturally focused on agriculture in his speech. But in ways that were more liberal than usually the case in such settings, he also spoke about the importance of organized labor to the economy along with related legislation he was working on in the state senate. One of the delegates, Nancy Brataas, who, like Redalen, went on to have a long and respected career in the legislature, decided at the last moment to vote for Quie, telling him, "Any Republican who would talk about organized labor that way was going to get her vote."

I asked how many ballots it took for him to win. This was one instance, however, where his memory failed him, and he had not a clue.

"So then we had that special election. There were just three weeks between the date Governor Freeman set for filing and the special election, time that included the endorsing convention, primary, and the election itself. Wow, did I pour it on during that time, hustling around the district."

His Democratic opponent was Gene Foley, a lawyer from Wabasha, whom he beat (Quie still remembers this particular detail) by 613 votes. The margin was small enough for a congressional subcommittee on elections to come out from Washington to investigate whether there should be a full recount. "But first, they were going to have spot checks in only some precincts. Foley and I each picked one precinct in every county in the district, so we each had twelve. In that recount, they found only a discrepancy in the precincts he picked, and that was where St. Olaf was located. One vote there had gone to me that should have gone to him."

"Not too bad," I said.

"No, not too bad. But there were discrepancies in every one of the twelve precincts I had chosen. The lowest was nine votes that

Gretchen and Al Quie, along with his father, Albert Knute Quie, on the steps of the U.S. Capitol in 1959.

should have gone to me and the highest was 58 that should have gone to me. Rather than continue and expand the recount, the committee went home."

I asked why he thought there were so many discrepancies in favor of Foley?

"In this one precinct in Fillmore County that had never gone Democrat, they gave all of my votes to him and they gave all his votes to me."

"Was that on purpose or was it an accident?"

"Oh, I assume it was an accident," he said with a bigger smile than usual. "Yes, I assume it was an accident."

For what it's worth, this turned out to be the only time in our 40 hours of conversation that Quie (in the words of the transcriber) broke out into "little sing-song sounds."

———— •◆• ————

The self-proclaimed "first person with a butch haircut elected to Congress since World War II," Quie arrived in Washington in March 1958, fourteen months into the 85th Congress. (Some people at the time, Quie said, viewed the "heinie" as too German.) I asked how his new career—which was to last more than two decades—started off.

"You go to Washington and don't know a blame thing. So the first thing was Walter Judd helped me. He said, 'Come stay at my house,' which was near the Capitol." A physician and a former missionary in China, the widely admired Judd wound up serving nineteen years in Congress, representing Minnesota's Fifth District. The fact that he was the last Republican to represent Minneapolis in the House says something about how the district has changed.

> What a great way to get started. I rode with him to the Capitol, and I got sworn in. Sam Rayburn swore me in. I held my hand up and pledged to uphold the Constitution of the United States. People came up and shook hands with me, especially the Republicans. That was a big deal. Things were going against Republicans bad at the time, and to have a Republican win a special election was really amazing to them, especially when it was a close election.

Moments later, as described two chapters ago, Rep. Cliff McIntyre, a Maine Republican, invited him to his first congressional prayer breakfast. Later that evening, Judd "encouraged me by saying that after my swearing in, Sam Rayburn pulled him aside and said, 'That young man is going to be here a long time.'"

I asked why he thought Rayburn, the legendary Speaker of the House from Texas, said what he did.

Al Quie, Speaker Sam Rayburn, and Minneapolis Rep. Walter Judd, minutes after Quie was sworn in on March 6, 1958, following his special election victory in February. The ceremony had been delayed because of a recount.

"I don't know. He must have seen something in me. Some people have an uncanny sense in seeing things in people that they don't know themselves."

Quie and I had this conversation seven months after the controversy surrounding the decision by Keith Ellison, a newly elected Democrat and Muslim, to take the oath of office, in January 2007, as Minnesota's Fifth District congressman (Judd's old district) by placing his hand on the Koran. I reminded Quie he once said he never actually held a Bible when he took the oath of office for Congress, which he did eleven times.

No one held any Bible or any other book in their hand. Except for people who win special elections like I did, the whole kit and caboodle get sworn in at the same time. Nobody has a desk in front of them except for a few in the leadership, so none of that. There's all this brouhaha about Ellison. Now, I've got to tell

Congressman Al Quie and his wife Gretchen entertain Dan, Jennie, and Fred in their father's office in the Rayburn Building in 1958. They were preparing for a TV spot to be used for the November election.

you, if I were in a Muslim country and I was the first Christian to be elected to their parliament, I would hope I had enough courage to say, at least for the photo ops, "I want to lay my hand on the Bible, because you folks elected me knowing I'm a Christian and a follower of Jesus Christ. I expect you to respect me and I'm going to respect you." Ellison is very liberal and all. But I have tremendous respect for people with intellectual honesty and how they come to it. That's who they are.

Quie's first committee assignment, the Committee on Agriculture, was not the one he most wanted. That would have been the Committee on Education and Labor, but he didn't ask for it, given the fact that southern Minnesota was and remains prime farm country, and his constituents, if offered the choice, doubtless would have wanted him working on agriculture more than anything else. But the impression should not be left that winning a seat on the agriculture committee as the single most junior member of Congress was small potatoes, as quite the opposite was the case. Yet since Andresen had been a member of the committee and Quie was experienced in farm politics and practice, his coming aboard as a freshman was not seen as wholly surprising. The fact that House Minority Leader Joe Martin also wanted him on the committee played no small role either. "I fit right in real fast." In a story to be told in the next chapter, Quie did wind up on the education and labor committee only a year later. On that occasion, the assignment, in fact, was a surprise.

In the fall of his first year in Congress, the Democratic chairman of the agriculture committee, Harold Cooley of North Carolina, invited Quie to join him and other committee members on a trip to Europe to look at farm policies there. Quie was enthused and looked forward to the trip, viewing it as a great "opportunity to learn," until the senior Republican staff person on the committee told him, "I just want you to know that two of Cooley's secretaries will be going . . . and they won't be doing any secretarial work." (For those interested in the minutiae of history, the two women were sisters, one had jet black hair, one was a blonde, and both were "really built.")

Not that Quie needed the admonition, but the staffer (also a crew-cut guy) warned the young Minnesotan that his reputation might be hurt if he went along. "So I went to Harold Cooley and said, 'If those two women go, I'm not going.' Well, of course, I wound up not going. Cooley had his priorities."

So, I said, "You're in Congress a handful of months and you're already challenging a senior member who would be traveling with two women improperly."

"Yes."

"What were people thinking of you at the time? Did they know you had done this; that you had stood up to Cooley?"

"Well, I bet it got around Congress, but nobody said anything about it. He just dropped me off the list."

———— •◆• ————

After staying a short time with Walter Judd, Quie rented a very small apartment on Capitol Hill. Figuring that Gretchen and the three oldest kids should visit "and have that experience at least once," they all came out, and "we had a marvelous time, all in that two-room apartment." Ben had not been born yet and "Joel stayed back home because as a two-year-old, he wouldn't remember anything."

As opposed to current arrangements in which members of Congress fly home at government expense whenever they choose, during all but the final two years of Quie's time in Washington, representatives were allowed only one expense-paid trip home a year, which meant that he got back to Minnesota only sporadically. While being stranded in Washington was not without familial costs, "it was also neat, because I could come to the office and leave as late as I wanted in order to keep studying and get my work done. To me, it was a great way to get involved and educated."

When he did go home, he would fly into Wold Chamberlain Field, get off the plane, and walk to his car, which he had left parked at the terminal weeks earlier.

"The car was still there?"

"Yes, the car was still there. No parking fee or anything." Towards the end of that first year and as traffic increased, the airport began charging for such close-in parking. But Quie discovered that he could continue parking for free, for another year or two anyway, at the Northwest Airlines employees' lot. "It was just a little longer walk over there. There were no parking ramps, none of that stuff. What a small-time operation." That's how he saved money. He saved time by taking late night flights back to Washington on the old Capital Airlines. "First, it was a prop plane, and then they got a jet. They were pretty slow airplanes. I'd get in there about six in the morning, catch a cab, and go up to the Hill." By "Hill," he meant his office, not his apartment.

"Did you sleep on the plane?"

"I always sleep on planes. I really have to have a lot of work to do before I work on a plane. They taught me how to sleep in the Navy, so I can sleep anyplace. I can sit in a hard chair and fall asleep."

Talking of free and cheap parking, Quie claims never to have been terribly alert to the various salaries accompanying his elected jobs. "It's interesting. I got paid $28,000 when I started in Congress, but I never paid any attention to what I was making, ever. I never checked what I was paid as governor, or what a state legislator was paid, or anything like that. I wanted to serve, and I probably would have done

Left to right, Gov. Orville Freeman, President Dwight Eisenhower, Sen. Hubert Humphrey, and Rep. Al Quie dedicating a new bridge in Red Wing, Minnesota, in 1958.

it even if they hadn't paid me anything." Left unaddressed here was how he would have supported his family if he had, in fact, opted to work for the government *pro bono*. Though he did say, "I made more money on the farm the year before I went to Washington than what I made that first year as a congressman." Constraining his income once in Congress was his refusal to accept any federal farm subsidies. "Before I would rent to anyone who worked the farm, they would have to agree that there would be no government payments."

———— • ◆ • ————

In opening a conversation one morning about his Washington work on civil rights, I stated, as I've done for a long time, that the two most important pieces of legislation passed by Congress in my lifetime were the 1964 Civil Rights Act and the 1965 Voting Rights Act. The former, I said, was significant for a slew of obvious reasons, and the second was just as important for reasons generally unacknowledged. For example, I would argue that the law guaranteeing African Americans the right to vote—beyond its intrinsic and manifest necessity—made it possible for fair-minded people to talk once again about "states' rights" as a non-pejorative. Once blacks in the south were assured the most basic of rights—or, more precisely, once politicians in the south could no longer ignore black voters—people all across the country, and all across the political spectrum, had reasonable confidence that African Americans would no longer be treated and cheated atrociously. Policy-makers and others, therefore, grew more comfortable and inclined to look to states and cities, and less to Washington, in addressing hard problems. This profound development, I would add, had much more to do with subsequent conservative successes, once again all across the country, than is hardly ever noted. With that as prologue, I asked Quie—who had been in Congress for half a dozen years when the Civil Rights Act was passed—if he would agree with the mountaintop standing I gave the two breakthroughs.

"I'd have to think about whether they were the most important or not," he said, though he had no hesitation in agreeing that "1964 and 1965 were great benchmarks in our nation." If the two seminal laws were not the most important, "they sure came close. It was a time Republicans stood proud."

"Republicans in the more 'conservative wing,'" as Quie put it, "had previously worked with southern Democrats in stopping certain bills but also in passing other legislation. This was especially true in the Rules Committee. When the Civil Rights Bill came up, Bob Griffin, Charlie Goodell, and I got together to talk, plan, and organize to get the bill passed. We worked on it every way."

"Are you saying," I asked, "that when it came to the Republicans in the House, you were the leading people pushing it through?" Griffith was from Michigan and Goodell was from upstate New York.

"Others were involved," he said, but he had no hesitation declaring, "We were the main three."

At a critical meeting of the House Republican caucus leading up to the historic vote on the Civil Rights Act, Quie recalls "getting up to talk with the passion I have for a lot of things." He also recalls, with no little pride, ending his speech by saying, "If you refuse to vote for this legislation, you're un-American . . . and you're not a Christian." Through laughter more than four decades later, it seemed to hit him, "Those were my words. Whoo!"

Especially given Quie's celebrated and well-deserved tolerance of all sorts, I was taken back at that moment as much as I was at any time in our months of conversation. Sensing he had been proud that he said what he said decades earlier, I asked if he was still happy about it. His comments were both unusually stark and uncommonly— some might contend, overly—nuanced.

> I'm glad I said it, because sometime you have to be as sharp and direct as that for people to really pay attention, though they can also get defensive. The people in the room had to look at what it means to be an American and what it means to be a Christian. I remember one colleague from Tennessee with whom I was in a breakfast prayer group. He was just so angry. He said, "You're saying I'm not a Christian!" So I said, "Listen, you've got to look at what Christian means. What is the nature of Jesus Christ? What is the nature of God?" He said he opposed the bill strictly because he thought it was unconstitutional. I respected him for holding that view, and we continued to be friends, but I just thought he was wrong.

"Let's say," I pushed, "Barry Goldwater, albeit a senator, was in that caucus with you. He opposed the Civil Rights Act, but only because he thought it was unconstitutional and not because of any racist or racialist reason, as he had, in fact, worked to integrate Arizona. What would you have said to Goldwater and people who voted like him for the reasons he did?"

"I would have said they were wrong." And a few minutes later, Quie made clear, "If there are things you have to change the Constitution for, and if they're right, change the blame Constitution."

"That's pretty direct," I said.

"I thought too many of them were like a woman in Rochester who was such an active Goldwater supporter. In a loud and angry voice, I once heard her say about people she disagreed with, 'You know, I get so upset with them. They don't understand. I feel like knocking them down and jumping on them and beating it into their heads.' That doesn't work, because you're dealing with ideas and human beings."

This led me to ask how he would distinguish what I described as his "sense of moralizing" from kinds practiced by some religious conservatives who at least leave the impression it's their way or the highway when it comes to abortion, gay rights, and similar questions. "I suspect," I said, "you're not real happy with some people on the right these days when it comes to those kinds of issues. But you yourself, back in 1964, said, 'It's my interpretation of the Bible and not yours.'"

"No, I didn't do that. No."

"You didn't say your interpretation of Christianity was right and theirs wasn't?"

"No, no. I'm just telling you of my understanding about the nature of God, which is different."

"I'm challenging you here, flat out. You said, 'If you don't vote this way, you're not a Christian.'"

Yes. At that time I was still calling people "Christian." I don't use that word now. Now I say, "Followers of Jesus Christ." So at that time, yes, I did say that. But when you have a confrontation of ideas, it can't be "my way or the highway," because when you add that, it means you won't listen. I would listen if somebody would say, "The nature of Jesus Christ is that slavery is still okay." Or if whites said their well-being is more important than that of blacks. Or if someone said, "I just don't believe that there ought to be sex between blacks and whites." Those are all wrong and terrible positions, but I'd be glad to engage in those conversations.

Months later I asked who the Tennessee congressman was with whom he had interesting words. "People will have to wonder," was the best I could get out of him.

Among conversations Quie had during the years of the Civil Rights Movement that left an impression was one with Andrew Young, who helped organize Resurrection City—"The Poor People's Campaign"—on the Washington Mall five weeks after Martin Luther King Jr. was assassinated in Memphis in 1968. Part of the impetus for the meeting, and for what turned out to be a friendship when Young was subsequently elected to Congress from Georgia, was a decision made by Quie five years earlier, in 1963, which he came to regret.

Old friends from Minnesota, a pastor and his wife, Carl and Joanie Groettum, had come out to Washington to participate in the March on Washington, and they stayed at our house. They were going to march with Martin Luther King, and Carl asked if I would join them. I said no, because as a member of the legislative branch I would be making decisions about issues related to the demonstration, and I didn't think it was appropriate for me to march. I knew it wasn't a very good answer, though that's what I said at the time. But now the pastor and his wife—who were childhood friends of Gretchen's—were losing their nerve, and he said that maybe he and his wife shouldn't go either. So I said to him, "Carl, some day this event will be talked about in history books, and your grandkids will say, "What did you do?" and you'll say, "I went to Washington to march, but I lost my nerve." So they marched while I stayed at our home, and I quickly regretted my own decision. I'm the one with the regret.

But I finally did something about it when Ralph Abernathy and the Southern Christian Leadership Conference set up a tent city on the Mall several years later. Charlie Goodell, Bob Griffin, and I went down there and said we were going to stand with them, and if they needed a Republican office to work out of, we'd open our offices to them. That's where my friendship with Andrew Young began. When he came to Congress [in 1973], I asked if he remembered that, and he said he did. Doing things like that builds relationships, and while he was a Democrat and he might do things differently than me in Congress, there was a human bond between us. I had respect for him for standing up with his people and for his people, and he saw in me a person who would actually come down there to meet with them. It would have been one thing for people living in the tents to visit me and my colleagues in our offices. But going down there and walking in Resurrection City with them, that was important.

When meeting with inner-city officials, Quie still makes it a habit to do so in their own neighborhoods.

———————•◆•———————

I mentioned a moment ago how I had been taken aback when Quie reported how he had told a congressional colleague how a vote against the Civil Rights Act would be both un-American and un-Christian. Staying with the broad subject, this is probably the right time to note the single most powerful emotional moment in our mornings together.

We had been talking about abortion, which we didn't do often. More specifically, I had just noted how, up until *Roe v. Wade* in 1973, the Democratic Party in Minnesota was more pro-life than was the state's Republican Party, insofar as Catholics were more likely to be members of the former rather than the latter. For a number of reasons, everything shifted after *Roe*, with a sizable number of pro-choice Republicans moving to the DFL.

"What makes me cringe," Quie said, "is when former moderate Republicans talk about all those kids who would have born in poverty in urban areas, but because they were aborted how it's better that we not have them." With more discomfort than I had ever heard in his voice, he added slowly, "*That* really hurts me. I feel it so deeply about what we did with the people who were here when the white man came. We tried to kill them with genocide. I feel so deeply about what we did with the people from Africa when we brought them over here on those slave ships. I can't help but cry thinking about it."

More than speaking haltingly, Quie now began to cry, and soon to sob, forced for a while to stop after every handful of words. (The ellipses that follow represent pronounced pauses.) "Can you imagine being in chains in a hold of a sailing ship? When I'm in a small room and there's any possibility that the door could be locked and nobody is around . . . I know the horrible feeling of claustrophobia. Think of these men and women . . . ."

I asked if he wanted to take a break.

"Mitch, I'll get hold of it. I've got to get my thoughts . . . ."

"Take your time."

After one of many sighs and a long delay, "We can't say to them, 'Snap out of it. That was in the past.'"

"Are you talking about African Americans?"

"And Native Americans. Everyone carries with them the stories. It wasn't all that long ago. There's a professor at Howard University who said that it takes 750 years for memories like those to leave a people, and that's only if nothing happens in that time to bring it all back again. I don't know if it's true, but it really strikes me, it really hits home. We're living in a culture that will be remembered by our offspring for a long time. That's what we're talking about."

Without saying exactly what the "it" in question was, he went on: "It will be resolved only if we consciously name it, talk with each other about it, and care for each other enough so that we walk with each other. It can't be done on a large scale. It's got to occur between people who have been cast together, whether as family or friends. But there's a host of people where that isn't going on at all."

"Men," he said, "because of our nature," have a hard time opening up in the way he was doing. "When I hear that a high percentage of men can't name anyone they can really share with . . . ," and his voice tailed off again. "I try to live my life vulnerably. If I were trying to put up a barricade or blockade for my own protection, it wouldn't have happened," meaning the way he had just broken down. "God made us to be social beings and for things like this to occur. So our relationship with God needs to be followed by relationships with other human beings. That's what we're talking about here, civility. Civility is to accept another person the way God made them."

After a concluding pause, he said, "Boy, I haven't gotten as emotional about this for a long time. You really, really released it in me."

"What in particular did it? You had been talking about African Americans, and right before that, the genocide of the Indians."

"What did it was that for some human beings, they believe it's better for their children, and other children, not to live. That's the way it comes out to me. Boy, what selfishness."

Months after this exchange, when I sent Quie a draft of this chapter for his review, I asked what he meant by the key word "it." How much did the two-letter word encompass?

'It' means the deep and underlying divisions between people that last for years, decades, and centuries: Divisions like those historically among Jews, Christians, and Muslims. Divisions like those historically between Catholics and Protestants. Divisions caused by one group taking away the land of another group. The deep divisions caused by genocide, slavery, and discrimination. In all these instances, the passion is so deep. Sometimes the distance gets shortened by intermarriage. In my time, Vatican II was very helpful. What are necessary are repentance, forgiveness, and love.

———·◆·———

Quie supported President Eisenhower's approach to fighting communism in Vietnam, which the Minnesotan described as providing advisers to the South Vietnamese. He later supported President Kennedy's policy of increasing American involvement. Congressional redistricting in 1962, following the 1960 Census, led him to lose rural Waseca and Freeborn Counties and pick up what was then exurban Dakota County farther north, but what has become the suburban southern rim of the Minneapolis-St. Paul metropolitan area. "One of the things that I noticed was that there were more radical people up there," by which he meant both left and right. At a public meeting in Dakota County soon after it became part of his district, he was asked what the United States should do in Vietnam. Referring to how the Nazis had murdered the parents of the "Jewish lad" he had befriended in high school, he said, "Here's my thinking. It comes out of my background. When Hitler moved into the lowlands, if we had sent troops in there and engaged him at that time, I think we would have ended the war fast. So I said I think Kennedy ought to send troops in. I got booed for that."

In August 1964, the Johnson administration claimed that three North Vietnamese torpedo boats fired on two American destroyers, the U.S.S. *Maddox* and the U.S.S. *Turner Joy*, in the Gulf of Tonkin, setting in train the massive escalation of U.S. involvement in the war. Quie, however, was skeptical to the point of becoming cynical about what really had happened at sea and the administration's truthfulness on the matter.

> We had to vote on the Gulf of Tonkin Resolution, which really would cause us to engage, and I absolutely didn't believe Lyndon Johnson. I thought he was setting this thing up to stimulate the American people's support for what he wanted to do there. So while I still, at the time, thought we ought to be helping the people in Vietnam, I also thought there might be something deceitful going on. I said to myself that if a person does what he doesn't believe, or if he doesn't do what he does believe, it corrupts his soul. There's got to be congruency between all of what you say and believe and what you do. So there I was on the floor of the House, and as all those votes were going up on the board, I wanted so badly to vote against that resolution. But I realized that if I was the only person to do so, it would put great pressure on me, and I didn't want that. So I went the other way and voted for it.

I asked if he regrets not voting against the resolution. "I've never ceased regretting it," he said. "I've never ceased regretting that vote where I put my political survival above my hunch about what was true. It has helped me, however, understand the internal pain of other people in politics."

The Gulf of Tonkin Resolution, which has come to be commonly understood as grounded at least partially in manufactured facts, passed in the House unanimously, provoking only two dissenting votes in the Senate—those of Ernest Gruening of Alaska and Wayne Morse of Oregon, both Democrats.

I asked Quie what made him believe, or maybe just sense, that Johnson was being deceitful?

"Just the way he was, the way he operated."

"Which was how?"

"I think all bullies are deceitful. It's truth that ought to prevail. Just the fact he had the reputation of grabbing his people by the lapel and shaking them. He just had a reputation for that kind of forceful nature. But I also recognize that some of my reaction might have been bias picked up from other Republicans talking about a president of the other party."

Secretary of Defense Robert McNamara didn't bolster Quie's confidence about the wisdom or execution of the war, either.

"Listening to McNamara increased my doubts. He would cite the number of Viet Cong, and he'd say that if we got those killed, then we'd be home free, we'd have victory. Well, the Viet Cong kept coming all the time. But I really didn't understand then who the Viet Cong were." Quie explained that it eventually dawned on him that the Viet Cong were not North Vietnamese, they were *South* Vietnamese.

But the widely held fear that the Domino Theory was right—that if the United States bailed out and left, neighboring countries also would fall to communism—was one Quie shared, leaving him wondering how "we could ever pull out." Also powerfully at work, as will be seen, was his inclination and preference to support administrations, regardless of party, whenever he could. Yet he was not impressed when Republican Richard M. Nixon came to office in 1969, wielding a plan to end the war "without ever saying what it was."

The next step in my thinking was when Ford came in, we pulled out of Vietnam, and he gave amnesty to all those people who had gone to Canada. I realized he was right, that someone had to have enough courage to say, "We're pulling up stakes. We can't do this anymore. We have to suffer the shame." But I felt an obligation to the people who had been with us, both the Vietnamese and the Hmong. We had a moral responsibility to take them in. So whenever the subject of their immigration came up, I spoke out in support.

Employing a farm analogy this time, the period reminded Quie of when he "was a young guy still in high school."

After my dad lost his arm, my younger brother Paul and I were doing more of the work around the farm, and we were cleaning out some pens and I said to him, "It's your turn to drive the manure spreader to the field, and I'll stay home." But he wouldn't do it, so I grabbed him. I was bigger than he was and I tried to muscle him up onto the seat of that manure spreader, but finally my strength gave out. I couldn't do it, and I had to back down. And I thought that's where we were in Vietnam. When it was over, we looked at where we were at the start and where we were at the end, and we had made no progress whatsoever. All those years, all that bloodshed. We might as well have just never started it in the first place.

I asked that when it was time for the United States to go, if he felt that our involvement in Vietnam had been justified, but that we had to get out, very practically, because we couldn't win any longer. Or if he thought that American involvement was intrinsically wrong to begin with.

"I think we should only have been advisers, as Eisenhower did. That should have been the extent of it."

"Did you believe that at the time, though?"

"No, that's where I am now, after the whole thing is over. No, I didn't believe that at the time."

"So at the time, you were supporting troop increases until we got to over half a million?"

"Yes, yes," he acknowledged, and to make a point about miscalculations of the moment and the brilliance of hindsight, he drew on Iraq. "When the first President Bush in that desert war didn't go on to Baghdad to get Saddam Hussein, I just knew in my bones we were going to fight there again. I felt he should have gone all the way to Baghdad. But now, when I look back, if he had gone all the way to Baghdad at that time, would things have been any different than where we are in Iraq now?"

As noted above, Quie endorsed Ford's granting of amnesty to young Americans who went to Canada to avoid the draft. (He was of different mind when it came to pardoning Richard Nixon for Watergate crimes, believing that prosecution is sometimes necessary for national healing.) But better than merely endorsing Ford's decision to allow the men to come home from Toronto and Calgary, as one might expect given how real, live people never get lost in his world of politics and policy, Quie was exceedingly thankful for that particular act of healing wrought by his longtime friend. The disorder, disillusionment, and disrespect of young people during the war "really cut me," and he continues to view Ford's decision to defuel some of the tinder as heroic.

———— • ◆ • ————

It occurred to me one morning that for all of Quie's devotion to bringing people together politically, spiritually, and the like, he nevertheless could be viewed as a caucus of one. Here was someone eager and equipped to work closely with others, yet not especially worried about standing alone or nearly so if need be; a person prone to examining the world from idiosyncratic angles. His comments about Vietnam are cases in point, though they would be even more clear-cut if he could have willed himself to vote no on the Gulf of Tonkin resolution. Of my suggested tag of a caucus of one, Quie said he never thought of himself that way, "but I do try to think things out, and I've gotten away from being fearful that my caucus or party might not support me. Maybe the reason is that when my party or caucus didn't support me, I still survived."

This brings us to the policy area where his contributions and, therefore, reputation were biggest: education. On no subject during his 21 years in the House of Representatives was Al Quie more successful in building teams. On no topic was he more prepared to vote surprisingly "no" with the express aim of improving bills later on. And in no area was he more singular in defining what constituted a successful program.

Chapter Six

Congress (II)
Education, the War on Poverty, and Challenging Your Own Team

Here's a real-life—and an equally equine—metaphor about teaching. It opens with Al Quie talking about Katherine Page, principal of Highland Elementary School in Columbia Heights, a first-ring suburb north of Minneapolis. As was frequently the case, the governor and I had been discussing the importance of human ties in learning. "I went to Highland with a study group," he reported, "and Katherine was talking about how the most important thing a child needs is a relationship." Many professionals in the field, Quie added,

> also say there needs to be a relationship between the teacher and student, especially if the student needs remedial help. They're right, of course, but what Katherine recognizes is that the relationship has to be with the parent, too. And more than in most schools, parents really were coming to her school and creating relationships. I wanted to figure out how this was happening, and I found out it started by teachers going to the homes of their students first, and not the other way around. Parents' comfort zone is in their home rather than at school.

> [Here's where the horses gallop in.]

> I use the example of training my horses. If there's anything in me that's tense, my horse gets tense and he can't learn. The horse can sense my tenseness. If I can't get rid of my tenseness, the only thing I can do is to get off and let it rest and walk until I'm calm. Then I get back on.

Horses are so eager to learn when you develop that oneness with them, when you understand where they are. If the wind is blowing and things are rough, you know they're going to be tense. If it's something strange for them, like the first time they go across a stream, they may not want to go. But if you just sit there and wait and have their head facing into it until they figure it out, they'll slowly take one step and then another. If it takes 45 minutes, be sure you told someone else that you might not be coming back for a while. I've done that.

Do you have the patience to listen? I had a horse that was an outlaw practically, because of what he'd done to his owner: broke his leg, kicked him in the head, jumped on top of him, all stuff like that. [Quie gave a cowboy chuckle here.] I just turned that horse loose in my pasture and I waited for him to come to me. I sat down at four o'clock in the afternoon and at ten o'clock at night, he came to me. Now if you've got patience to wait from four till ten . . . ."

Lacking in patience, I interrupted at this point and asked what he did for those six hours.

"I just sat there and waited. Just sat there and waited."

"No book or anything?"

"No book or anything. I just sat there and made sure I didn't look him in the eye. He kept his back to me all the time in the corner, so I couldn't look him in the eye. Now teaching in many schools, it's the same. This horse, because of things that happened to him, I'd have to say he was damaged. Many kids are also damaged early in their lives. And, you know, their parents are often damaged, too."

The risk in these stories is that they may leave the impression that Quie is a weeded-over flower child when it comes to how boys and girls learn and thrive; that he might be excessively occupied with soft feelings and insufficiently interested in hard work. Be assured he's not, and not just because Republicans en route to 90 are usually tougher-minded and more earthbound than that. Nonetheless, metaphoric lessons and other examples like these are telling in how he views education—the field that has been his policy passion above all others.

———•◆•———

In celebration of his 80th birthday in 2003, Center of the American Experiment, the Minneapolis-based think tank I've led since 1990, staged four events in Quie's honor. The finale, in conjunction with several other groups and individuals, was a big bash in September attended by about a thousand people of all stripes and plaids. "Man of faith, public servant, lover of life and adventure" was how the invitation described him. His many friends hoped to put on the biggest birthday party ever for a former Minnesota governor, and we believe we did. It was a wonderful evening—even if the hotel refused to allow Quie to enter the ballroom on horseback. That really was our plan and he was more than game, but for unfathomable reasons the hotel said he'd have to walk in, on his own two feet, like everyone else.

The other three events, earlier in the year, were more intellectually animated. At each a top-tier scholar talked about a main theme of Quie's professional—and no less his personal—life: faith, families, and education. For education, the governor and I chose Chester E. Finn Jr. an old colleague whom I've long described as the nation's most incisive critic in the field. Checker (as he's known) is a veteran observer of Congress and, not incidentally, a former Senate and White House staffer in both Republican and Democratic settings. His introductory remarks, in which he used another metaphor to summarize Quie's conception of education policy, are perfectly on target.

While the governor only occasionally uses the good Catholic word "subsidiarity," Checker opened with it, while also noting that, "there is nothing more private, more intimate, more local, and less of anyone else's business than rearing one's own children."

"The doctrine of subsidiarity," he explained, "teaches that the entities nearest to a social challenge should do their best to meet it before resorting to larger or more distant groups for help. You don't hoist things higher up the organizational ladder unless you absolutely must." When it comes to education, Finn asked, at what level should various decisions be made, and by whom? Who should have lead responsibility? Parents? Teachers and principals? Superintendents? State policy-makers? Federal officials? More than an everyday five-layer cake, he argued that a richer and more accurate way of picturing American education is that of a *marble* cake, five-layers tall. Or, if you will, imagine a high-caloric world in which everybody is constantly swirling around on sugar highs. (This last word picture is mine; not Checker's.)

"I want to suggest," Finn continued, "that one lens through which we can reasonably view Al Quie's approach to education these past 80 years is that of a person [who has] patiently and assiduously tried to re-bake the cake with neater layers and less marbling by sorting out, in a more rational and efficient way . . . the various responsibilities for educating children and making decisions about schooling. He has sought to assign to the family those education responsibilities that it can most appropriately and successfully fulfill. He has done the same at the school, district, state, and even the federal levels."

Quie framed the sequencing this way in one of our conversations:

The federal government can take money away easier than anyone else can. And state government can take money away from people easier than local levels of government can. There ought to be some way that you have a clear balance where the federal government does the least amount of harm, and state government does the least amount of harm, and people locally have the greatest voice. They aren't going to have as great a voice as they used to have because we've consolidated school districts in Minnesota from about 1,600 when I was on the Oak Grove board to about 350 now, and I'm convinced that big districts aren't going to work. What we need are smaller districts, smaller schools, and smaller classes.

Quie's focus and confidence in parents, however, were less of a given when he arrived in Congress in March 1958.

A year after getting there, he participated in a White House conference on families and found himself disagreeing with a nun who contended that government officials often were too quick to take children away from their parents and place them in foster care. "How I ever in the world had the *audacity* to do so, but I stood up and took her on and talked about how horrible parents were at times. Because of my work in special education in Minnesota, I had developed a lot of confidence in the skills and knowledge of professionals in the field and I just figured that if parents were doing lousy jobs with children, let's find people who could do better jobs and put the kids with them. Let's put more of this in the hands of professionals. Boy! Have I ever done a 180."

It was a reversal, it goes without saying, that should not be interpreted as suggesting that Quie believes kids who have been seriously neglected or abused should be forced to stay in dangerous and unacceptable situations just because a biological parent lives there. Of course he doesn't. We'll talk more about boys and girls living in circumstances that are a million miles different from the one in which he grew up in Chapter Twelve on early childhood education.

About two years after the White House conference, Rep. Edith Green, a ten-term Democrat from Oregon and a major figure on the House Education and Labor Committee, put together a group to visit the Soviet Union and study education there. Both she and Quie thought the focus would be higher education, but the scope expanded along the way. "We first flew into Frankfurt and went to the Berlin Wall, where we went through Checkpoint Charlie, and I could see immediately the enormous difference between West Berlin and East Berlin, just in the construction of buildings. On the east side of the Wall, there were nets on the buildings to keep bricks and other debris from falling off and killing people. As I could see it, there was no pride in their work, as opposed to the West where there was pride."

After describing a flight into Moscow featuring restrooms on the plane "worse than those at a gas station," and then sitting on the plane "forever" as officials checked their passports, Quie and the delegation visited the likes of Moscow State University before moving on to the Soviet equivalent of elementary and secondary schools as well as preschool programs. In addition to Moscow, they traveled to Leningrad, Uzbekistan, and Kazakhstan, the latter two in Soviet Central Asia.

When I was in Kazakhstan, I spent time at an *Internot*, a residential institution where children lived away from their parents, having been taken there when they were very small, between about two-and-a-half months of age to about two-and-a-half years old. It was the kind of program, frankly, that I thought we should have for parents who were not able to handle their kids or who handled them wrong. So I visited this particular Internot outside the city of Almata, and I was impressed with what the kids were doing. As the Soviets said at the time, they were "developing the new human being for the socialist society." I talked to a mother and father who had a child there. They were really impressed, too. I asked if their child ever came home over the summer, and they said, "No, no. He could, but he didn't." (I don't remember if they had a boy or a girl.) You had to watch that business about how people in the Soviet Union said they *could* do things back then. What did they really mean by it? They said they didn't bring their child home for the summer because officials at the Internot "were doing such a good job" and they didn't want to "interrupt or interfere" in development. Something just struck me that there was something wrong about all that.

I sensed the same thing about the word "could" when I was in the Soviet Union in 1985, as it turned out, about two months before Mikhail Gorbachev came to power. Could Jews in Moscow attend synagogue on a regular basis if they so chose? Sure they *could*. I was there on a Friday evening and saw them. But who was to say KGB agents wouldn't mark the Sabbath in their own way, by taking photos of Jews gathered to pray? And once the shots were developed, who really knew if congregants had a fair chance for finding new jobs or better apartments?

Before the trip, Quie had visited with famed child psychologist Urie Bronfenbrenner at Cornell and did the same on his return. Dr. Bronfenbrenner had studied children in the Soviet Union, among other many other places, and Quie wanted to compare notes and review the visit with him. "It was really insightful," he said.

If I had to guess, the legendary scholar said something like the following (as he did on at least one other occasion): In order to develop, a child needs the enduring, irrational involvement of one or more adults in care and joint activity with the child. When asked to restate what he meant by "irrational involvement," Bronfenbrenner's Ivy League response was, "Somebody has got to be crazy about that kid!" Places with names like Internot wouldn't seem hospitable to such exuberance.

"Several years later," Quie said, "the Soviets just quit the whole Internot because it was such an absolute failure. By that time I had learned some things, especially from Urie, about how important parents are. All of this was a learning experience for me."

———— • ◆ • ————

I opened our conversation one morning by asking Quie if he had always been on the Education and Labor Committee while in Congress. He had not, as the practice was for members of the House to serve on only one major committee at a time, and he had won a prized seat on the Agriculture Committee immediately after arriving in Washington. But that's not to say he wasn't interested in a spot on Education and Labor, and a fortuitous flight from Washington back home in early 1959—a year after his victory in a special election and three months after re-election to his first full term—led to the assignment. "I was getting on a plane to fly back to Minneapolis for a Lincoln Day dinner when Carroll Kearns, the ranking Republican on the Education and Labor Committee, and I saw each other, and he said, 'Let's make certain we sit together.'" The Pennsylvanian was to speak at the dinner, now called the Lincoln-Reagan dinner, and still a major annual event for Minnesota's Republican Party. Not incidentally, Quie won re-election in November 1958 even though Republicans in the House lost 48 seats, reducing their caucus to 153 members in the 435-person chamber. "Kearns and I were talking about my interests," Quie continued,

> and I said the committee I'd love to be on was Education and Labor because I had some ideas for making labor legislation fairer and that I would love to work in the whole education area. I told him about my experience with handicapped children in the Minnesota Legislature, and then getting engaged right away after getting to Congress in helping students go to

college. So Kearns said, "As soon as we get to Minneapolis, I'm going to call Charlie Halleck [the House Minority Leader] and I'll get you on that committee." I mentioned the rule about not being on two major committees at the same time and that I didn't want to drop the Agriculture Committee. He said, "We'll work that out." He also said the reason there was an opening on the Education and Labor Committee was because "after the passage of the Taft-Hartley Act," the committee was "too hot for Republicans." A seat on it, Kearns said, was "practically tantamount to defeat," as Republicans "would go on there and they'd lose in the next election."

I asked why membership was so dangerous for Republicans.

"Organized labor," Quie said, "was much stronger then, as you know, and they would pour everything they had in getting rid of Republicans on the committee."

"So it was a matter of labor attacking Republicans," I said, "rather than the party's base attacking them for votes they may have cast or for simply being on the committee?"

"Yes, it was labor attacking. That's the way I understood it. Taft-Hartley was just disastrous for organized labor, or at least that's the way they saw it. But I told Kearns that it was safer being in the eye of a hurricane than at the edge and that if a person was straightforward and honest he would be safe. But if he did lose, it would be an honorable defeat."

The Taft-Hartley Act, officially known as the Labor-Management Relations Act, was passed in 1947 over President Truman's veto. It constrained unions in various ways, including giving the federal government power to obtain 80-day injunctions against any strike it deemed a danger to national health or safety.

"When I returned to Washington after the weekend in Minnesota," Quie continued with the story, "I got a note from Carroll Kearns saying I was on Education and Labor. I was really delighted. But I quickly came to recognize, as I thought about organizing myself, caring for my family, serving on the Agriculture Committee, as well as spending some time on other interests, how difficult it is for members of Congress to do their jobs right if they're on more than one major committee." Fortunately, the education and labor workload was slowing down at the end of the Eisenhower administration, and Quie eventually left the Agriculture Committee in 1967.

A main dynamic on the Education and Labor Committee during this period, according to Quie, was "absolute opposition on the Republican side to the federal government assisting in K-12 education — absolute opposition. There was no equivocation on that one. The Republicans on education were like labor unions on labor legislation. They weren't going to let any more legislation go through because they were afraid of what it might do to them. The only Republican interest in education was in higher education, especially in matters of scientific research."

Along with research, there also was House Republican interest in helping finance buildings and facilities at colleges and universities. The federal government had been underwriting the construction of dormitories as campuses began to grow dramatically following World War II. But now, President John Kennedy recommended that Washington also help pay for academic buildings, though his plan called for federal dollars going only to public colleges and universities, not private ones.

That's when I started my study to see if that was the right philosophy or not. I went back to the Northwest Ordinance and to the Morrill Land-Grant Act in 1862 and determined that, at least in higher education, we should not discriminate between public and private institutions. So with the help of Edith Green, who had some things she didn't like about Kennedy, we passed a bill in the higher education subcommittee, which she chaired, that included private colleges and universities as well. We then got it through the full House and did the same in the Senate, but when it came back to the House after the conference committee report, the National Education Association mounted a campaign in opposition and defeated it on the House floor.

At the beginning of the 1960s, the NEA was still much more of a professional organization than a union, with administrators, rather than teachers, continuing to hold largest sway. I asked Quie why it had opposed federal funding for academic facilities at private institutions, though it was the kind of question to which anyone halfway involved in education would know the answer even before uttering the question.

"They were opposed to the bill," Quie said, "because it might somehow lead to vouchers. That was the main thing. That was their bogey man, and it's the same to this day. But then, in 1963 we were able to pass it, the Academic Facilities Act. People picked up on the idea and after a while they said, 'Hey, the NEA is wrong,' and we were able to do it."

A few months after this conversation, Quie added a postscript about Al Shanker, the longtime president of the rival American Federation of Teachers who died in 1997, saying, "In retrospect, Shanker may have helped in getting the Academic Facilities Act passed in 1963. I got to know him well later on, and he became one of my education organization heroes."

———— • ◆ • ————

Came the War on Poverty, and President Lyndon Johnson proposed by far the largest federal involvement in American education ever: the Elementary and Secondary Education Act of 1965, which still serves as the foundation for Washington's financial support and reach into the nation's schools. No Child Left Behind, for example, while radically different in many ways from the original ESEA, is but the latest reauthorization of that seminal legislation.

The superb historian Diane Ravitch has written in *The Troubled Crusade: American Education 1945–1980* about how Kennedy, in 1961, had tried to get Congress to pass a federal aid to education bill, but failed because of the "usual conflicts over race and religion." After Johnson's mammoth victory in 1964, which was accompanied by now truly immense Democratic majorities in Congress (68 to 32 in the Senate and 295 to 140 in the House), Johnson was both determined and now equipped to win what Kennedy couldn't. "With this kind of legislative support," Ravitch has argued, "no group was powerful enough to block a bill. Previous bills, phrased in terms of helping the schools or raising teachers' salaries or meeting the nation's needs, had foundered. Johnson's bill was cast as an antipoverty measure, and its largest benefits were aimed at improving the schooling of poor children." The focus on poverty made a compromise possible between partisans of both public and private schools, for while only public agencies would receive federal dollars, poor kids attending nonpublic schools would be eligible to share in services and facilities.

The biggest part of the first ESEA—five-sixths of it—was known as Title I, whose aim was to meet the "special educational needs of educationally deprived children." Programs designed by local educational agencies using Title I funds, according to Ravitch, included not only improvement in academic performance, but also "the provision of socialization skills, cultural enrichment, social work, parental involvement, libraries, speech and hearing therapy, nutrition, clothing, and medical services." The goals were diffuse to the point of global, yet as one observer (quoted by Ravitch) put it: "Title I . . . asked schoolmen to launch an activity in what was essentially an uncharted area and to implement successful programs for the very group of children the schools historically had seemed least able to help."

People who think about such things almost surely assume that Quie voted for the 1965 iteration of ESEA. But he didn't — for three main reasons, one of which was conventional, with the other two more distinctive.

In order to maintain Catholic support for the bill, provisions were included that allowed for a modest stream of dollars for instructional materials to be used in religious schools, as well as other accommodations that pleased Catholic educators and leaders. But because the coalition pushing for this radical expansion of federal power was novel and, therefore, fragile, managers of the bill, according to Quie, refused to accept any amendments. In fact, "People at the time said they didn't even correct grammatical errors because they figured doing so might hurt the coalition. So it passed both houses with those mistakes, and I voted against it—although not because of its grammar." Keep in mind that because the South was almost uniformly Democratic at the time, and that Southern Democrats were regularly less enthused than other Democrats about getting the federal government involved in neighborhood education,

A meeting of the House Education and Labor Committee in 1961. The pipe-smoking man in the middle is Rep. Adam Clayton Powell, a Harlem Democrat with whom Quie worked well. Others at the table, from left to right are Representatives Edith Green of Oregon, Carl Perkins of Kentucky, Powell, Peter Frelinghuysen of New Jersey, and Quie.

the coalition was "fragile" despite overpowering Democratic majorities in the two chambers. The same deep reluctance generally applied to southerners' views about Washington's participation in matters of parochial education and, of course, race overwhelmingly.

The unexceptional reason Quie voted against the first ESEA was that he thought it would wind up costing much more than Democratic leaders were saying that it would. He voted against Medicare in 1965 for the same reason, and needless to say, he has been proved wildly correct in each instance. "I figured they were being duplicitous with both pieces of legislation, and I also thought both bills imposed the federal government's will on people much more than they should. It was in future years that I developed amendments that would bring the education law more in keeping with what I wanted."

It was at this point in our conversation that I expressed surprise that he had voted against the original ESEA. He had left the hint of an impression that he would have been happy, 40-plus years earlier, if the legislation had never come to be, with or without his amendments. But the realist in him recognized, both now and then, "once a program becomes part of the warp and woof of our society, I don't think you can be a dog in the manger and say, 'Let's repeal that bill.'"

"There were two things," he said, "I wanted to have done in order to support the program. One was to give parents a voice, and the other was to determine more accurately what children really should be covered by it."

As for the former interest, and in another instance, Quie pushed for stronger citizen participation in local, federally underwritten Community Action Programs. And as was the case with ESEA, he originally voted against omnibus legislation containing CAPs until he prevailed on the issue. In the matter of ESEA, he argued that for any school district to receive Title I funds, it would have to have a parental advisory committee. He later upped the ante—or more precisely, lowered it on Checker Finn's ladder—by urging that each school, not just each district, have such a group. Quie succeeded on this score by working closely with the chairman of the Education and Labor Committee, Adam Clayton Powell, a Democrat and African American from Manhattan, whom I remember as being quite flamboyant and controversial.

Before Quie even got to Congress, Powell had been pushing amendments of his own that encouraged racial integration and the greater involvement of minorities in American schools more generally; a direction in which most southern members of his party had no interest in going. So Quie went to Powell and said Republicans were prepared to vote for an amendment of Quie's and that its stipulation of more parent involvement would mean more black parents could become involved in ways that Powell sought. Key, I should add, to understanding how such an interesting bloc of bedfellows came be, is the earlier noted fact about how a higher proportion of congressional Republicans than Democrats voted for the Civil Rights Act of 1964. The same was true for the Voting Rights Act of 1965.

When it came to determining who qualified for Title I help, as originally passed, ESEA counted the number of *economically* disadvantaged children (based on Census data that was three years old before it could be used, but which then would not be replaced for another decade), rather than the number of *educationally* disadvantaged children (based on annual testing). Quie acknowledged the sociological fact, both then and now, that economically needy students are more likely to be academically behind than are boys and girls from middle class and affluent families. But that did not mean, Quie emphasized both then and now, that students from families without much money are always unsuccessful in class, or conversely, that students from more fortunate families always do well in their school work. All this was perhaps obvious, but not necessarily the stuff of blunt federal formulas—formulas that just happened to disproportionately benefit New York and Kentucky, the respective homes of the two most powerful Democrats on the Education and Labor Committee at the time, Adam Clayton Powell of the Empire State and Carl Perkins of the Bluegrass State. Their Republican colleague from the Gopher State never prevailed on the point and Title I funds are still distributed on the basis of economic rather than educational well-being.

But most centrally and viscerally, Quie had problems, as he still does, with an implicit tack in programs such as Title I. "By this time, I had come to the conclusion—though it grew even stronger later on when we were working with handicapped kids—that you shouldn't have to put people into a box in order to help them. There ought to be a seamless flow. As soon as children fall behind, there ought to be programs to help them catch up and keep up, because if they don't have such assistance, they will do even worse, and then they really will fit into boxes and need special programs."

A few minutes later he put it more painfully, "It's tough when a person is suffering so badly that they become mentally ill." And a short spell after that, as an example of the depth and mystery of parent-child bonds and a preview of our subsequent conversations about early childhood education, he explained why he and his siblings could never sing a note. "My mother, who had a beautiful singing voice, as did my father, used to say the reason none of her children sang is because she was almost always sick when carrying us so she couldn't sing. I didn't understand this at the time, it just passed over me. But the child in the womb is feeling and hearing these things. *It's alive.* It's picking these things up."

————•◆•————

I personally and professionally have an impossible time imagining any public program that *doesn't* put people in boxes—better known as "categories," each one weighted with codified rules for entry and aid. And for good measure, I would suggest that "seamless," by definition, is bridging too far for immense bureaucracies of any sort. Yet nuance is in order here. To contend that the federal government has been of near-empty service to American elementary and high school students during and subsequent to Quie's tenure in Washington, as critics particularly on the right sometimes do, is criticism spread too facile and far. It's a barb too severe, for example, if one simply considers the better lives enjoyed by millions of disabled boys and girls and their families because of federal mandates regarding equal educational opportunities for all children—legislation that Quie had important things to do with, perhaps most notably, leading the way in expanding the notion of "handicap" to include learning disabilities. And it's impossible to imagine how efforts to lessen cavernous academic disadvantages and differences across the country would have been launched and propelled when they were, and with anything approaching the seriousness of purpose and resources they were, if the Elementary and Secondary Education Act of 1965 had not been enacted. Those who sculpted the seminal law made both history and a difference. To acknowledge, however, that improvements wrought by federal educational policies in the lives of children, scholastically and in other ways, have not been nearly consequential enough is equally true, and Quie concurs, of course. Just look at much of inner-city education or the embarrassing and dangerous ways that American teenagers of all places and backgrounds stack up against adolescents in much of the rest of the world. To a provocation of mine concerning the ability of Washington ever to devise and implement such beneficial policies, Quie readily said, "Well, they've proven so far they can't do it on a large scale."

———— • ◆ • ————

The story has been different in higher education in many ways, starting with the frequently cited observation that while very few parents from around the world have sent their children to attend American elementary or high schools, many millions of international students have attended colleges and universities in the United States. More important than Quie's role in making it possible for private and religious institutions, not just public ones, to receive federal dollars for academic facilities, was his subsequent leadership in getting Washington to expand collegiate access primarily by underwriting students (who could "vote with their feet") rather than institutions themselves.

Bob Andringa was the lead Republican staffer for the House Education and Labor Committee and worked with Quie from 1969 to 1972 on the "first significant package of amendments to the Higher Education Act of 1965." While Quie and Congresswoman Edith Green teamed up on legislation regarding academic buildings, they disagreed on whether federal aid ought to flow to campuses based on enrollment (the Oregonian's position), or to students based on their financial need (the Minnesotan's position). Quie's approach proceeded to lose three times in a row: first in subcommittee, than in full committee, and then in the full House. But all was not dead, as according to Andringa, Sen. Claiborne Pell, a Rhode Island Democrat, "was looking for a good idea." This led to Andringa working with Pell's staff in constructing a Senate counterpart to what Quie had sought unsuccessfully to pass in the House. It did, in fact, pass in the Senate, and only 59 conference committee meetings later, the two bills from the two chambers were reconciled.

"In the last late-night committee session," Andringa reports, "after weeks of working closely with Democrats Carl Perkins, John Brademas, and Frank Thompson, Al was able to 'recede' to the Senate on what was really our program for grants to the neediest students. That program, which later was named 'Pell Grants,' has grown to over $8 billion a year. This was another example of Al's bipartisanship; tenacity at pursuing what he saw was right, and leadership on education while very much in the minority."

Referring to that final session, Andringa wrote on another occasion, "I will never forget returning to Congressman Quie's office at 4:30 a.m. after a brutal conference committee meeting at the Capitol. He had just surprised a Democratic leader [Green] by swinging enough Dem votes to win a huge program. 'We won!' I was elated after two years of hard work. Yet even though bone tired, Al said, 'Let's take a minute and pray for Edith. She's probably hurting right now.'"

Quie agrees with Andringa's sequencing of events and recalls in particular how his experience with the GI Bill shaped his views about having federal funds follow students. "I could have used it to go to either St. Olaf or Cornell; the choice was mine. Other students back then deserved similar options." In our conversations, he also drew a connection between the freedom of choice inherent in the GI Bill and his preference for market-based early childhood programs which afford parents significant latitude in the kind of settings they choose for their young children.

————————•◆•————————

Returning to Quie's acknowledgment of the federal government's scholastic inadequacies, he likewise reported how he had been angered (albeit sometimes also perversely amused) by the ease with which flat-out corruption could poison its educational and antipoverty programs. Angered and offended, yes; surprised, not at all. Take, for example, a summertime school lunch program in the early 1970s that "was feeding more kids in New York City than there were kids in New York City." Quie introduced the story by first noting that, "People need to keep in mind that when I went to Congress in 1958, there was no school lunch program in Minneapolis at all. All the schools were neighborhood schools and parents took care of meals. Children either would take their lunch to school, or they'd come home. They had that hour at noon."

As for what was going on in the Big but pilfered Apple, Quie got the General Accounting Office to investigate (it's now the General *Accountability* Office). "On the last day of summer vacation, just like the police, GAO officials staked out a site and watched as some guys sold school lunches out of their truck to construction workers and other adults. The men from the GAO were going to see that arrests were made after what they thought would be the criminals' last run, but they never came back, and I was told they sold their trucks and took off."

This was one of the scams he found to be "hilarious," though he presumably wasn't laughing when he and Republican colleagues sought to pass legislation aimed at cutting back on such fraud. "We tried several amendments, but boy, the Democrats' opposition was so strong. I guess they saw voting for it as an admission of guilt on their part and the Johnson administration." Though in a typical jab (actually more of a rip), he said the way in which current Republican members of Congress have been loading up bills with non-debated earmarks shows they're "crooks just as big." Human nature, he would argue, is nonpartisan.

It's a losing game to list more than a few aspects of American education in which Quie was *not* immersed once he was appointed to the Education and Labor Committee a year after arriving in Washington. One not-yet mentioned sphere was vocational education, where he again called on the GAO, this time to research what percentage of graduates of vocational programs were, in fact, working in fields for which they trained (putting aside how many actually were graduating to begin with). The numbers came back with more than 60 percent not finding jobs in their skill areas, which led to his leadership in the passage of the Vocational Education Act of 1968. Vocational education organizations were upset, he said, wanting to prevent performance and outcome evaluations. But the law, he wrapped up, did in fact make vocational training more relevant to occupational needs.

Quie remained engaged in national education circles after being elected governor of Minnesota in 1978, most notably by his participation on the Reagan-appointed National Commission on Excellence in Education, which issued the famous "Nation at Risk Report" in 1983, shortly after he finished his sole four-year term. For a politician who never spent much time on stylistic packaging, it nonetheless was his suggestion to print the document in a height and width smaller than the norm so that officials and other key players—

like people who organized doctor and dental offices—would be apt to keep it atop piles of books and papers rather than buried below, as they did with *Reader's Digest*. The plan worked, though the document's language, remarkably crisp for a government task force report, had something to do with it, too. ("If an unfriendly foreign power had attempted to impose on America the mediocre educational performance that exists today, we might well have viewed it an act of war.") Not constituted to leave not well enough alone, at the 2003 Checker Finn forum cited above, Quie—spurred by two decades of self-critical hindsight as well as only puny national progress in reforming American education—criticized the work of fellow panelists and himself as having been "arrogant and inarticulate." He and other commissioners could have made a much larger difference, he said, if they had done their jobs more boldly and "addressed problems of the inner person."

———·◆·———

Quie, in other words, and as demonstrated many times already, is not bashful about challenging his own team—and just about everyone else if he believes it constructive to do so. And he expects the same directness in return, frequently saying such candor is one of the best favors people can do for him. "When I'm at the top of an organization, the first thing I say to the people in it, 'I want you to challenge me, challenge me straight.'" But also as seen many times and as will be addressed more completely in Chapter Nine on congenial disputation, energizing his assertiveness is an interest in better understanding other people rather than rhetorically pummeling them. (For a good laugh, try imagining Al Quie ever getting into a shouting match.)

All of this is aligned with his history of prodding hesitant Republicans when he thinks politics and policy demand it, his conviction that politicians are obliged to seek common ground, his recognition that Republicans and Democrats need to talk to one another and, when it comes to the nether reaches of the two parties, his fondness for quoting Carl Albert, a Democratic Speaker of the House, who said occupants of the respective fringes are really more alike than different. "I think they make up a circle, not a straight line," the fifteen-term Oklahoman said. "Those two extreme groups come together."

As for prodding and pushing colleagues, two chapters ago we read about a congressional Republican who said he'd continue following Quie's lead in education, but did the crew-cut farmer from Minnesota really have to go so fast? On another occasion, a particularly conservative colleague warned, "Al, I've got to quit going to the subcommittee on higher education." Quie asked why.

"Because you and others are starting to change my mind."

"That's good," Quie responded.

"No, it isn't," his colleague shot back, fearful of what his more ideological counterparts would think (he had been an official of a major conservative organization) if they knew he was, in fact, modifying his mind. To the largely non-ideological Quie, figuring out new ways of fixing problems, within a well-thought-out frame, is the whole idea. To his colleague, the exercise was fearful enough that he really did stay away. "Mossback conservatives" is a term Quie used occasionally in our conversations, never as a compliment.

One of his favorite examples of how he nudged both Republicans and Democrats was his role in the passage of the Metallic and Non-Metallic Mine Safety Act of 1966, a compromise grounded (not incidentally, by Quie's lights) in friendship and respect born and strengthened by faith and prayer.

Jim O'Hara, a Democrat from Michigan, was a colleague on the Education and Labor Committee who, according to Quie, was "totally supportive of organized labor." He never participated in any of the regular prayer groups Quie was involved with, "because his children were going to parochial school, and he drove them there in the morning, which was naturally more important to him. He obviously was a man of faith, and we worked together." They did attend one special prayer breakfast together, with a visiting head of state, and then went back to O'Hara's office and prayed. Hubert Humphrey attended another such breakfast, at Quie's invitation.

People read and know all about black lung disease now, but conservatives in the mid-'60s were preventing passage of legislation that would deal with the problem, and it just tore

Congress apart. The bill was just languishing there. Then Jim O'Hara got interested in getting a bill for non-coal mines passed, so I decided to write one that would fit with my Republican philosophy of having more enforcement at the state, rather than federal level. I introduced it and then testified on it before a subcommittee Jim chaired. In doing so, I not only pointed out what a dandy piece of legislation I had written, but I also highlighted the shortcomings of his bill. But I had messed up in two spots; I had the intent of his legislation wrong, and Jim, in the most loving way, corrected me. I just knew he did this as a friend, because I had heard him excoriate not only Republicans but Democrats, and he would have been justified in doing that to me. I appreciated that, and the final legislation went through both the House and Senate without a dissenting vote. The *Wall Street Journal* wrote that the bill passed because of a "prayer." Jim must have told them that.

Quie is also very fond of a story about Barbara Jordan, a Democrat from Texas, perhaps best remembered from her stately membership on the House Judiciary Committee that voted to impeach Richard Nixon. Quie had an amendment on the floor that would change the formula by which states and congressional districts received federal Title I dollars. As Jordan was entering the chamber for the vote,

she came over to me and said, "Al, I just respect what you're doing, and I'm going to vote for your amendment." Hers was a very important vote, and I had tremendous respect for her. One of the things I had the ability to do then was look at various congressional districts and be able to remember if they'd get more or less money if a formula changed. For some reason, numbers stick in my head. But after thanking her, I realized that her district would get less money, and I also realized that she didn't know that. It would not have been right to let that slide so I left my post where mostly Republicans were coming in and went over to her and said, "Barbara, I appreciate what you said, but I want you to know that you'd get less money for your district, and you have to take that into consideration." "Oh," she said, and thanked me . . . and then changed her vote from "Yes" to "No." By the time I got back to where I was standing, lots of members had gone by, and I wound up losing my amendment. But it was the right thing to do and as it turned out, I did get the amendment through a few years later in large part because Carl Perkins was willing to take less money for Kentucky. [In the matter of how "numbers stick" in Quie's head, the late Bob Renner, who was his chief legislative aide during his governorship, was once quoted as saying his boss was "one of the few guys I know who doesn't round numbers."]

Perkins, as noted, was a Democrat and the consequential chairman of the Education and Labor Committee. By then, he and Republican Quie had developed a good relationship, and while it would be wrong to attribute the bond only to the fact Quie had successfully trained several of Perkins' horses (remember he was from Kentucky), it probably didn't hurt either. The amendment, by the way, had to do with Quie's interest, described earlier, in tapping more current data for allocating Title I funds around the country.

A week earlier in our series of conversations Quie was speaking again, with extra feeling, about the need for the two parties to talk with one another, for no other reason than to "test your ideas against their ideas." Republicans and Democrats, he said, had to talk about reaching common goals and helping "people live more in grace with one another."

"You've been just terrifically engaged and passionate in discussing this," I jumped in when I had a chance.

"Yes, you can tell my passion."

"Your voice," I add, "is simply faster right now than it has been on other subjects, so this is clearly close to your heart. But questions just occurred to me for the first time: Would you have been so comfortable in working collaboratively with Democrats, not worrying very much about who had the upper hand and receiving the bulk of credit, if you were not in such a safe district? If you had to fight off Democrats all the time, would you have been as interested in seeking truth and

Quie and Rep. Carl Perkins, the powerful Democratic chairman of the House Education and Labor Committee. Their relationship grew closer after Quie trained several of the Kentuckian's horses.

understanding as opposed to doing politics in more conventional ways? Would you have been such a nice guy?"

After a pause and a sigh, Quie said, "Yes." I said, "Good," and we both laughed.

"What causes me to be what I am, I don't think, was a safe district." He went on to explain that he didn't always have one, as he won his first term to Congress with only 613 "official" votes (he really received more), and he had to beat an incumbent to win his state senate seat four years earlier in 1954. This might have been the only time in our conversations where I thought I offended him, suggesting as I did that maybe his political style was at least partially the product of fortunate geography.

———— •◆• ————

Before getting to the most historically significant way in which Quie—along with Gerald Ford and a few other "younger, more dynamic men"—challenged a very senior Republican colleague, we need a quick word about what he thinks about some of the current ways of Congress.

There's too much money in politics for his taste, and he would prefer a system in which only individuals living in the same congressional district as a congressional candidate could contribute to his or her campaign. A parallel rule would apply to legislative districts and legislative candidates running to serve in state capitals. Same thing with gubernatorial candidates: All dollars would have to come from supporters within that state. As for the presidency—since "we don't elect presidents, we elect 'electors'"—he similarly thinks all money spent in a state in a presidential campaign should come from that particular state. Limits on individual contributions would be erased entirely, but everything would have to be posted on the Internet immediately so people better understood if certain gifts possibly influence how politicians vote. "If you put things out in the light of day, where everybody can see it, then people in public office feel more like they're being watched, and they're more careful." As for the constitutionality of all this, Quie's answer mirrors his response to the routine claim more than 40 years ago that the U.S. Constitution and the 1964 Civil Rights Act were incompatible with each other: change the Constitution.

Even though he's "not against" lobbyists and recognizes their importance, Quie nonetheless has problems with the way in which legislators, both at federal and state levels, are excessively dependent on them. This issue is inseparable from what he sees as the more fundamental problem of an excess of committees and subcommittees, which started in the U.S. Senate.

Take a look at books and directories that list all the members of Congress and see all the committees they're on. You know everything is not coordinated perfectly, so members wind up scheduled to be at more than one subcommittee at a time. This leads to staff members attending committee meetings in their place and playing too large a role of their own. It gets even worse because in developing legislation and working things out, staff members often spend too much time with lobbyists and not enough with their bosses. All this leads to a situation where the men and women who actually are elected aren't as engaged in solving problems on their own when time and other pressures are great.

For an example of how he thinks Minnesota state legislators are not as good as they once were in working collaboratively under stress, he pointed to their failure to work out a transportation bill that could have avoided a gubernatorial veto; a failure that nullified any chance of a special session shortly after the I-35W bridge collapsed in Minneapolis in August 2007.

The kicker to this chapter is a particularly great old kick, going back to 1965 and a headline in the old *Minneapolis Tribune* that blared, "Quie Helps Lead GOP 'Rebellion.'" I first read the story when doing research for an article about him that had been commissioned by a local magazine, *Minnesota Law & Politics*, in honor of his 80th birthday. The article, printed in the August-September 2003 issue, was called "A Governor Turns 80: Al Quie is just like you remember him, only older (and even wiser still?)."

"The rebellion of young House Republicans continued on Wednesday," reporter Nick Kotz wrote, "and at the center of it as a rising leader was Rep. Albert Quie of Minnesota." The young Republican "inner group" of about seven, Kotz continued, "achieved its initial success Monday when Rep. Gerald Ford of Michigan defeated Rep. Charles Halleck of Indiana as House minority leader." Quie was head of a Republican committee at the time that sought "changes in the distribution of power" in the House. According to Kotz, the group's first objective was to "break up the concentration of power now in the hands of a few older men and distribute it among young, more dynamic men." Of their broader goal, Quie was quoted as saying, "Republicans are seeking to improve the national image of the GOP from one of reluctant opposition to [Johnson] administration plans to one of constructive leadership."

A kinder and gentler prairie version to be sure, but I wrote at the time (only partially tongue in cheek) that Al Quie was Newt Gingrich before Newt was Newt himself in challenging party orthodoxies and old bulls. (I later learned from Quie that Gingrich concurred and once told him, "I'm just copying you, Al.") Like all politicians who serve seriously, Quie had

Left to right: Rep. John Rhodes of Arizona, President Gerald Ford, Quie, and Secretary of Defense Mel Laird. Their prayer group had just met in the Oval Office.

no interest in second-string power. Back then, as now, he had a copiously considered and deeply felt take on the world and the role of government, and he had no interest in being part of a perpetually peripheral minority. Politics was his calling, in the most compelling and demanding sense of the term, and as such he was determined to have his party make a discernible difference, not just an interminable pain of itself.

Beyond old news clips, I asked Quie how Ford got to be minority leader.

Charlie Goodell, Bob Griffin, and I—all of us were members of the Education and Labor Committee—were the kinds of people who looked ahead and we saw how the Republican Party had all these difficulties and how it was in decline. We thought that Republicans were only reacting to what Democrats proposed and did and that we had no real plan of our own about improving both the party and the country. All the chairmen of all the committees were Democrats, of course, and they provided the Republican ranking members with very little staff help, though our people didn't take advantage of even that small amount of research help. So the three of us decided we ought to have better leadership to bring changes about. We knew we couldn't take out Charlie Halleck, who was still too strong, so we started out with Charlie Hoeven who was chairman of the Republican Conference Committee and who we thought was weaker than Halleck.

We first asked Mel Laird if he would run against Hoeven, as Mel was very smart, very capable, and he knew politics, but he didn't want to do it. Being confrontational that way and challenging leadership was not what he was all about. We asked who might do it instead and Mel said Gerry Ford, who he described as low key and having the ability. So we went and talked to Gerry, and he just said, "Yes, I'll do that." Just like that. I *love* leaders who say, "I'll do that," when you challenge them and then they actually go and do it. They don't have to weigh things forever. Gerry, as much as he might have been maligned, that's the way he was. He knew it was something that needed to be done. He defeated Charlie Hoeven, and that was the beginning. A little less than two years later, after we just kept talking to other Republicans about ideas, Gerry defeated Charlie Halleck for minority leader. We won by very few votes, but we won. If you're going to take on the king, be sure you kill him, not just hurt him. [Note: Quie chuckles here.]

I asked what side had been more conservative and what side was made up of more moderate Republicans. He said ideological distinctions didn't apply, as it was much more a matter of colleagues who wanted to focus on ideas as opposed to those less enthused by the prospect. "Non-orthodox" Republicans versus "orthodox" Republicans seemed closer to the mark. Nevertheless, more conservative members of the caucus, including those who were elected during the next cycle, had their rhetorical day when they realized that efforts by Ford, Goodell, Griffin, Quie, et al. to devise "constructive" alternatives to

Democratic policies invited the problematic acronym *CRAP*—Constructive Republican Alternative Proposals.

After Ford's victory as minority leader, Quie said, "Goodell and Griffin moved up in leadership, but I told Gerry I didn't want anything because I wanted to continue focusing on my work on the Education and Labor Committee. But, I added, if he wanted to put me on the Ethics Committee, I'd do that, and he did."

"That must have been a fun committee," I said.

Quie quickly agreed, possibly because the Abscam scandal didn't hit until he left the committee after a year or two of service. During the short time he was there he urged colleagues to disclose anything that might be even close to suspect or un-kosher. But when the *New York Times* reported that he had received courtesy gifts of a business suit along with a "ring with a stone" during a trip to South Korea—even though the suit didn't fit, the ring was worth less than $4, and the meeting at which he revealed it was theoretically private—Quie correctly recognized the committee's leaky staff mitigated against members eagerly divulging all.

———— • ◆ • ————

A postscript to this story: Quie supported Charlie Halleck for Minority Leader in the 86th Congress, which convened in January 1959, when he ran against incumbent Joe Martin, the same Rep. Joe Martin who previously helped Quie get on the Agriculture Committee as a new freshman. Quie voted the way he did because he thought Halleck would do a better job than Martin and that it would have been irresponsible to choose someone for such an important post because of a political favor or personal tie. Within the year, Halleck helped Quie get on the Education and Labor Committee. Yet half a dozen years after that, Quie voted against Halleck because he thought Ford was better qualified to be Minority Leader. Most important to his conception and practice of politics, Quie says, are matters of principle, increasing justice for people without power, and the wisdom of actual outcomes, of course. Personal ties are also important and he's acutely alert to matters of mutual obligation, but not in logrolling ways removed from considerations of merit when it came to the work of Congress.

Chapter Seven

Governorship (I)
Running for Office and before the Budget Crashed

I n their 1999 book, *Minnesota Politics and Government*, political scientists Daniel Judah Elazar, Virginia Gray, and Wyman Spano write about how Al Quie, of the "seven governors examined here," was the only one who faced a "genuine crisis," correctly describing the economic downturn of the early 1980s as "the most severe since the Great Depression." They don't even attempt to capture the pain. Not incidentally, my own twenty months as Quie's speechwriter, from May 1981 through the end of his term in December 1982, coincided perfectly with that period, and in perversely self-aggrandizing and melodramatic moments, I've been known to describe my role back then as the "voice of doom."

It truly was a tough stretch. Quie, in the midst of the budgetary siege, confided to friends in a prayer group how he feared he had let God down—only to be revived in strength and hope moments later when he was alone, and with tears in his eyes, recited Psalm 51: "Create in me a clean heart, O God, and renew a right spirit in me." He was "alone" in the sense that his friends in the regular Tuesday morning prayer group had just left. But as Quie described it, he was anything but alone, in that, "I felt the presence of Jesus Christ right there beside me like I never had before, and I was renewed. From that time on, the governorship began to be a joy."

Asked to encapsulate Quie's years as governor, those whose political memories of Minnesota reach back more than a quarter century are likely to focus on the final two years of his term and the unprecedented string of special legislative sessions he was forced to call in order to close—and as it usually turned out, only temporarily—gaping wounds in the state's biennial budget. The budget, it's crucial

Quie's celebrated billboard during his 1978 race for governor satirizing Wendell Anderson's 1976 resignation as governor and his appointment to the U.S. Senate by his successor, former Lt. Governor Rudy Perpich.

to point out, was required by state constitutional mandate to be kept in constant balance; no projected deficits were allowed at any time over the 24 months. Quie's recollections of that period—both agonizing and uplifting—will be the subject of the next chapter, the second of two on his governorship. As for this first one, we begin with his decision to leave the Capitol in Washington and his hopes of returning to the Capitol in St. Paul 21 years after serving three years as a state senator.

———————◆———————

Not that Quie's retirement from Congress was premised in his running for governor, as his decision to leave the House of Representatives was in train, quietly and privately, before he decided to seek the top job in state government back home. "I remember right after the 1976 race for Congress and Walter Johnson saying to me, 'Well, how does it feel to have just run your last congressional campaign?' It was amazing how this guy could see that within me." Johnson, who was a businessman and a key member of Quie's kitchen cabinet, remains a good friend.

Quie traces his decision to run for governor most directly to a conversation he had in 1977 with an old friend of Hubert Humphrey.

I was coming back from the floor of the House of Representatives and returning to my office in the Rayburn Building when I got off the elevator and ran into a friend of Humphrey's who I hadn't seen for quite a few years. He was getting off another elevator and after we greeted one another, he asked, "Are you going to run for governor or the Senate?" Walter Mondale had been selected as Jimmy Carter's running mate and there was an opening in the Senate. Though I had been thinking seriously about leaving Congress, I did the usual thing by saying, "Oh, no, I've got seniority in the House, and I'm going to stay there." Then it just hit me, and I said, "If Wendy Anderson steps down and Perpich appoints him to the Senate, I'd be so incensed, I'd run for governor." And this guy said, "Well that's what's going to happen." I said, "Eh? No, they're not going to do that." And he said, "Yes, they are." I walked back to my office, and I knew right then that's what I ought to do: run for governor. And I knew I could win.

Wendell Anderson, who would become a good friend of Quie's, had been governor since 1971. Rudy Perpich, a DFLer like Anderson, was his lieutenant governor. Their job-shift "arrangement" would lead eventually to one of the best political billboards of all time, Quie's award-winning, "Something scary is going to happen to the DFL. It's called an election." Quie still enjoys the heck out of it, calling it "really neat."

"Let me back up for a second," I said. "What made you think you could win?"

"It was a feeling I get in my heart that says, 'Hey, this is the way things are going to unfold.' Sometimes it means something good is going to happen, though sometimes there's a pain and it means there's something in my life that's dishonest. On the good side, I felt the same thing at the end of Tim Pawlenty's campaign for re-election in 2006. When I saw him on election night, I congratulated him and said, 'You've won. He didn't believe me at all. He didn't think he was going to win. I can't explain it. Sometimes things like that just come, though people probably are more likely to remember them when they're right than when they're wrong."

After getting back to his office, Quie knew "there were two people I had to work with," his wife Gretchen and their youngest child, Ben. Gretchen "had come to love Washington and her work with the International Club and all the other things she was involved with there," and she also was concerned about the effects of an all-consuming campaign on Ben, who was a high school sophomore at the time. The other four children had already left home for college and adulthood. To think things through, the three of them went on vacation in a "remote part of Maine" in August, accompanied by Doug Coe, an old friend from Quie's early prayer group days in Washington, and his wife Jan and their son Jonathan.

"Gretchen just said to me, 'If you want to do it, I'm going to go with you.' I often yielded to her when we had important decisions to make because I could see her wisdom. In this instance, she had to get her head around the situation, but she realized I had to run. It was the same kind of thing as when I bought her an easel when we were first married and I said God wanted her to be an artist. Meanwhile, a "draft Quie" committee led by Republican activist Len Nadasdy—to which Quie had given the go-ahead in June—had been building support for an eventual campaign.

As for Ben,

He and I were talking and walking down this country road in Maine, and he just said to me, like a wise sage, "Dad, I know how your heart is set on running for governor—that you believe you ought to do it. You'd never be satisfied with yourself if you didn't make the run. I'm going to be with you. I'll be okay through that."

What I had done prior to the trip to figure all this out was to talk to a friend at Harvard who was head of the psychiatry department there, Dr. Armand Nicholai. Doug had introduced us several years earlier, and we had been in a prayer fellowship and had traveled to England together. So I called him, and we talked about how people make decisions. He said that when he was in medical school and seemed to be called to psychiatry, he wondered what in the world it meant, so he put out a fleece. I didn't know what his fleece was, but I figured if Armand Nicholai put out a fleece, and Gideon in the Bible put out a fleece, then maybe it was okay for me to do so, too. My fleece was that both Gretchen and Ben would be supportive, and if that happened, then I would go for it.

They were, and he did.

A fleece, I should add, can be understood as a test, or the seeking of a sign.

One day Gideon was threshing wheat in a secluded place, so as to escape the notice of the Midianites [we learn from James Dearmore in *Favorite Bible Stories in Simple English*], when an angel from God appeared to him, bidding him to go and save the Israelites from their foes. Gideon obeyed the command; but before commencing the battle, he much desired a sign from God showing that He would give the Israelites the victory. The sign Gideon asked for was, that when he laid a fleece of wool on the ground, if the victory were to be his, then the fleece should be wet and the ground dry. He placed the wool on the ground, and taking it up the next morning found it wet, although the ground was dry.

———·◆·———

Meanwhile, Walter Johnson had urged Quie not to seek the new job, prompting the then-last-term congressman to call him from Maine and announce, "Well, I got your letter, but I'm not taking your advice. I'm going to run." Johnson had written that Minnesota was fundamentally a DFL state, there were other strong Republican candidates, and Quie had been away too long. The hill, in sum, was too steep. Yet to demonstrate still exceptional rapport, Quie soon after asked Johnson to chair his campaign, and Johnson agreed.

Quie then called Ray Plank, a businessman who had helped him in a congressional race fifteen years earlier, in 1962, saying, "Ray, do you want to change your life?" Plank asked what he had in mind, and Quie asked if he would help with fund-raising for the campaign. Once he was back in Minnesota, Quie upped the ante and asked Plank to chair his finance committee, and like Johnson, Plank said yes. Quie and Plank actually first worked together in 1956 in a group called Young Men of Minnesota. "Can you imagine," Quie said, "an old guy like I am now starting an outfit called Young Men of Minnesota?" The organization aimed to invigorate the state's Republican Party with new ideas. "I used to say, I don't care what party someone was in, if they got involved, in two years they were going to be a Republican."

Here's a seemingly forgotten historical footnote (at least I hadn't known it before our conversations): Several people, including Plank, pushed Quie hard to run for governor a dozen years earlier, in 1966, and he gave it more than serious thought—actually allowing friends to start organizing in all of Minnesota's 87—before deciding he still had a lot to accomplish in Congress.

Next he had to find a campaign manager. Quie offered the job to an experienced person who had formerly lived in Minnesota but had moved to Indiana. "He thought on it but turned me down." So the candidate turned to someone from Washington who had no ties to Minnesota but was an exceptional head of the minority staff of the Education and Labor Committee, Bob Andringa. "Bob," Quie said, "is just such a naturally organized person. He also was a fellow believer and we had spent time in prayer together as we worked in the committee. I realized he had no knowledge of Minnesota whatsoever, but I came to the conclusion that no one in the state had the skills he had, so he and his wife Sue picked up and moved to Minnesota, and he became my campaign manager." For a novice, Andringa did quite well, bringing home a winner, and after the election, he would serve for about two years as Quie's director of policy research before being named executive director of the Denver-based Education Commission of the States.

Those were three people I dealt with, along with my chairwoman, Carolyn Ring. They all had organizational skills way beyond anything I had and had proved what they were able to do. Bob was able to both lead the minority staff and work well with the majority staff on the Education and Labor Committee, even though he was the most junior of them when I moved him up to be the head of the minority staff. Walter was able to take corporations that were failing and help them become successful again. He also built a successful business of his own. Ray had been successful in the oil industry and shopping malls and all. And Carolyn was chairwoman of the party. They had the skills, and they knew how to enlist people who were better than themselves as well. That was our team as we began running.

I asked if he remembered how and where he declared his candidacy for governor. For someone who can still vividly recount what it felt like to be lifted onto a horse when he was two, Quie strangely doesn't recall very much about the day and moment he announced his run for governor. "Some way or other, I suppose we went up to the Capitol. There's sort of a press room there. I suspect that's what we did." Actually, he declared at a news conference a short ride down the hill from the Capitol, at the old St. Paul Holiday Inn in St. Paul. The date was August 31, 1977. For what it's worth, he had no problem recalling campaigning a while later at a Renaissance Festival on a steed. "Good jousting horse," he told me.

Early on the campaign trail in 1977—before precinct caucuses, followed by the statewide endorsing convention, and then the primary, all in 1978—Quie found himself up against several contenders, including a comparatively new and exceptionally impressive player in Minnesota politics, Dave Durenberger, a lawyer who had served as chief of staff for a former Republican governor, Harold LeVander. Quie remembers this part of the contest well.

The Republican Party sponsored a series of debates, and I sat there one time and listened to Dave and I thought to myself, "Why in the world am I running against a guy as articulate and able as he is? Why am I running for this job?" But something in me said that was where I ought to be and I ought to stay in the race. So I kept pressing away, which pushed me into thinking about how I could express things as well as Dave or perhaps even better. As we got to December, from all the press

I was reading and all the spin Dave's people were putting on it, it just sounded to me like he was going to win.

It probably was Bob Andringa's idea for me to record a three-minute [audio] tape and then find a person in each precinct around the state who would ask permission to play it at their caucus meeting. Well, the party had decided they would do straw polls in 100 precincts to see what people were thinking. The press didn't trust the party, so they picked another 100 precincts to do straw polls of their own. I was in the Twin Cities that evening visiting two or three precincts when word came in that I had won against all of my opponents by a margin of eight to one in the precincts the party had selected and by ten to one in the precincts the press had picked. Frankly, the race for the nomination was over then, and Dave's friends convinced him to change gears and run for the Senate instead.

Durenberger did switch after the precinct caucuses, and Quie prevailed easily at the subsequent statewide convention in June and then in the primary in September. Howard Knutson and Bob Johnson, two legislative veterans, were the other Republicans in the race, with Knutson dropping out after the convention and Johnson staying in through the primary. Jumping ahead to November 1978: Durenberger won election to the U.S. Senate, where he served for fourteen years, and Republican businessman Rudy Boschwitz also won a Senate race that night—the rarity of two Senate seats being open simultaneously having been caused by Walter Mondale's election as vice president in 1976 and by Hubert Humphrey's death earlier in '78. Quie was elected governor that night as well. This constituted what quickly became dubbed as the "Minnesota Massacre"—a remarkable Republican rebirth in a presumably liberal state just a handful of years after Watergate.

Shortly after writing this chapter, I was asked to ask Quie if he had considered running in 1978 for the Senate instead, and if he had done so and won, how things might have worked out. In keeping with his critiques of congressional life in the previous chapter, his answer was a quick no.

I had no interest in the Senate, as I didn't believe in the way it had become organized. Staff members were doing senators' work too much. Senators were on too many committees so they would look good, but that meant they were on too many subcommittees that met at the same time with each other. In addition, the federal government had gone too far in usurping power from states and local jurisdictions. I wanted to start correcting this by taking action at the state level, starting with taxes and public education in particular. I soon realized in the campaign for governor that we could do a lot about environmental laws and the judiciary at the state level, too—devising strong but not harassing laws in terms of the environment and demonstrating respect for the law, justice, and love when it came to the courts.

————— • ◆ • —————

In the campaign, this time against DFL incumbent Rudy Perpich—who would die in 1995 at age 67—I asked what his "basic answer" was in those first days when reporters asked why he was running for governor. It wasn't as thought-through as what he said 30 years later.

"My basic answer was a mistake."

"Why was it a mistake?"

"Early on I would say I wanted to return home to serve Minnesotans. But that didn't resonate with people at all. They didn't want people to *serve* them. They were looking for someone to solve problems."

According to press accounts, perhaps the closest Quie came to citing a theme or issue in announcing his candidacy was when he said in a prepared statement, "Although my activities in the Congress continue to be extremely challenging and rewarding, my desire is even stronger to work here to make Minnesota an even better place to be employed, to raise a family, and to find personal fulfillment." The statement handed out to journalists never mentioned Perpich by name. Six weeks later, on a campaign swing in Greater Minnesota, reporter Betty Wilson was still writing about how Quie was emphasizing national issues and sidestepping state ones, talking about Jimmy Carter as frequently as he talked about Perpich. Quie admitted, she wrote, that he needed to bone up on state matters "before I can give an intelligent answer."

Recognizing that additional specificity and crispness were in order, "I came back with what developed into a principle of my life: decide what the three most important issues or ideas are, and then tell people what you're going to do about them." Polling, Quie said, had shown that "nothing was overwhelmingly important to voters except one thing: They thought taxes were too high." But in a major rub, he added, perhaps especially for a Republican candidate, "I never really cared if taxes were high or not."

With both of us laughing, I said, "I won't tell the Taxpayers League we've had this conversation."

"I always wanted enough in tax revenues to pay for the things government ought to do and then cut out all the things it shouldn't do. That was my view. But now I had to figure out how to talk about taxes in the campaign in a way that made sense and was effective and was true to myself. How was I going to handle that?"

The answer came in a conversation with a school janitor during a campaign stop in St. Cloud.

"I asked, 'Hey, what are your biggest concerns?' He said his taxes were too high and for a person whose income wasn't big, I was amazed what he told me he was paying in state and federal taxes. But inflation was very high then, and that was moving him up in the tax brackets even though his income remained low. His purchasing power was going down, and his taxes were going up, and nobody had voted on it."

The national inflation rate in 1978 was 7.6 percent, increasing to 11.3 percent in 1979, and 13.5 percent in 1980. It was never lower than 5.8 percent in the five years leading up to Quie's election.

I asked Quie if that was the birth of income tax indexing, which prevents taxpayers from artificially graduating into higher brackets, and which turned out to be one of his major successes as governor.

"That was the birth. It was just upsetting to me that people's taxes were increasing without them realizing what was going on. You ought to put everything out in the open for everybody to look at. So that's when I decided that indexing personal income taxes was going to be my number-one issue."

A few minutes later I said that when I joined his staff in 1981 my sense was that taxes clearly were important to him in intrinsic and philosophical ways. Quie agreed but said that was the case not in terms of the size of taxes but rather what he saw as the need for "integrity and fairness in how they're levied."

So it seems to me, I replied, in regards to taxes, there was a difference, at least in emphasis between himself and other "more hard core" conservatives and Republicans.

"Yes," he answered in a word.

The second issue Quie came to stress during the campaign was making it easier for people to observe environmental laws "without those laws harassing them, without making them jump through all kinds of hoops, and without causing businesses to give up on Minnesota and leave the state."

When I started campaigning, I found out there were an awful lot of people who were very upset with environmental laws in Minnesota as well as some environmentalists, especially when it came to the Boundary Waters Canoe Area. The battle at the time was whether people should be allowed to use motorboats on the bigger lakes in the BWCA, and it seemed to me, why should anyone care if someone wanted to have a motorboat on a huge lake? If people just wanted to canoe without motorboats around, there were hundreds of other lakes where they could portage and do all that. I was once rated one of the twelve top environmentalists in Congress, but I saw what some people who called themselves "environmentalists" were doing to people in Minnesota. So I decided the next principle was that we were going to have strict and tough environmental laws, but we were going to make them clearer and easier for people to follow.

Officially the Boundary Waters Canoe Area Wilderness, the BWCA is located in the northern third of the Superior National Forest in northeastern Minnesota. Huge at approximately 1.3 million acres in size, it contains over 1,200 miles of canoe routes and about 2,000 designated campsites.

Quie's third, virtually ordained major issue was education—specifically, his growing belief, prompted in part by Ben's educational problems a few years earlier, that students needed more individual attention. "So, if I could pick just one thing in education that I could talk about, it was lowering class sizes, especially in the early grades. I went to speak to the Minnesota Education Association, and they unsurprisingly endorsed Perpich because he was a DFLer. But I remember an article in one of the Minneapolis papers that said that while Perpich may have gotten their endorsement, I got their heart. I was thrilled at that."

In listing key issues, Quie mentioned a fourth about which he actually said little during the campaign but a great deal after he won: picking and appointing judges. We'll get to it at length in Chapter Eleven and his current work on judicial retention.

———— • ◆ • ————

Another nearly forgotten historical footnote: Quie had run statewide once before, albeit with an asterisk. For a period in 1961 leading up to the 1962 elections, before a new redistricting plan based on the 1960 Census became official, all congressional candidates in Minnesota were technically competing against each other from Roseau in the northwest to Rochester in the southeast. But in terms of statewide efforts actually lasting until November, his 1978 campaign for governor was his first—and as it turned out, only—statewide race lasting longer than a footnote. What was it like?

"Hard to get my head around it," Quie said, as running in 87 counties was radically different than running in only a dozen. "So I just decided I was going to carry the vision and let other people plan the strategy about where I should go, where to meet the press, that kind of thing."

One of his early and gutsy steps (some might describe it as an early and entirely out-of-character step) was showing up at the governor's residence, bereft of any invitation, during a Saturday afternoon meeting Rudy Perpich was having with farmers and other protesters who were upset with plans to build a power line in Stearns County, about an hour's drive northwest of the Twin Cities.

"Guess who came to Rudy's luncheon?" was the headline in the *Minneapolis Tribune.*

"Perpich was giving them an audience, and for some reason I couldn't even get a phone number for the residence. It was unlisted, so my people said, 'You've got to go there.' Well, that was going to be kind of uncomfortable for a reserved Norwegian, to butt into somebody else's party. But I did. I went."

An upshot was that Quie, who had little sympathy for the protesters when the meeting began, changed course considerably once he learned from the Department of Agriculture in Washington that original plans had the line running over big farms. When those farm owners and operators protested, the line, Quie said, was refigured to run through the land of much smaller farmers, a move he viewed as "simply unjust." The power line likewise was designed to avoid state-owned parkland, "so you'd have to say that birds were more important than people."

To Quie's relief, the controversy—which included vandalism such as the cutting of bolts and the toppling of towers—eventually died down and "I never had to send out the National Guard." To his regret, the line was in fact completed right through protesters' property, although if it had been up to him, "the power line would have run right down the median of an interstate or else at the edge of it."

For the record, the *Tribune* reported that "Perpich and Quie chatted briefly in a corner during a pause in the action while protesters and news media representatives hustled upstairs for the buffet. Otherwise, they managed not to cross paths."

The only significant question about Quie's campaign in need of answering at the Republican convention in June was who his running mate as lieutenant governor might be. For one of the few times in his life, he was agnostic, allowing delegates to choose between Lou Wangberg, a young and politically engaged superintendent of schools in Bemidji in northern Minnesota, and Nancy Brataas, the legislator who had supported Quie in his long-shot and accelerated quest for the Republican congressional nomination two decades earlier. The convention chose Wangberg, who in recent years has taken to calling himself the "last male lieutenant governor in Minnesota history." After the two were elected five months later, "everybody said, 'You ought to put your lieutenant governor to work.'" Having been there, I can vouch that Lou worked hard, but, "frankly," Quie continues, "I never figured out what the lieutenant governor should do."

Despite all this activity, Quie contends that the two Senate races—Dave Durenberger against DFLer Bob Short and Rudy Boschwitz against the appointed Wendell Anderson—"sucked all the air out of the gubernatorial campaign, just totally. I practically had fallen to where the attorney general and state treasurer were."

Asking and answering his own question about how he finally got "traction in that whole blame thing," Quie acknowledges he was helped by a report that was "a bit derogatory towards the Perpich administration." To his credit, according to Quie, "Perpich said, 'Let everybody see it.' But others in his administration held back, which led to stuff leaking out. It was the stonewalling that brought attention to the gubernatorial race. You just got to thank them for doing it that way. If they had let all the information out right away, the issue would have been over immediately. But they didn't, so I benefitted."

I asked if he recalled what the controversy was all about. He largely didn't, just remembering "there was a suspicion of corruption or something like that. Somebody got money they shouldn't have."

Yet while the Quie team picked up some traction, that didn't mean the campaign was humming. As described earlier in the chapter on his religious motivations, the Republican challenger garnered a bit of buzz when, during a debate, he held up a copy of *Time* magazine that called Perpich "Governor Goofy." Quie also won the support of a number of groups and individuals unaccustomed to favoring Republicans, including (he thinks) Veda Ponikvar, the publisher of an influential newspaper and a major political activist in Chisholm, in northern Minnesota's very heavily DFL Iron Range—not far from Rudy Perpich's Iron Range hometown of Hibbing. But the general sense in various quarters in the weeks leading up to November, Quie recalls, was that he would lose. The "Minnesota Poll," for instance, released by the *Minneapolis Tribune* the day before the election, had Perpich winning by 49.5 percent to 45.5 percent for Quie.

"I realized that my whole campaign was trying to make me into somebody I wasn't. I remember calling the whole campaign staff together and saying, 'Everything looks like I'm going down the tubes.'

Everybody knew it. I said, 'I don't want somebody defeated who really isn't me. I'm going to be me.'"

I asked what they were trying to make him into, and beyond vaguely suggesting that some people wanted him to "look at some issues from a different perspective," the much more scandalous answer was that several tone-deaf and misguided souls wanted him to stop wearing cowboy boots.

"So two weeks before the election, I said to all the volunteers and staff, 'Bob Andringa has been leading you very well. But I say to you right now, you're free. You do what you believe. Just like I'm going to be myself, you be yourselves. Just go for it. You don't have to check with Bob or anyone else.'"

It's impossible to gauge the effects of their bureaucratic liberation, but one quite unattractive initiative some people in the campaign pursued was putting fliers on the windshields of cars parked near Catholic churches on the Sunday morning before Election Day that falsely claimed that the pro-life Rudy Perpich was pro-choice on abortion. Rather than being outright malicious, it's possible the campaign workers really did think that Perpich endorsed abortion rights, confusing him with his brother who in fact did. Nevertheless, if one had to guess, Quie won more votes by the mistake (or worse) than he lost, and it prompted Perpich's wife, Lola, to charge angrily that Quie carried a Bible in one hand and a bucket of mud in the other. Quie continues to lament the incident, feeling bad for Perpich, who more than three years after the election told his successor that losing had felt like "falling off a cliff." It was the first time the two men had spoken since the campaign. "I wanted to see him and talk with him after the election, but Rudy wouldn't see me. It just hurt him too much."

Sunday night right before the election, Quie assembled his five children at dinner and said, "I originally called you all together because I wanted to prepare you for my defeat." But he was now feeling great, having just returned from an encouraging stop in Duluth, which, like the nearby Iron Range, was and remains a DFL stronghold and an intriguing place for a Republican gubernatorial candidate to spend a final electoral weekend. ("Here's my principle," Quie told me later. "Candidates should start their campaigns in territory where they're the strongest and enlist the help of people there. Then they should end where they're weakest. Republicans who do the reverse have failed.") He felt so great, in fact, instead of soothing his family, he reversed course and announced, "I'm going to win. I know it in my bones. I'm going to win."

In the same way Quie had aimed to comfort his kids, his friend Chuck Colson had come to town to comfort him. But a little after nine o'clock on election night, shortly after some media outlets had declared Quie the surprise winner, he went to his friend's room at the headquarters hotel, the Registry in Bloomington, and said, "Well, Chuck. I won!" Colson, goes Quie's recollection, was "dumbfounded." The final margin was by more than 110,000 votes: 830,000 for Quie to 718,000 for Perpich, rounded off. It was the largest number of votes ever won by a Minnesota governor.

One key ally, though, was not at the Registry, as he was certain Quie was going to lose and the prospect of being even in the vicinity of an electoral wake was too painful to entertain. So he left not just town but the state for the evening. Quie refuses to say who it was.

What about Gretchen during the final days of the race? What was she doing? "Good Gretchen campaigned solidly right through those days," Quie said. "A friend told me she was getting on a bus late Monday afternoon in Minneapolis, the day before the election, and there was my wife, all cold and all, campaigning for me. The woman said, 'I got on the bus, and I was so overcome by what she was doing that I actually cried.'"

———— •◆• ————

"When I realized I had won," Quie allowed, "I also realized I hadn't put together any plans for naming commissioners, and I had no real plans for how we were going to implement the ideas we talked about during the campaign. We had done none of that."

I asked why not.

"We were just rushing from one place and problem to another to win the election. A lot of my people thought I was going to lose, so too many of us figured, why spend time planning for the future if we were going to lose? In fact, most of them thought I was going to lose."

Al Quie with an undersized sweatshirt after his 1978 victory as governor.

The admission begs questions, which have been raised regularly over the years, about whether Quie was better equipped, temperamentally and in other ways, to be a congressman rather than a governor, a legislator rather than a chief executive. And at several points in our conversations, he agreed with a portion of the assessment, at least as it applied to early in his term. "You know," he acknowledged one morning, "here was a guy who spent all his time in the legislative arena and, frankly, I was not fully prepared for the executive branch. It was a huge learning curve. But I learned. I learned. And I'm pleased that people look back, especially on my last year, and they say, 'Hey, that guy did a pretty good job under the conditions.' That makes me feel good."

He also had great fun pointing out that some people simply "have the audacity" to run for a job like governor, having had only legislative experience beforehand.

An area in which he believes he improved over time was in evaluating and appointing commissioners and other officials.

One of the things I had real reservations about was my ability to read people well enough to pick the right individuals for the right jobs, but I came to have confidence in it. I was increasingly able to see connections between the traits I saw in people when I interviewed them and how they did their jobs later on. I learned that if you have people who are dependable, you should give them their head and just let them run their departments. But I also insisted that they keep me informed about everything they did that affected other departments. To the extent that it was possible, I wanted department heads to make decisions as if I was dead. And when it came to appointing women and minorities, because of the barriers many of them had faced, I tried to focus more on their innate abilities than on their resumés, which might have been shorter and less impressive because of discrimination.

In respectable time, though not as fast as some in the media and other critics viewed as fast enough, Quie filled his cabinet. Early in the exercise, in addition to naming Bob Andringa his lead policy adviser, he chose as his chief of staff Jean LeVander King, who had been working for Dave Durenberger and was the daughter of former Gov. Harold LeVander. The two of them, plus Dick Bragg and Rob Stevenson, two friends and colleagues with whom he was spiritually close, led the way in staffing and organizing his office. Jean was the first woman in Minnesota ever to hold the job.

But well before all the interviews—actually, the very first thing Quie says he did when meeting with the press the day after he won— was to make an announcement in the company of his family. "One thing I want everyone to know is that if you ask me to do anything on

The new governor and first lady at their inaugural ball in 1979.

Sunday, I'm not going to do it." It was a Sabbath pledge born obviously of his faith, but it also was rooted in advice offered by the Democrat whose unelected trek to the U.S. Senate riled him into running for governor in the first place, Wendell Anderson.

In related movie news, when it was released in 1981, Quie adored "Chariots of Fire," the Oscar-winning film about a Scottish sprinter who gave up a chance for a gold medal by refusing to run on a Sunday at the 1924 Paris Olympics.

———— · ◆ · ————

In the interregnum between his victory on November 7 and his swearing in on January 2, Quie took self-evident advice from the National Governors Association seriously. Namely, learn everything he could about the state budget, both income and outgo, and try to reach rough consensus with other key players, from both sides of the aisle, on projected revenues for the next biennium. That two-year budget period would start on July 1, 1979, following a legislative session that would run from the first week of January into the middle of May. Having a strong facility with numbers, and despite having spent the previous two decades-plus in Washington, he became better steeped in the state's programs and finances than his critics later would either believe or acknowledge when the economy had a nervous breakdown.

But even before then, DFLers in the legislature, particularly the House, were anything but inclined to exercise "Minnesota Nice" in their dealings with him. Though in fairness, Quie readily concedes he could have been more solicitous of Democrats and generous in recognizing their collaborative good works. (As we'll see next chapter, supposedly friendly Republicans also could be brutal towards him.) Say and condemn all you want about heavy-duty ideological and other fights in Minnesota and national politics currently; the political and partisan environment a generation ago was much more alike than different. This would prove to be especially the case during the economically disastrous days to come.

It decidedly didn't help that the 1978 elections, in a roundabout but complicating way, resulted in an exact tie in the number of

Independent-Republicans and DFLers elected to the Minnesota House: 67 each. The deal struck in the chamber was for Republican Rod Searle to be elected Speaker, but for Democrats to control a majority of committee chairs. Grizzled legislative veteran that he was, Quie had more than doubts. "'Oh, man,' I figured, 'This isn't going to work.'"

Drawing on what he learned in Washington, "I invited leaders from the House and senate to the residence for breakfast once a week so we could talk things over. We were congenial with each other, but there weren't trust relationships." The four men at the time were Republican Searle and DFLer Harry "Tex" Sieben in the House, and Republican Bob Ashbach and DFLer Nick Coleman in the senate. Coleman, who was a particular power, would soon develop leukemia and pass away and be succeeded by Roger Moe, with whom Quie eventually would develop an unusually close and trusting relationship during exhausting negotiations and special sessions aimed at fixing budget chasm after budget chasm. Speaking of the original four, he said,

> We would get along pretty well at breakfast, but then the Democrats would often go out and slam me in the press. But it wasn't just their fault; it was mine as well. Republicans had been out so long I was too conscious of making certain they got most of the credit in being authors of bills and things like that. As I look back now, I would let Democrats get credit, too.

> Also I didn't realize at the time the reason I could get along so well with Democrats in Congress was that I never ran in any of their districts. But back here, I kept saying I would run for re-election as governor, so that meant I would be running in all the DFLers' districts. It also meant every week they were having breakfast with the enemy. But the enemy—me—was not giving them an opportunity to develop strengths and achievements that would help them in their next campaigns.

In no area, other than later budget aggravations, did such strained relations stymie and frustrate Quie more than in his signature, first-year education initiative: attempting to reduce class sizes significantly in kindergarten through third grade.

———— • ◆ • ————

There was not as much data available when Quie became governor as there is now pinpointing how well American students actually were doing in school—how much they really were learning, or not. Still, enough research and information had come to light during Quie's last years in Congress for him to realize that teenagers and other young people in the main were not doing nearly as well as they needed to do. In general, they weren't performing nearly as well as most adults assumed they were. Whole groups and grades of kids were more apt to perform worse, rather than better, than earlier cohorts. Students in other parts of the world, including those in quite unexpected places, were increasingly learning more math and science, as well as reading better, than American boys and girls. And international students also were quickly catching up and frequently passing their counterparts in the United States in both high school graduation and college participation rates. As for the state he was now leading, Quie was convinced that Minnesota kids were falling behind, too.

In my work on the Education and Labor Committee in Congress and in looking at statistics, I saw that Minnesota was resting on its laurels. People here were glorying in the fact that reports showed we were ahead of other states. But the whole of elementary and secondary education in the United States had been declining for years, slowly. We were still on top of the other states, but we were declining just like they were.

So I figured if I was going to try and do just one thing, it would be to get lower class sizes in kindergarten through third grade. Two things led me to do this. One was a study by Dr. Gene Glass at the University of Colorado where the researchers showed that for smaller classes really to work, they had to get down to no more than fifteen students and preferably even fewer. The other motivation was Ben's experience when he was having a hard time in a public school in Maryland and how much better he did when there were only eight students in his class in a private school. But I ran into a buzz saw in the legislature.

One of the problems there—and many legislators have admitted this to me—is they had absolutely no clue that education was declining to the extent it was, no clue at all. But the other, much bigger problem was that since I was "Mr. Education" in Washington, Democrats here just didn't want me to chalk up a victory. I was just astounded that every DFLer in the House voted against reducing class sizes. It just shocked me. I also was amazed that all the Republicans there voted *for* it. I was just trying to figure this whole blame thing out. DFLers said the proposal was too expensive, but most of all, it was a matter of their saying, "We're not going to give the governor this one." The bill passed in the senate; that was okay with them. It was a deep, deep disappointment.

DFL legislators described their opposition a bit differently in the press, contending that "our plan is a kindergarten through grade 12 program," while Quie's was "just K through three." They also argued that their way led to a lighter property tax burden and, in a brilliant act of jujitsu, argued that their approach afforded school boards and educators *at the local level* more discretion than did Quie's initiative.

While I come to the issue in significantly different ways than Democrats in St. Paul did almost 30 years ago, I've long been of the mind that spending a lot of money on reducing class sizes is almost always one of the least cost-effective ways of improving academic performance—if doing so can improve learning at all. For example, whatever improvements in student achievement that might result from smaller classes are likely to be nullified by the need to hire large numbers of teachers who are not as expert in subject matter or skilled in pedagogy as those already working. So of all my disagreements with Quie—there isn't a rash of them, but a number—the wisdom and efficacy of major efforts to reduce class sizes is near the top of the list. Though in fairness to him, his conception of what needed to be done was substantially more nuanced than simply changing ratios of teachers and kids. For example, he argued then (and still argues now) that a major problem in class-reduction plans is that most teachers teach basically in the same way regardless of how many students are in front of them.

If teachers keep doing the same things in both bigger and smaller classes, then students are not necessarily going to do any better, even if there are fewer kids around them. What I wanted to do is figure out how education colleges could do a better job of training new people in the field to teach more effectively in smaller classes. I thought, for instance, we should get regular teachers to learn from special education teachers because they know how to work with much smaller groups of students. It just doesn't make any sense that class sizes for pre-fourth graders don't make a difference. It's just like people who think that one parent can raise children just as well as both parents.

A news account at the time referred to how Quie stressed that he was "calling for more than simply reducing class sizes." He was also "proposing fundamental changes in education, including more individualized instruction, new teaching methods and more parental involvement." However, none of this was to be during his first legislative session because, as Quie claims, "for the Democrats, power to stick it to me was more important than anything else." Although also pivotal were soon-to-be financial exigencies that radically tightened everyone's policy and innovation leeway.

In reference, by the way, to his often-cited tag as "Mr. Education," there was speculation on several occasions in the 1980s that the Reagan administration was interested in possibly appointing Quie as secretary of education. There were, in fact, conversations, though he says no offer was ever made nor was one ever likely since he disagreed with Reagan's interest in returning the Department of Education to non-cabinet status. He also assumed White House staffers would have too much to say in how he might run the department, and he had no interest in being nibbled or constrained like that. A number of years earlier, during the Ford administration, there was speculation about his perhaps being named head of what was then the Department of Health, Education, and Welfare or being chosen as Ford's vice president after Nixon's resignation. Nelson Rockefeller wound up with the job, albeit not for long.

We're saving economic, budgetary, and tax (including indexing) issues for next chapter. We're also saving what turned out to be one of Quie's proudest accomplishments—merit selection of judges—for Chapter Eleven, which will also focus on his current and passionate efforts to keep partisan and expensive politics as far away from Minnesota courtrooms as possible. So to conclude the chapter at hand, on what other issues did Quie seek to be of service as governor? Here are several raced-through blurbs.

Streamlining regulations. The Department of Natural Resources provided an excellent vehicle and example for cleaning up rules and regulations, with Quie's interest provoked while campaigning at the State Fair in St. Paul, as holy a secular institution as there is in Minnesota.

> When I was running for governor, I went over to the Department of Natural Resources building at the Fair and there were an enormous number of people either wanting to ask a question or criticize something the state was doing, and they were waiting in a line that stretched all the way out of the building, onto the sidewalk, up to the corner, and halfway down the next block.

"Personally," I said, "I'd do that only for french fries or pork chops on a stick. And even then, I wouldn't."

"I wondered," Quie continued, "what in the world they were doing."

> The problem, I found out, was that if a person had a local issue with something the DNR was responsible for, they would have to speak to someone like a game warden, who would then have to speak to his regional supervisor, who would then check with someone at headquarters in St. Paul, and then, after a decision was made, it would have to work its way back again. That just frustrated people terribly. So we short-circuited all of that and gave much more discretion to DNR officials at the local level, and by the following year when I visited the same building and its exhibits, there were a grand total of six people waiting on line. Citizens were now able to

get their questions answered and their problems resolved right in their local communities.

Governor Perpich had appointed Joe Alexander commissioner of DNR not too long before I was elected, and while I had wanted to change all commissioners, I interviewed some who had been with Rudy anyway. Joe was a former game warden who knew the department and who agreed with my idea of governance. I decided to keep him, and it was one of the best decisions I made.

Ending strikes. Quie dealt with three significant strikes as governor, involving truckers, community college faculty, and state employees en masse. In keeping with his need and drive to put human faces on issues, he was known to get out of his state trooper-driven car and talk with strikers. If he was advised that it wasn't the safest course, he would reply that it was safer than possibly driving over someone's foot, and at any rate, "We've got a good lieutenant governor if something happens to me." He found it strange and unhelpful that he was prevented, by law, from talking to the head of the faculty union. Just as he was amazed when he found out that the president of a packing plant in southern Minnesota, and the president of the striking union there, had never talked with each other before a "Presbyterian pastor got those two together, and they started resolving their differences." As always with Quie, just about everything reverted back to relationships. Though on one occasion, the truckers strike, he realized he had no option other than to call out the National Guard.

The truckers went out on strike and they weren't delivering gas, so there were big long lines at filling stations. It was really tough. We were struggling with that, and it was hurting the economy. We discussed calling out the National Guard and stopping the strike, but Orville Freeman had problems when he did that when he was governor, and other people, especially on the DFL side, had trouble with the idea. I remember Jim Sieben, my adjutant general, said he would do it, but he also didn't think it was a good idea. Adding to the problem, frankly, was that a lot of truckers, especially the independent ones, supported me when I ran for governor, and I was still planning on running for re-election then. Calling out the Guard to stop them from striking would not be the best thing I could do politically. But I realized that stopping the strike was important to the economy, so we called out the Guard and the truckers complied.

But then I made a mistake. I should have just let people wait in line one more weekend, but I got on the air and announced to everyone in the state, "Now, you're going to get gasoline, but for this weekend, it won't be delivered to the pumps fast enough, so please wait and don't take any trips this weekend." Boy, did resort owners get upset with me. Man, were they ticked off that weekend.

Transportation safety. Quie and I had the second of our regular weekly conversations the morning after the Interstate 35W bridge across the Mississippi River collapsed in Minneapolis on August 1, 2007. He talked of the horror people on it must have felt at the time and of how he wondered, on hearing the news, if his son Dan or Dan's wife or Ben or any of their children might have been there when it went down, because they traveled that route all the time. We then quickly went on and talked about other things. But nearly three months later, in a conversation about the importance of taking long views, he used funding highways and bridges as an example of planning prudently for the future, and in so doing, added to what he had first thought when he heard about the I-35W disaster.

When a Department of Transportation study came in during my term, I wanted to know if we were going to be able to maintain highways and bridges as they aged. People in the department said that with the amount of revenue they saw coming in, we were going to have serious problems in 25 to 30 years. So I proposed that we increase the gas tax and also index it to inflation. But the idea didn't catch on at all. So while the "first thing that hit me" when I heard about the bridge was the horror people must have felt and the anxiety of their families, the second thing was that I knew it was coming. After I left office I did nothing about it. I felt guilty, even though I've been a private citizen all this time.

When I asked if there was ever an actual bill filed to index the gas tax., he said no, as "legislators were not about to be preemptive. I did, however, always support a gas tax increase whenever it was proposed."

Yet just about the same time that Quie was admitting to feeling guilty, he was being saluted in the media for the freedom he had given his transportation commissioner, Dick Braun, to do what he needed to do to protect public safety, politics be damned.

"It was poignant," I said, "what you just said about how you felt. But as you know, of course, there's been a lot of attention recently to Dick's leadership and the vision and courage he showed, for example, in closing down the High Bridge." (The old High Bridge was a vital span across the Mississippi River in St. Paul that Braun deemed unsafe and shut down to all traffic. It was later demolished and replaced.) Braun, I continued, "has said very nice things about how he spoke to you before he issued the order and you simply told him, 'Do the right thing.' He also has been telling reporters and others about how he once showed you a map of Minnesota and how various things the department might do or not do would make various legislators around the state unhappy, and that you again simply said, 'Do what's right.'"

After we discussed how Elmer Andersen might have lost his bid for a second term as governor in 1962 by a grand total of 91 votes out of over 1.3 million cast because he had said the same thing to his highway head—who proceeded to anger a whole town by closing a regional office there—Quie allowed that if Braun had come to him, say, two weeks before a re-election bid of his and said that a bridge needed to be closed down, but that it would be safe to delay doing so for a month, he might have said, "Hey, wait a month. I think I would have been politically savvy enough to do that. I also expect that Dick would have understood that without even having to talk to me about it. I don't think I would have been strong enough to close it just before the election."

Chapter Eight

Governorship (II)
Crisis, Resurrection, and Farewell

Towards the end of several conversations about the budget crisis that dominated more than half his term, I made reference to bringing the topic to "closure."

"The closure," Quie answered quickly and with emphasis, "is that we solved the problem and gave Perpich a surplus."

Having lost to Quie in 1978, Rudy Perpich returned to the governor's office, this time for two full terms, first defeating Republican Wheelock Whitney in 1982, and then Republican Cal Ludeman in 1986. More precisely, according to Quie, Perpich was able to start his new stint with a budget reserve in the vicinity of half a billion dollars, which grew, in reasonably short order thanks to a radically improving economy during Ronald Reagan's two terms, to a neat billion, give or take a few bucks. It's clear Quie is proud of that achievement and his largely above-the-fray leadership, which was central in making it possible. The fact that we had this discussion just a couple of weeks after the Minnesota Republican Party had honored him, added a measure of energy and satisfaction to the moment.

We've dealt only sporadically with those very difficult years; it's time to appraise them more completely. Though to start, let's spend a few moments spotlighting headlines and pulling from newspaper stories and editorials of the time, as doing so will provide both context and sequencing.

As you note the enormous amount of spending that needed to be cut out of budgets, or newly raised in taxes, or shifted around by means of advanced accounting, keep in mind that total general fund expenditures in the 1980-81 biennium, the first for which Quie was responsible, wound up at only $7.2 billion. They wound up under $8.2 billion in 1982-83. Given the variety of adjustments that had to be made, this was not very much money with which to work. By comparison, expenditures from Minnesota's general fund budget for the 2008-09 biennium (in non-inflation-adjusted dollars) are estimated to finish off at about $34 billion. In percentage terms, according to an excellent package put together by then-reporter Dane Smith of the Minneapolis *Star Tribune* in 2003 (during Gov. Tim Pawlenty's own budget crisis), total shortfalls during the 1982-83 biennium constituted 16.8 percent of projected revenues.

For further perspective, here's a remarkable excerpt of a speech Quie delivered to a live television audience around the state in November 1981. He had just said Minnesota faced another shortfall, this time $768 million for the biennium ending June 1983.

> I must impress upon you how much $768 million is. If we were to shut down—completely shut down—for the entire biennium, all the institutions run by the Department of Public Welfare, including hospitals for the mentally ill; the whole Department of Corrections, including all the prisons; all seven campuses of the Minnesota State University system; and all eighteen campuses of the Minnesota Community College system, we would save less than $500 million. And this assumes that these shutdowns started not today, but at the start of the biennium last July.

A few moments later he gave a snapshot of similar shortfalls in other states, including $655 million in Washington state and $1.6 billion in Ohio. The problem was national, not provincial.

Also keep in mind, as just suggested, that many of the adjustments that Quie and legislators were forced to make occurred deep into budget periods; stretches of time after huge sums had already been spent, further choking their latitude. In reviewing the chronology that follows (which wound up by necessity running longer than I had anticipated), consider the near-ceaseless water torture of rotten news that saturated well more than half of his term and the toll it had to take on everyone involved, not just Quie.

————·◆·————

I might have missed something, but in reviewing thick loose leaf binders of news clips in the Legislative Reference Library in St. Paul, the first reference to the impending disaster seems to have been a story on June 19, 1980, by Robert J. O'Keefe in the *St. Paul Dispatch* headlined, "If surplus dwindles, Quie could face voters' wrath." The former congressman, O'Keefe opened up,

> appears to be in good political shape midway through his first term as the state's chief executive, but a problem lurking in the background could provide trouble when he tries for re-election. . . . The state treasury isn't lined with cash the way it has been in recent years. The problem is starting to get serious, and by the time Quie runs again in 1982, it could be much more serious.

Rather than "midway through his first term," Quie was only eighteen months into it, actually.

The month of May, according to O'Keefe, had been "tough" for revenues, as they had run "well below expectations." Revenues had rebounded in the early days of June, "so it's still too early to say that a deficit is actually developing." O'Keefe attributed part of the problem to a national recession then under way, but also "ironically" to the income tax indexing that Quie had run on in 1978 and got through the legislature in 1979. The result, O'Keefe wrote, has been to "reduce state income well below what it would have been otherwise."

It was interesting to the point of ironic that O'Keefe's analysis came only two months after Quie had garnered some of the most encouraging stories of his governorship. Under the headline, "Quie comes out as clear winner in final round," Bill Salisbury of the *St. Paul Pioneer Press* wrote, "When the 1980 Minnesota Legislature adjourned Saturday, the clear winner was Gov. Al Quie," with the state senate, "controlled by a lopsided DFL majority," placing a distant second, and the evenly split House coming in "dead last." An Associated Press story in the *Worthington Daily Globe* made much the same point, albeit with the less flattering headline, "Bland, dull, and dumb Al Quie shows he is in charge of state."

A dozen days after the O'Keefe column, a headline in a *Minneapolis Tribune* editorial talked about "Recession in non-metropolitan Minnesota." And a dozen days after that, a headline in a story by Gary Dawson in the *St. Paul Dispatch* read, "Quie could face $200 million deficit, Moe says." According to DFLer Roger Moe, chairman of the Senate Finance Committee and soon-to-be Senate Majority Leader, Quie had "created a fiscal 'mess' out of the state budget and may face a $200 million deficit at the end of the current budget period a year from now."

On July 21, 1980, an article in the *Minneapolis Tribune* by Steve Brandt talked of how "there's no question Gov. Al Quie pushed through the 1979 legislature the largest state tax cut in Minnesota history" but that "there's debate aplenty" on whether that indexing provision "will allow Quie to fulfill the second half of his campaign promise: improving state government."

Two days later, on July 23, a headline in a story in the *Mankato Free Press* announced, "Quie doesn't regret tax relief." Reporter Vic Ellison wrote, "Even though Minnesota has a budget deficit of $90 million, Gov. Al Quie says he doesn't regret pushing and signing a $730 million tax relief bill during the 1979 session. And if he had it to do over again, he adds, he would. . . . Even if the deficit reaches $200 million by the end of the biennium next June, Quie said he will not regret the decision."

On July 24, O'Keefe wrote, "It is becoming clearer and clearer that a new era in financing state government has started."

An August 2nd story by Gary Dawson (in a combined Saturday issue of the *Pioneer Press* and *Dispatch*) reported that revenue collections "slightly exceeded estimates." Nevertheless, the headline in a story by Steve Brandt and Joe Kimball in the *Minneapolis Tribune* on August 20 said that Quie "hinted to school officials Wednesday that he might be willing to approve a sales tax increase [to help cover a shortfall] if the education lobby could push it through the 1981 legislature."

A September 8th editorial in the *Dispatch* titled, "Deficits, indexing and common sense," argued that a "deficit, if one does appear, will have been caused primarily by the state of the economy, with tax indexing being responsible for only a fraction of the shortfall."

Intimations about taxes grew stronger in a story by O'Keefe on December 8. "In a sharp turnaround from his earlier position, Gov. Al Quie hinted today that a tax increase may be necessary at the 1981 Minnesota legislative session. Quie said that high interest rates and a recession could take a bigger toll than expected on revenue coming into the state treasury."

Came the new year of 1981, and a January Minnesota Poll in the *Minneapolis Tribune*, perhaps surprisingly, had 61 percent of Minnesotans giving Quie a favorable rating, down only seven percentage points from a year earlier. Good news like that would not continue.

About ten days later, in a story in the *St. Paul Pioneer Press* about Quie's proposed budget for the 1982-83 Biennium, reporter Bill Salisbury quoted a DFLer who termed the plan "downright Reaganesque." It was not meant as a compliment. The budget called for deep cuts but no new taxes.

A headline at the same time in the *St. Paul Dispatch* read, "Quie happy he's off tax spot—for now." He wouldn't be for long.

On April 2, a headline in the *Minneapolis Star* announced once again, "Revenues fall short, set Quie scrambling." Revenues in March had fallen $42.7 million short of estimates.

A week later, a headline in the *Daily Journal* in Fergus Falls made the new damage explicit: "Quie must cut $503 million."

And a week after that, a headline in the *St. Paul Pioneer Press* described the basics of the governor's new attempt to stop the bleeding: "Quie asks tax hike, more cuts, curbs on city-county spending."

A couple of days later, a headline in the *Minneapolis Star* said, "IR lawmakers leaving Quie on limb."

A month later in May a headline in the *Minneapolis Tribune* reported that "Legislators, Quie to plan special session." And two weeks after that, the *St. Paul Pioneer Press* was able to announce, "Quie, DFL agree on sales, income tax hikes"—$555 million worth, more precisely.

Two months later in August 1981, a headline in the *Mankato Free Press* was punchier than most, "Quie: 'Stupidity' reason for cash shortage." The Department of Finance had made a $16 million error in estimating sales tax income, swelling a July shortfall to $40 million. "I put that as stupidity," said the governor.

A day later in the *Minneapolis Tribune*, an editorial said, "The buck stops with Quie—or should."

"Quie likely to call 3rd special session," read a headline in an October edition of the *Minneapolis Star*.

"Quie in political cellar," read an editorial a week later in the *Red Wing Republican Eagle*.

A week after that, a headline in the *St. Paul Dispatch* informed readers that "Quie will detail state cash woes in speech."

Two days later he did so, with a *Minneapolis Star* headline announcing, "Deficit put at $860 million; Quie calls for special session."

A little under three weeks after that, two days before Thanksgiving, a story by Bob O'Keefe in the *St. Paul Dispatch* opened: "Gov. Al Quie today recommended reductions of more than $775 million in state spending, opening the way for increased property taxes and more borrowing by public agencies."

The year ended with Lori Sturdevant writing in the *Minneapolis Tribune* that the governor's "hard-line opposition to an increase in state income taxes appeared to soften a bit Monday as Quie aides and legislators began talks aimed at breaking the deadlock over how to balance the state budget."

A week into 1982, a headline in the *Minneapolis Tribune* let it be known that "Quie would back tax increase if spending is cut [by] $460 million."

And then there was the headline: "Quie decides not to run" in the afternoon *St. Paul Dispatch* on January 25. "Gov. Al Quie," Bob O'Keefe wrote, "has decided against running for another term and planned to make his announcement at a news conference in the Capitol today."

"Allies, except Gretchen, are glum," a headline in the morning *Minneapolis Tribune* claimed the next day.

"Deficits in advice, budget got Quie," a headline in the afternoon *Minneapolis Star* claimed later in the day.

"Quie shows class," an editorial headline in the *Mesabi Daily News* claimed the day after that.

But six weeks later it was back to the old routine, as a March headline in the *Owatonna People's Press* read, "Rumors were right—state is having financial trouble again."

Al and Gretchen Quie in the governor's residence in 1979.

Yet those problems evidently proved to be of the garden variety, as news clips don't contain much more about major budget disasters for another eight months, when in November 1982, the AP's Gerry Nelson wrote in the *Faribault Daily News*, "Gov. Al Quie and legislative leaders were back in familiar roles Thursday mulling over a $312.5 million shortfall in state revenues that threatens the state's credit rating and apparently will mean higher income and sales taxes."

All was resolved on Quie's watch a couple of weeks later, with the *Sunday Tribune* in Hibbing announcing, "$342 million bill ends week of political drama."

Much has been made of the seven special legislative sessions held during Quie's four years in office, 1979-83, in part because none had been held since 1971. However, of the seven, only four (cynics would say "only" four) seem to have dealt directly with cutting spending and/or raising revenues in order to balance the state's books. Those sessions, as cited by the Legislative Reference Library, lasted one day in June 1981; two days in July 1981; forty-nine days from December 1981 through January 1982; and three days in December 1982. The other three special sessions addressed issues such as workers' compensation, energy and transportation appropriations, and short-term emergency jobs for unemployed men and women on the Iron Range.

———•◆•———

"So you wake up one morning," I said in one of our conversations, figuring I might not be able to ask another glib question for a while, "and you read a report and think, 'Son of a gun, the state is running out of money and there's a recession about to hit or already under way.' Could you walk me through all of that again?"

"It started earlier," he assured me.

Quie decided at the start of his term that the Finance Department would publicly report every month—more frequently than the norm—how well state income and spending were tracking compared to budget and projections. "I think it was about May of 1980," he recalled, "that it became clear revenues were not keeping up with expenditures."

I asked why he had made the decision to be more open than either law or past practice required.

I wanted to be totally transparent in government. I was advised not to do it because people supposedly wouldn't understand if the numbers some months didn't look good. But my theory always has been that people are emotionally and intellectually competent to know the truth and I just figured that some day we were going to have some financial troubles and people needed to know that.

Right at the start, when we were preparing the budget for the 1980-81 biennium [that started on July 1, 1979], it was understood that inflation was helping balance the books because as people moved up into higher tax brackets they kept on paying more in taxes. DFLers told me, "We've got the greatest system here with the graduated income tax. You'll always have more money coming in, and you can find ways not just to spend it but to protect yourself." But, of course, we indexed income taxes in our first legislative session, so revenues weren't going up that way anymore, which pleased me, even though it took away a cushion.

I asked if he knew of any calculation that contrasted the amount of taxes *not* collected because of indexing and the size of revenue shortfalls at various stages. He said he never saw any such numbers, though in light of oncoming deficits and their severity, it's understood that revenue losses caused by indexing were comparatively minuscule. At any rate, to Quie, indexing was more of a philosophical imperative, an end in itself, rather than a conventional economic device or means.

So levels of decreased revenues because of indexing were an accepted given; what wasn't anticipated was the loss of largely unknown reserves Quie had been told were buried in the bowels of the budget. "As we were finalizing the budget during that first legislative session, someone on my staff said to me, 'I just want you to know that DFLers are saying they've spent the hidden cushion, so if the economy doesn't stay up, you're going to have trouble.'" Compounding matters was that Quie had already agreed to have the state pick up additional welfare expenses in Minnesota's 87 counties, as he assumed there would be enough money. "That's where we lost it, right there. I figured, well, we'll go along and work this thing out. But an alarm bell had gone off in my head."

The bell chimed for real about a year later, in May 1980, when Finance Department officials informed Quie that revenues were beginning to fall seriously behind projections.

I asked what they thought would happen in June. They didn't know, but they urged that we not announce anything until we knew more. I went along, but it was a mistake, as I should have let people in Minnesota know right away that we were having difficulty in May. People need to know what a problem is before they hear what a solution might be. One of the things politicians and others in public life often do when they get into office and get to be leaders is try to protect people's emotions so they don't get so upset about things. It has caused me to say to people in all kinds of organizations that I've been involved with that, "Your emotions are your problem; they're not mine." And that, "My emotions are my problem; you don't have to worry about them." But I didn't follow my own advice, and I wasn't candid enough with people in the state when I should have been. Then in July, we found out the problem not only was continuing, but that it was exacerbating.

Insofar as the Department of Finance had been issuing numbers all along, I asked how it was that people in the state were largely unaware of emerging budget problems until Bob O'Keefe wrote what he did in June 1980. Quie said the monthly data released by the department came without interpretation and that it took an insider like O'Keefe to translate them. "Finance officials and I had decided to wait one more month before properly interpreting the numbers ourselves. It was like waiting to tell your loved ones you're sick. It was a mistake."

I toyed with the idea of calling a special session of the legislature to solve the matter but decided finally not to. That was another mistake. One reason I should have called legislators back to St. Paul was that they were involved in making the mistake of leaving the state with no reserves whatsoever. But Republicans had come so close to gaining control of the House, and I thought I could help us win a majority by taking the issue pretty much off the table for the November elections. So I decided I would make all the cuts myself, without any legislative help, and un-allotted $195 million in state spending. But man! Not only did DFL legislators turn against me, but Republicans were upset with many of the cuts and tried to save their own hides, too—if you want to call it hides instead of some other part of their anatomy. So those are two of the things I should have done differently at that point. I should have called a special session, and I should have let all 201 legislators share in the pain and struggle with me and take ownership of the problem.

One of the many petitioners who visited with Quie seeking the softest possible landings for his programs and constituencies was Don Hill, the president of the bigger of the two teacher's unions in the state, the Minnesota Education Association. (The MEA has since merged with the smaller Minnesota Federation of Teachers.) Hill argued for no cuts at all in elementary and secondary education and instead urged increasing the state sales tax by one percent. Quie was not yet nearly prepared to recommend a tax increase of any kind, but he wanted to protect education as much as possible, as it was "my love, my baby." Yet because K-12 education spending constituted the largest part of the state budget, having it escape unscathed was practically impossible, though Quie did make certain it took a proportionately smaller hit than other activities.

"The media," according to Quie, "started camping out at the door of the Finance Department at the end of every month to get the reports, and they waved them all over, showing how the numbers had missed again."

I asked if despite getting beaten up in the press if he also was getting praised for taking on so much of the burden himself. Might any editorial writers have been calling him a hero?

"No, they sure weren't calling me a hero, by far. They were really beating me up pretty seriously. It's so long now that I don't have any of those feelings. But I was pretty upset at times." According, for instance, to an April 1981 editorial in the *Mankato Free Press*, "Gov. Al Quie's solution to the state's budgetary problems is, to put it kindly, amazing. He has managed to alienate almost everyone in the state."

A couple of points about the media environment in the late '70s and early '80s are useful here.

In reading through clips about when he first took office, it's clear that editorial writers, in the decided main, respected and liked Quie. But especially in those first days of his term, he took a fair number of silly hits from commentators who argued that he was wrong in not allowing the press to attend virtually all meetings in his office as Rudy Perpich had permitted—and who also had pledged to remove the actual door to the governor's office if he were re-elected. Never mind that if Perpich, or any other politician, really wanted to keep something away from reporters, all he had to do was communicate

Al Quie and Henry Kissinger, shortly before the sitting governor introduced the former secretary of state at a Minnesota dinner in the early 1980s.

with officials and other folks by phone, or in a dozen additional ways, rather than face-to-face in his office. But Watergate was still a reasonably fresh memory, and sunshine and open-meeting laws had been adopted all over, and some journalists got carried away on the subject. Quie understood that while substantial openness is essential, the people's business simply cannot be addressed wisely if officials are compelled to conduct it exclusively in "Macy's window," as organizational theorist Warren Bennis put it at the time. He took lumps for this. And then there was the suspicion in some quarters that several senior staff members constituted not just a conventional palace guard but a closed-off "God Squad." Add to this sour mix a terrible train of budget numbers, plus the media's natural skepticism of people in power, and there's no way coverage in those years could have been fun to read first thing in the morning.

———•◆•———

To be expected under the circumstances, Republicans seeking to retain old legislative seats and win new ones in the 1980 off-year elections did poorly, further weakening Quie's clout. I asked if he thought that DFLers, and sometimes Republicans, were jumping on him because he had been weakened and, therefore, was fair game in their eyes?

"Yes. Oh, yes. Yes. You'd be there in a meeting with them and it would be civil, but then they'd go out and meet the press and slam me."

Al Quie is anything but a whiny paranoid, so it's interesting that he believes Democrats ganged up on him on the budget in no small way simply because they could. And that they opposed his plan to reduce class sizes in K-3, not on educational grounds, but primarily to stick it to him. And likewise, he believes that when it became necessary to close a mental hospital, majority DFLers in the legislature picked the one in Rochester in sizable measure because it was in his home congressional district. Though in making such charges, he was quick to note how he had been equally culpable of playing such hardball during his own career—for example, publicly calling for the firing of Sargent Shriver and Henry Kissinger. "I'm not totally innocent myself. It's not that I'm some super righteous person saying, 'Tut, tut, tut.' I'm just pointing out the way human nature and political nature work sometimes."

In regards to urging LBJ to fire Shriver as head of the Office of Economic Opportunity, Quie said "not quite" when I asked if he had felt comfortable doing it. And as for Kissinger, at a dinner in Minnesota several years later Quie introduced him as a "great American" while also privately confessing to the former secretary of state that he shouldn't have called for his ouster during the Ford administration. For his part, Kissinger admitted that the former congressman had been right on the foreign policy issue in question and that he himself had been in the wrong. The admission impressed Quie, and no, he no longer recalls what the actual matter was.

As for where Minnesota and much of the rest of the country stood economically in the early 1980s, "All this was a growing emotional problem for me, trying to figure these things out. What should I do? What should I recommend?"

We had reached the stage where the cuts we needed to make would be really severe. And then there was the question of raising taxes. I had run for governor promising that I would not seek re-election if I couldn't improve state government while also cutting taxes. But now I realized that raising taxes was going to be unavoidable. That was really a tough one for me to bite the bullet on. At first I thought we'd do it by increasing the income tax. But then I changed my mind and decided it had to be the sales tax.

I asked Quie, "Why the switch?"

If you increase income taxes when people's incomes are down, you don't get much money. But even with the fact that food and clothing are exempted from the sales tax in Minnesota, everybody has to buy things, so we'd be better off with an increase in the sales tax. Now, why was I having a struggle with that? I had watched arguments about the sales tax for a long time and thought the political religion in Minnesota was that people would just plain oppose it. I was surprised when the legislature was able to start a state sales tax over Gov. Harold LeVander's veto, but I still thought opposition to it was stronger than opposition to the income tax [in the mid-1960s]. And since I was still planning on seeking re-election, this was affecting my judgment, and I thought the income tax was the way to go. But after thinking it through, I realized it had to be the sales tax, and I actually wound up vetoing a bill that had my earlier recommendation for an income tax increase. That was embarrassing.

As you may recall from the recitation of headlines above, Quie and legislators later on had no choice but to accept an income tax surcharge, which eventually was repealed.

"So this was the 1981 legislative session," I asked, "before the really bad stuff hit?"

"Yes, yes. It just kept getting worse as we went along."

It was at this point, in May 1981, that I joined the administration as the governor's speechwriter.

———— •◆• ————

The next revenue forecast, as mandated by state law, was in November, "and it showed that we were way off in our revenues, both currently and projected." It didn't help that "the gifted person we had inherited in the Department of Finance who had been making budget projections died, taking all his theories and ways of doing things to the grave with him. He had not written out his formulas or trained anyone. Boy, was that ever a struggle."

I asked if the numbers were off because no one fully knew how to calculate them or because the economy was deteriorating further. He said both, refusing to fix blame on anyone, but instead noting the problem humans have in consistently telling people like their boss the whole truth. The episode furthered his view (he considers it an axiom): If you're my friend, challenge me and give me the unvarnished truth.

> There's another thing, looking back, that I find really interesting. Gretchen and I were at a National Governors Association meeting in New Orleans in November 1981, and all this was so much on my mind that I couldn't sleep, so I got up at 2 a.m. and took out my pen and started working on a solution. Thinking about it and praying about it, it came to me how we ought to resolve the state's financial problems. I said, "Gretchen, we're going home, we aren't going to stay to the end of the conference." I got back to St. Paul and laid out my ideas for my staff and the department heads, but nobody agreed with them. But as things turned out, the basic solution that everyone finally reached at the end of the 49-day special session was almost exactly what came to me that morning in New Orleans.

If my own memory is correct, he and Gretchen didn't get a flight out right away, because he didn't arrive at the Capitol until very late the next night, well after midnight. Quie remembers returning in comparatively good spirits; I remember the opposite.

"You may think you were in a good mood," I said in one of our conversations more than 26 years later, "but you really weren't."

"I wasn't in a good mood?"

Again I reported that by my lights he wasn't, though hindsight suggests, given how long we had been waiting for him to return, and how I had personally eaten far more White Castle hamburgers that night than ever before or since, maybe a bit of greasy projection was going on.

"I guess," he said, "I got over my good mood in a hurry once I found out how everyone disagreed with my plan."

That early morning meeting provided the grist for a speech Quie was to give within days specifying how the administration would seek to fix the newest revenue shortfall. It would be the second major budget speech he would give during this period, the first having laid out how serious the state's economic problems were (the one cited earlier about closing down hospitals, colleges, and the rest). Yes, I was privileged to work on both, though I can't say doing so was great fun, especially since Quie originally seemed just as unenthused about the prescriptive second one as he had about the meeting preceding it. Though in fairness to him and in gratitude on my part, he did tell me several days later that while he didn't like the speech at first, he had warmed up to it. If there's a single, painful line that has stuck with me from the two addresses all these years, it's about how no one should be discouraged about the state's future because Minnesota still had timber stands reaching to "God's heaven" (among other fine attributes).

———— • ◆ • ————

A short time later, in January 1982, in what would turn out to be his last year in office, Quie was scheduled to be interviewed on a Friday afternoon by Betty Wilson of the *Minneapolis Star*, who doubtless would ask him if he planned on seeking re-election later in the year. It was a question he was not prepared to answer, but an approaching blizzard bailed him out, as rather than contend with her interrogation

A button marking former president Gerald Ford's appearance at an Al Quie salute at the old Minneapolis Convention Center. A month later in January 1982, Quie announced he would not seek re-election that November.

(as reporters go, she could be particularly persistent), as well as being forced to "pace the floors" at the residence in St. Paul, he and Gretchen drove up to their property on Marine on St. Croix, northeast of the Twin Cities. They had bought the old home during his first year as governor after having sold their home in Silver Spring, Maryland.

"That's where I came to the decision," he said, "not to run again."

Whenever someone would ask if I planned to run again for governor, I would say yes, but I would have a pain right here on the left side of my chest telling me that there was something wrong with the answer. All the time in those first three years whenever somebody asked me, the same pain would be there. So I faced it, and it took more courage than I ever had before, but I decided not to run again.

I did it for three reasons, including that pain in my chest. Another was that I had come to realize that the reason why I could work with Democrats in Congress was that I didn't run in their districts. But as governor, I would be running for re-election in all their districts, so they had to treat me as the enemy. So I decided I'd better bite the bullet and not run again. You could call it "dying to your political self." You know, that was my *life*. I knew that being in politics was what I should be doing in my life, but now I would have to hang it up. The third reason for deciding not to run was that I had been dreaming for a long time of riding the Continental Divide from Canada to Mexico and living with my horse for all that time. With the stress I was facing, I figured I would be too old and infirm to do that if I stayed another term.

In discussing the three reasons, the last line about creeping age and infirmity was the only part that made him laugh.

Gretchen and I got back to St. Paul on Monday morning. I remember I had a pardon board meeting in the forenoon. It was one of the most fascinating cases we had, about a wife and some other stalwart citizens who wanted to get a guy who was a triple murderer pardoned. I made sure we got done on time, because I was going to have a press conference at 1:30 at which I was going to announce that I was not going to run again. Within me, it was like the resurrection. I began a new life as governor from that time on.

———•◆•———

Before finishing up with 1982, let's go back to the fall of 1981 and a speech Quie gave at Concordia College in Moorhead, on the western edge of Minnesota. He had expected to speak about the state's economic situation to a large group of Concordia donors, but in looking over the large crowd at the Lutheran institution, "I thought they must know something about the whole experience with Jesus Christ and the Holy Spirit because they were so generous to the college. So instead of talking about the budget and economy, I said I was going to talk about the Holy Spirit."

After his spontaneous remarks, Roger Moe, the senate's DFL Majority Leader, came up on the stage, and after speaking to someone else, walked over to Quie and shook hands. Moe lived north of Moorhead in the small town of Ada, and suffice it to say, relations had not been entirely cordial between the two men, with the senator, for example, having been quoted in the press as describing the governor as a "cunning political animal." It was not meant as a compliment. Nevertheless, when Quie was first elected, he had asked former DFL governor Wendell Anderson, who, among legislative Democrats, might be best equipped and most inclined to collaborate productively with a new Republican governor, and Anderson had named Moe. Roger was chairman of the Senate Finance Committee at that earlier time, causing Quie to be particularly disappointed that their working relationship had been as contentious as it was.

"When I shook hands with him on that stage," Quie said in one of our conversations, "I knew something different was happening, and I asked that he come see me when we both got back to St. Paul."

I remember the next part of the story well, because as I walked just outside the governor's inner office one day, there sat Roger Moe, whom I had known and liked since 1975 when I worked at the University of Minnesota and whom I now greeted and (politely) asked what he was doing there. He said he didn't know, just that Quie wanted to see him. Many years later I reminded the governor what he had said that day to his executive secretary, Esther Allen, when she inquired why he wanted to see Roger, "I just wanted to tell him I love him." When asked about the highlights of his governorship, Al Quie invariably mentions his relationship, both political and personal, with Roger Moe over the last portion of his term. "After the Concordia speech," he said, "that's when we really began talking with each other."

That was 1982. In reviewing this chapter, Quie added this 2008 postscript.

"Roger just recently told me that he was looking through papers stored in his basement and he came across the prayer he had written in longhand for the Concordia gathering. He prayed for people in trouble and he prayed for 'my friend Al Quie.' After all these years, I now realize it was me who the Holy Spirit changed that night."

———— • ◆ • ————

It's 1982 again and the last of Quie's 28 consecutive years as a state senator, U.S. congressman, and governor. Between his new friendship with Moe and his decision not to seek re-election, "that was the beginning of a year where we had true governance trying to solve our budget problems."

There was less backbiting than there had been before by a long ways, and even some DFL legislators, who previously seemed to have no time for me, came in to thank me, which was something. Then Roger Moe came in towards the end of the year—the economy was still causing us difficulty with revenue forecasts—and he said, "Governor, if you lay out not only how we can solve this current shortfall, but how we can fix the problem into the future, I'll commit my caucus to you." He did. I got nine Republicans in the House to vote for it. We got things straightened out and gave my successor, Rudy Perpich, a $500 million surplus, which before long, with the improving economy, grew to a billion dollars.

In talking about the period, Quie mentioned how he had suffered and how some Republicans wanted Democrats, along with DFLer Perpich (this was now after the November elections) to suffer in return. But what we really hadn't spoken about, I said, was the suffering of citizens who lost welfare, health care, and other benefits, as well as state and other employees who lost jobs, because of the cutbacks.

"We really haven't talked," I said, "about the human dimension of the cuts. But there were people showing up at the Capitol in wheelchairs protesting what you were doing." I asked that he talk about them and others who had been hurt, and he focused first on his decision to end a health insurance program that protected people from potentially huge expenses.

We had a catastrophic insurance program in which the state would pay for everything after recipients paid for a certain amount on their own, but costs were mushrooming way beyond what anyone had estimated. I thought about changing the formula, but came to the conclusion after talking to several people in the administration that we would have to end the program completely, at least for a while.

As it happened, I went to church that next Sunday down in Nerstrand and a friend of mine I had known from grade school, a farmer, came up and said how he had cancer and how wonderful that program had been and how much he had benefited from it. I told him I was sorry, but we needed to end the program and that he'd have to spend down even further on his net worth.

Quie continued talking about the human toll of cutting back on "goodhearted" governmental programs, especially the effect on low-income people. But he also emphasized the way in which such programs—including the big three of Medicare, Medicaid, and Social Security—have a habit of growing far more expensive than initially predicted by their architects and early advocates. And correspondingly, he noted how people have a habit of being less careful with dollars other than their own.

"I recall when we were coming out of the Navy and how some of the guys were trying to figure how they could take their luggage home without paying for it. I talked to them and their answer was along the lines of, 'Oh, it's *just* the government.' I'll always remember that. 'It's just the government.' That stuck with me."

The moment also proved right for him to repeat how income tax indexing had been helping lower-income people just as it had been helping higher-income people and how Rudy Perpich—at Quie's later urging—would come to agree.

But I needed to push harder, as one of the toughest aspects of the budget crisis for me was the number of state employees who lost their jobs and livelihoods, with the same happening to educators and other local employees because of reductions in state payments to counties, school districts, and the like. This led to one of the few times I was surprised and taken aback by what he said. Yes, of course, he was pained by the effects of benefit cutbacks, including increases in college tuitions, on people, especially those "on the edge," as he put it. But as for the layoffs, he said, "I've always figured if a person has skills and ability, he can find a job someplace, and we didn't have anywhere near the unemployment other states had. No, frankly, the layoffs didn't bother me as much as they did you."

———— • ————

Wondering how a speechwriter might earn his keep for almost a full year working for a politician not seeking re-election, I went to see Quie a couple of days after his announcement in January 1982 and asked what he planned on doing for the rest of his term (or words to that forward effect). It was during that chat in his office that we agreed he would host a series of public meetings at which smart people would dig into tough subjects. That conversation led to what became known as the "Governor's Forums"—five to start, later expanded to eight after he enjoyed the first several sessions so much.

I had forgotten most of the topics until I spent time in the library working on this chapter. We opened in June with a program on housing and followed with forums on crime, mental health, soil conservation, education, physical infrastructure, education again, and ended with a final session in November on public-private partnerships. What I also forgot was the good press the project generated. And what I didn't know until recently, frankly, is the significant role the series played in helping him view his final year in office as a success. "That was just the most ideal way," he said in one of our morning conversations, "to bring people together on controversial issues. Otherwise, they wouldn't be talking to each other."

Al Quie resonates much more to policy broadly defined than politics narrowly practiced, and he finds congenial disputation (as he puts it) infinitely more appealing than grown-ups yelling at each other. Serious—which is not to say always scintillating—discussions and analyses were exactly what the forums succeeded in achieving. "I plan on taking full advantage of the freedom for straight talk and unfettered debate that my non-candidacy allows," he had said in announcing the project. "I will leave office, not in silence, but to the clash of ideas and dreams."

What kind of questions and problems did the governor, along with scholars, activists, and others, pursue? It's impossible to read the titles of four morning panels at the October 1982 forum on infrastructure without thinking about a bridge that fell into the Mississippi River a quarter century later.

First was, "Chicken Little was Wrong—Everything *but* the Sky is Falling."

Followed by, "Public Works: Pay Me Now or Pay Me Later."

Succeeded by, "Is it Wise to Mortgage the Future?"

And right before a panel discussion where participants were to pull everything together: "Who Should Pay to Rebuild Our Infrastructure?"

Quie's farewell address, which I was honored to work on, was of similarly textured cloth. Delivered at the Hubert H. Humphrey Institute of Public Affairs at the University of Minnesota before an embarrassingly small crowd, reaction to it by the media was nevertheless stunningly good.

"Governor's speech displayed courage," read a headline of a *St. Paul Pioneer Press* editorial.

Drawing not just on the speech, columnist Leonard Inskip of the *Minneapolis Star Tribune* (the papers had recently merged), wrote of how Quie was exiting "at his peak," with his "last few months hav[ing] been his best: leading the state through a fiscal emergency; organizing a series of thoughtful forums on future problems; delivering a farewell speech that, if widely heeded, could elevate the tone and quality of political discourse and help Minnesota make the difficult adjustments that lie ahead."

Columnist John Camp (who was soon to win a Pulitzer Prize) wrote similarly in one of the St. Paul papers: "Retiring Gov. Al Quie has shown us a class act the last few weeks."

What was it about the speech—which the *Star Tribune* reprinted nearly in full—that critics found so apt and on target? How better to conclude Al Quie's nearly three decades in elected office than with a reprise of portions of what he had to say nearly as long ago.

I entered public life with a strong belief in the sanctity of the individual, the centrality of the family, and the compassion and good sense of people in neighborhoods and local communities. I believed that all people have infinite worth and that all people possess gifts that can be known fully by no one.

My belief in these ideas gained strength as the years passed, and I better saw their worth, and as they withstood the doubts of skeptics and the strain of great change. Nothing, but nothing, has challenged my early—and lasting—belief in them. And, most certainly, nothing has altered my belief that it's through love which we share with family and friends—and, yes, even extend towards enemies—and the hand we hold out to those in need, that God's grace is most apparent.

This constellation of family and community provides a good backdrop for what is perhaps the basic dilemma and quest of our people: How can we, in a nation of over 200 million people—in a society in which both public and private institutions continue to grow relentlessly in size and scope— how can we escape anonymity and inhuman scale and feel that we are in charge of our lives? . . .

We seek, as a people, purpose and community. We seek to be true to ourselves and good stewards for our children. Our longing, at root, is spiritual, for we are seeking clearer, fuller meaning to our lives.

In political terms, we are looking for ways of distributing power and control more broadly. And, when we are wisest, we are also looking for ways of making our outlook more global. . . .

Out of the tugs and turmoil of this period, I believe, are emerging common understandings about organizing the body politic. They have to do with individual and group responsibility, trust in the competence and compassion of our fellows, and the expectation of accountability from those who represent us. . . .

Whatever explanation one offers for this changed view of government's role, I believe it is real and will last. I believe this

will be the case even if someone other than Ronald Reagan—
or someone other than a Republican—is president after 1984.
This will be so because of the fiscal incapacity of the public
sector to continue adding to its obligations in the same way it
has done for the last 50 years.

The abridged passages above, while they were quintessential Quie
in terms of his soul-deep devotions, were largely ignored by the
media. Emphasized, instead, were extended portions that followed
about poorly performing political parties, excessive partisanship, and
"dogmatic bunkers."

We have much to do to make our dreams work. Unfortunately,
our political debate generally doesn't contribute enough to the
task. I have grown increasingly disenchanted with the
shallowness of our debate of public issues. . . .

I don't think people have understood well enough the
complexity of our state's economic situation. The fact that it's
absurd to talk about Minnesota's problems as removed from
those of the rest of the nation and world hasn't stopped many
from posturing that they nevertheless are.

Political gamesmanship, of course, not just intellectual
inadequacy, has had much to do with this simplistic tack.
Nevertheless, we who are in public life have not distinguished
ourselves in terms of helping citizens—or ourselves—
understand the nuance and interdependence of our
predicament. With few exceptions, we have not engaged in
that kind of debate. . . .

We do not lack in Minnesota for studies, proposals, and
inquisitiveness. We are rich in institutes, citizen groups, and
editorial writers free of bashfulness.

What we do lack is participation by elected and other officials
in substantial discussion of public issues. And nowhere is this

shortcoming more pronounced than within our two major political parties. My opinion of our party system has changed during my career.

As when I entered political life, there are today many excellent people active in the Independent-Republican and Democratic-Farmer-Labor parties. And it's obvious that our entire political system depends on them. But I have lost confidence in the capacity of our two parties to strike the imagination and reflect the real interests of our people. This applies to both parties, at both the state and national level.

A good question is whether parties have ever met such a severe test. Perhaps not. Still, I have come to the conclusion that parties today are more extraneous than integral to most people. They are viewed by many of their leaders as ends in themselves. And their grasp on the issues of the day is only randomly firm. In hindsight, the primary defeat of both parties' endorsed candidates for governor [in September] was not surprising. . . .

And then there is the matter of partisanship. Politics in Minnesota suffers an excess of it, and I deplore it. My argument is not with firmly held beliefs, as I urge conviction, not timidity. My argument, rather, is with orthodoxy based on pettiness.

As opposed to the most recent budget deliberations, and those of last March as well, the negotiations of last December were dreadful because we were all drawn—some of us obliviously, some of us eagerly, none of us wisely—into dogmatic bunkers which we defended as if they guarded the very honor of our parties. We were able to overcome this silliness only when I decided not to seek re-election, when the gravity of our problem finally took hold and when legislators realized it was better to be any place *other* than St. Paul if they wanted to *return* to St. Paul.

If I were to cite the biggest difference in state government now, as opposed to when I served in the state senate in the 1950s, I would be forced to choose the often unbending partisanship of politics that has developed in Minnesota. . . .

He then began to conclude by talking about what he was most proud of achieving as governor.

I am very proud about a number of things my administration has accomplished, two in particular: indexing of state personal income taxes and the merit selection of judges.

Because indexing prevents tax revenues from rising faster than inflation, politicians have less room to hide. Public officials should be put on the spot, not only when it comes to determining the services their constituents receive, but also when the taxes they pay are increased. I will leave it to others to judge the political import of the fact that my largest achievement as governor—indexing—is a concept difficult to grasp, whose resulting tax cuts are invisible. But what is most important is that it holds public officials accountable.

As for the merit selection of judges, I take enormous pride in the caliber of the men and women I've appointed to the bench. At no moment is a governor more aware of his capacity for long-term influence—good or bad—than when he's appointing a judge. I hope future governors will retain the program we have designed for merit selection in conjunction with the bar, the courts, and others; a program that assures the selection of superior individuals, free of disproportionate partisan consideration. . . .

Looking back over the last four years, I would have done only a few things differently. I would have been more aggressive earlier in working for a sounder job climate. I misread how intractable a mountain needed to be moved. . . .

From left to right: Gretchen Quie, Al Quie, Mark Balma, Gerald Ford, and Minnesota Governor Arne Carlson, sometime in the 1990s. Balma is a portrait and mural artist and the occasion, in the governor's reception room at the state Capitol, was a viewing of a painting Balma had done of Ford with the leaders of France, England, and Germany.

And in education, rather than isolating the issue of reducing class size in kindergarten through third grade, as I did in 1979, I should have used the occasion also to urge basic changes in the state's entire funding formula for elementary and secondary schools. . . .

I've enjoyed my public career immensely. As a young man, I saw public life as an opportunity to serve others. I still do. Politics is a noble profession. For all the criticism directed at people in politics—fair and unfair, leveled by others as well as ourselves—there is honor and integrity in this service. I have been honored to be part of it.

"I leave office and public life," he summed up, "confident, strong, happy, and at peace. I also leave as I entered: convinced of God's presence and his spirit within us."

Chapter Nine

A Note on Civility and Congenial Disputation

As politicians go, Al Quie was commonly viewed as a "civil" one, and he was. As for current politicians, as opposed to being *Quiesque*, they're commonly viewed as *quiescent* on the issue—albeit in noisy and rude ways. This may or may not be a fair reading of men and women presently in public life, though it would be hard to make the case that those with whom Quie served during the budget crises of the early 1980s were particularly polite and pleasant by contrast. Not quite. Burr and Hamilton aside, politics is the way people settle disagreements without shooting each other, but that doesn't mean it isn't a full-contact sport, as it always has been and always will be. Often, in fact, it's best understood as a collision sport.

Incivility was a main theme in Quie's 1982 farewell address, and it was one of the concerns that led several people to approach him and me in 2007 about writing this book. One of them was the social critic Os Guinness, an old friend of Quie's, whose own 2008 book, *The Case for Civility*, correctly argues that civility is "not to be confused with niceness and mere etiquette or dismissed as squeamishness about differences." Rather, Guinness writes, "It is a tough, robust, substantive concept that is a republican virtue, critical to both democracy and civil society, and a manner of conduct that will be decisive for the future of the American republic." In similar spirit, Yale law professor Stephen L. Carter, in his 1998 book, *Civility: Manners, Morals, and the Etiquette of Democracy*, wrote of how civility has two parts: generosity, even when it's costly; and trust, even when there is risk.

This is precisely the kind of civility—political and other kinds— that Quie has favored and sought to practice: much sturdier than saccharine, more demanding than acquiescent, much riskier than lying low. Here's an example from one of our conversations. I had just asked him if he agreed with those who believe politics is broken and grimy.

"Yes," he said, "but I believe it's redeemable."

So I asked that he make believe he was on *Almanac,* a long-running public affairs program on Twin Cities Public Television, and that he had 45 seconds to say how he would fix politics.

"Ha! Fix it in 45 seconds?"

"Okay," I said. "It's public television. You've got a minute and 45 seconds."

"If I had 45 seconds, or even less, first thing I would say is, 'Go find your enemy and become his friend.'"

"Even though," I asked, "your closest political supporters might be displeased with you?" We had just been talking again about how it's usually much safer to challenge and anger your political opponents in regards to legislative and other controversies than to challenge and risk angering members of your own team. Doing the former is automatic and applauded by friends; doing the latter can be wrenching and applauded mostly by foes and strangers, if at all.

"Yes, even though it might displease your closest allies. You must introduce your enemies to others, to your family and friends. You must be seen with them. You don't just do it in private. You must walk with them. You must physically walk with them."

"So it's not just a spiritual or metaphoric walk?

"No," he said.

"You show up at the same places?"

"Yes, that's right," he said. "The spiritual becomes the physical," and he repeated a story from a previous conversation about how an African American woman once told him how happy she was to be in Washington and out of the Deep South (this was in the 1960s) until she was in a Saks Fifth Avenue one day and a white friend pretended she didn't see her.

"That African American woman," Quie said, "taught me a lesson. If you've built a relationship, when you get to that point, let other people see you together."

Reasonably confident that he had indeed done so, I nevertheless asked if he had ever gone out of his way to make certain other people saw him in this way with someone in particular.

"I don't believe," he said, "that the denomination I belong to, the Evangelical Lutheran Church, should have pastors on their roster who engage in open homosexual relationships. But I have no problem with people whose sexual orientation is homosexual. At a large meeting at Central Lutheran Church in Minneapolis in 2006, I went up to a gay friend and his parents who were in the front of the room and embraced each one of them for all to see, as they were being ignored."

Earlier in that conversation, I had asked, "How does a candidate who doesn't have a strong base, perhaps who's running for the first time or is an incumbent not in a secure district, how can he unilaterally disarm when it comes to the caustic side of politics if his opponent is going to continue beating the hell out of him? You can make an argument that the person who tries to be more civil is more likely to lose."

If you run for office there are two things you do. First, you point out what you're going to do, if elected, to benefit people, and you also point out the dangers of your opponent. You can't just ignore your opponent entirely. But when you do this, you shouldn't run a campaign that's primarily about demonizing your opponent so that people will be voting for you only to get rid of the other person. Focus on what you're going to do to help people meet their needs by having government do only what it ought to do. When you deal with your opponent, don't skew or slant what you say about him, but rather make sure you're totally honest. There's nothing wrong with pointing out the weaknesses in his arguments. Just go for it. That ought to be done.

The second thing I used to do, once I found out who my opponent would be, I prayed every morning for him. I prayed for him more than for myself. I needed to talk to God about him. You know, if you pray for a guy, you're sure not going to start saying or doing something dishonest about him.

I asked Quie exactly what he would pray for. "Did you pray for his good health? Or for him to see the light as you would like him to?"

"I prayed," Quie said, "mostly for his well-being and that the campaign would be a rewarding experience for him. I also prayed I wouldn't do something that I'd be ashamed about afterwards."

———•◆•———

Halfway through our 17th conversation I noted that while he had used the word "philosophy" many times in the previous months, he had never mentioned the word "ideology." As far as I'm concerned, the two terms can be used interchangeably, as long as "ideology" is not conceived in rigid ways—though that's precisely the way many people, including Quie, tend to view it.

"I sure do have an ideology," Quie said, "but I don't know if I'd be called an ideologue. What probably expresses it better is that I have a 'world view.' As much as possible, I believe decisions should be made at local levels, as close as possible to where the action is. I guess you could call that an ideology. Though you might call it a philosophy, too—a political philosophy. You tell me what the differences are."

This I attempted to do, in a disquisition starting with World War II, stretching through the War on Poverty, then *Roe v. Wade*, on to Reagan, finishing off the previous week. "Would you," I asked, "agree or disagree with that?"

"After listening to you," Quie said, "I'll deal with it in a different way," and upon drawing ideological and philosophical distinctions of his own among political, economic, and spiritual realms, he moved the conversation to single-interest groups that pushed no-tax and other pledges he'd never sign and political consultants who urge their clients to run nasty campaigns. In terms of their contributions to civil discourse and civility generally, he wasn't admiring of any of them.

"I remember when I was in Congress I was asked by a senior citizens group to sign a pledge saying I would support some issue or bill they wanted. I actually was angry and said that if they didn't trust me well enough to use my best judgment on their behalf, then they shouldn't have me in office."

"Do you think," I asked, "single-issue organizations and impulses are stronger now than when you were in office?"

"Oh, yes, by far," he said, "by far." His answer was virtually the same when I asked if political consultants were causing campaigns to become too vicious. I asked if paid consultants had ever pushed him in a barbed direction he didn't want to go. No, he said, what he had said and done were his own decisions. This included, he said and as noted in an earlier chapter, the time when he held up a copy of *Time* during a 1978 debate with Rudy Perpich and reminded viewers the magazine had called his opponent "Governor Goofy." I've always thought that was a little edgy on Quie's part, though if I recall correctly, he never raised his voice discourteously.

A kicker to this section was Quie's response to a partial explanation of mine for the rise of incivility in political life; namely, that once states like Minnesota adopted near-absolute gift bans, legislators and other public officials had fewer opportunities to get to know each other while collegially grazing at shrimp and egg roll lines sponsored by organizations employing lobbyists. As realpolitik analyses go, I've been particularly fond of this one, though Quie (who doesn't drink, by the way) brusquely dismissed it by saying, "I've never had anything meaningful happen at a buffet."

————•◆•————

On another occasion, after acknowledging that current political invective pales in comparison to routine eighteenth- and nineteenth-century slurs, I asked, "How, beyond appeals to the Lord, can we get people in politics to cool their rhetoric a bit?"

"Well," Quie said (and despite the organization of this chapter), "if we put civility number one, we're going to lose. Disputation comes first. If we put civility first, it will be pabulum and fluff."

Four months earlier, in talking about the importance of being "absolutely open in every way" when discussing politics and other matters, he referred to his "passion for congenial disputation." People, he said, not only have to dispute each other, "they have to be given permission" to do so.

Albeit already teased in earlier in the book, this was the first time he used the term "congenial disputation" in our conversations. It has an intriguing ring, so much so that on hearing it initially, I said, "I think we may have the title for the book."

"It's not going to sell," he retorted, "if we do that."

Nevertheless, I did Google it and found that no other publication title contained the phrase "congenial disputation"—the locution, in fact, was nowhere to be found in the ether—but it lost out to the more straightforward thumbnail you see on the cover.

Quie assumed the term was his, having personally married the two words when he finished reading Thomas C. Oden's *The Rebirth of Orthodoxy: Signs of New Life in Christianity*. "I don't recall Oden using those two words that way, but when I was done with the book, one of its main ideas gelled down to congenial disputation."

In the same way civility, properly pursued, is not a spindly or easy virtue. Congenial disputation, as pursued by Quie, is neither a casual nor comfortable chat, as the aim is understanding and sometimes reconciliation, not laughs. Take, for example, how Quie views his job as a board member, a role he frequently has played since leaving elected office.

"The way I interact with people at board meetings, a lot of them actually don't think it's congenial at all, though when I got off the Prison Fellowship board one person did write and said how much he appreciated the fact that I asked hard questions and probed. I absolutely do put people on the spot, and for some of them the discomfort is enormous. But the issues these organizations deal with are so important, and I have such passion for them, we have to be forthright—though I always try to smile and chuckle when I push the way I do. I can't help but do that."

Chuck Colson, founder of Prison Fellowship Ministries, several years ago said how much he appreciated Quie's tenacity and tough questioning at board meetings, even if not at those exact moments.

In order to engage in congenial disputation, Quie argued, "People need a sense of big pictures; they need to think about issues." People more interested in trivialities and gossip need not apply. "But," he contended, "because of this whole postmodern period we're in, we tend to think more with our feelings than with our intellect." Feelings, obviously, are crucial, he acknowledged, even though earlier in his life he tried to "rid" himself of some of the more uncomfortable ones before "realizing God had created them." But as he likewise and immediately noted, "God also gave us the ability to reason." So in order to meld heart and head, he concluded,

> There needs to be *intentionality* in the way we reason together that lessens the chances of people getting hurt. The biggest reason why people don't engage in this way is because they're afraid of getting hurt. They figure other people won't be reasonable, and it's threatening to them. And it's not just words that can be frightening, but a person's tone of voice or the way he moves his body—his body language. People also can be frightened, of course, by how serious conversations of this sort can hurt their friendships or even their economic well-being.

There also needs to be fortitude. In another thematic continuation from his farewell address 25 years earlier, Quie spoke of how political parties are less hospitable to vigorous differences of opinion and debates among adherents than they used to be.

> When parties [referring to both Republicans and Democrats] are controlled by ideological extremes, it means that those who believe differently either leave, or keep quiet, or get knocked down. I remember we used to have *amazing* debates in the two parties. John Ashbrook, for example, was the most conservative Republican on the House Education and Labor Committee, and Ogden Reid was the most liberal Republican on the committee, but I helped get them in a relationship with each other where they could be open and straightforward with one another. I go to precinct caucuses and we can have those discussions, but you've got to stand up and do it.

"And be real brave," I added.

"Yes, you can do it if you're real brave. That's right. I used to be the governor; I can be brave. But how can another person who just graduated from high school and goes to his or her first precinct caucus be expected to do that? I've seen in our caucus a young person get bold and decide they would engage. Now, that's a beautiful sight to me."

On another occasion, he spoke of how it's not a good idea for people in congenially disputatious moments to be solicitous of others' emotions to the point of everyone clamming up. "I learned I can't be responsible for someone else's emotions, and they can't be responsible for mine. We can only be responsible for our own."

Quie's notion of "intentionality" is pivotal. Men and women must be purposeful, he argued, in engaging with other people—especially with those who are different from themselves in significant ways. Exchanges like these, he said, need not be face to face, as many people prefer pursuing them in writing—though Quie is a face-to-face guy, not because it's safer, but because "it just takes me forever to do it in writing." Intentionality, more specifically, as he made clear, is a disposition and determination that needs to be taught, as it usually doesn't come naturally. It certainly didn't come naturally to Quie, whose curiosity has always competed with his shyness. Yet as noted several chapters ago, he has worked hard, and I would argue remarkably successfully, in shifting his temperamental center of gravity from someone who stared at girls' shoes to someone who now seeks out frank and respectful conversations, for instance, with gays and lesbians on issues like same-sex marriage.

———————•◆•———————

"Over the course of your public lifetime," I asked, "who are the politicians who have been the most civil, open, congenial, and intellectually interesting in the ways we've been talking about? Is there anyone who strikes you as just absolutely first rate?"

"The first one who comes to mind," he said, "was Charlie Goodell. When he came to Congress [in 1959, a year after Quie arrived], right off the bat he started asking me questions about philosophy and ideas and where I was trying to go. He just probed hard and asked all those challenging questions. He came from Jamestown, New York, and at the time I thought he was way too conservative."

Quie was laughing at this point, thinking back to how liberal Goodell became once he was appointed by Gov. Nelson Rockefeller to fill Robert

F. Kennedy's unexpired Senate seat after he was assassinated in 1968. I was a college student in Binghamton, New York, at the time and remember the metamorphosis of the upstate Republican well.

"Another person," Quie said, "was Bill Steiger of Wisconsin. He was just a brilliant guy who was ambitious and ready to go right off the bat. Both of those people had total integrity and I told each of them, 'Don't wait until you get seniority. Pursue the things you're really good at with vigor.'"

"Now, over on the Democratic side, John Brademas of Indiana might have been the best. He also was a brilliant person. We were very much involved in education together, and he challenged me in everything I was thinking and doing. That's how we started out, and we became very close. We had great respect for each other. He thought enough of me that when he was meeting with people like Margaret Mead and Hans Kung—he dealt with people like that—he invited me to be with them."

Brademas, who went on to become president of New York University, was one of about a dozen of Quie's old Washington friends who participated in a video-taped luncheon conversation in 2003 as part of the Minnesotan's 80th birthday celebration. In talking about the years they served in the House together, Brademas' voice caught as he recalled the stressful battles and close, trusting friendship he had with Quie.

"Jim O'Hara of Michigan was another Democrat I came to appreciate so much on labor issues. But it's interesting that I didn't have that kind of relationship with anyone when it came to foreign affairs. As I look back on my conversations in that area, the most meaningful were with President Eisenhower, as he had the most marvelous grasp of the relationships and understandings among nations, which surely came out of his work in World War II with our allies."

"How much time did you spend with him?

"There were times in the White House, but the best times were after he left office, up on his farm in Gettysburg."

I asked what the common denominator was in the exceptional relationships. "The easy answer," I suggested, "is that you all could be cordial and honest with each other, and learn from each other, but was there something else?"

"Bob Poage," Quie said, "wasn't exactly a cordial person."

Poage was a Democrat from Texas with whom he "could engage intellectually," but who got sufficiently irritated with Quie at a meeting of the Agriculture Committee one day to threaten, "If you persist in that, I'll cut you."

Laughing at the memory, Quie said, "I can just see him with a knife and he's going to get me. I just looked at him in shock because nobody had ever said that to me before."

Cordiality, Quie and I agreed, wasn't necessarily a first requirement. "I did come to understand Bob Poage better when I had dinner at his home, and he was a pussycat around his wife."

So what were the most important things, he asked himself, about the special relationships he had in Washington, as well as the treasured one he came to have as governor with the DFL Majority Leader of the Minnesota Senate, Roger Moe? Relationships that epitomized what he describes as congenial disputation?

"Being straightforward with one another was a large part of it, and the tremendous respect we had for each other. But there was something *invisible* between us, too.

"*That* was it," Quie wrapped up in what sounds like a eureka! moment on the page but was no surprise to him at all. "It was respect, but it also was spiritual."

Chapter Ten

Prison Ministries
"The people God lays at your gate"

---◆---

Most people familiar with Al Quie's ministry to prisoners probably assume it began with his friendship with Chuck Colson. They also likely assume the two men became brothers in Christ only after the latter's life began unraveling in the whirlpool of Watergate. Both assumptions are wrong, as all started earlier. How much earlier? In a stretch, back to first grade.

---◆---

"How," I asked in our fifteenth session, "did you first get involved working with offenders?"

"I used to stay away from anyone like that," he said. "Did I ever tell you the story of seeing the guy in the one-cell jail in Nerstrand?"

He had broached it several months earlier, but he expanded this time.

When I was in first grade our teacher took us on a field trip to visit the local grocery store and bank and places like that. We had a community building in that small town of 270 people that had a jail with just one cell inside, and as we were looking around, we saw a man in it. I can still see him. Other than looking sad, he looked like he had no emotion. He just looked at us. Because his beard looked to be several days old, I figure he was probably arrested on a Friday and it was now about Monday and the sheriff hadn't come to get him yet. I still remember how I felt when we were walking back to school, which was about two or three blocks away. I thought to myself how horrible it would be to be cooped up in a cage like that and not see the sunrise or sunset. One of the marvelous things in my bedroom was that I could hear the wind through the trees. There was a huge maple tree outside the window and I loved the sound of the wind in its leaves. But someone in that jail would never hear those things.

I also imagine that my sense of claustrophobia had something to do with it, and I resolved that nothing like that was ever going to happen to me. Plus my parents always talked about living a straight and moral life and the importance of staying away from temptation. So it was all ingrained in me. I just turned away from people who were incarcerated or prisons or anything about them.

When he repeated this story, I realized I had never asked him how someone who was claustrophobic could be a Navy pilot.

"It never bothered me then," he said, "because I was in control. But it bothered me a lot when I was in a tank we used to experience low-air pressure at high altitudes. I spent my time praying in order to get through."

Jumping decades ahead, Quie was now in Washington and both starting and participating in prayer groups in Congress, but he also was interested in branching out to the executive branch by starting fellowships "in the departments downtown."

"So I talked to Harry Blackmun about starting something in the Department of Justice and he said he'd pull some people together. But since he was on the Supreme Court at the time, he didn't feel he should be part of it, and he wasn't." A decade before being appointed to the high court by President Nixon in 1970, Justice Blackmun was resident counsel for the Mayo Clinic in Rochester.

One of the people who got involved in the group was the chief U.S. marshal, who not much later was convicted of keeping some weapons from a raid in Chicago and then selling them and not paying taxes on them. So he was sent to Leavenworth. Emotionally and intellectually, I turned my back on him because, you know, he was in the pen. I couldn't do anything about it.

But the day I found out about it, I came home late that night and Gretchen was already asleep. I had not done my devotion in the morning because I had left so early, so I debated with myself about whether to do it then or wait again until the next morning. Something, though, caused me to do it right then and I was in the last part of Matthew 25 where Jesus talked about judgment day and feeding the hungry, giving drink to the thirsty, welcoming strangers, clothing the naked, and visiting people when they're sick. I was patting myself on the back for what I had done—I had sent food overseas, I had given drink to the thirsty, I had clothed the naked, I had paid attention to strangers, I had visited people when they were sick. But then Jesus also said we had to visit those who were in prison. I said, "Nah! He can't mean somebody who's *guilty*. He must mean visiting people like Saul when he became Paul and went to prison. He wasn't guilty at all." So I tried to convince myself it wasn't anyone like the convicted marshal. I also probably thought if somebody was going to visit him it ought to be someone who was old, like I am now, and not somebody who was busy in Congress. So I read on, but when I came to the end, I sat there condemned. I just knew I was wrong. That's when it came to me that I was wrong.

It was perhaps only two weeks later when Quie got a call from two friends who had been visiting prisoners regularly at Lorton Penitentiary, John Staggers and Stu Murtoff. Located in Virginia, Lorton served as the District of Columbia's prison.

John was black and Stu was white, and it said something that the two of them would visit Lorton together, as inmates there were mostly African American. They said they wanted to bring someone by the name of Pat Patterson to visit me and it turned out he had been the leader, the Godfather of all the black criminals in Washington. I still remember when they came into my office in the Rayburn Building: I glanced at everything of value so I could check to see if it was still there when Pat left.

They had met when Pat was still at Lorton. John and Stu said they didn't push their religion on anyone, but one day John gave his Bible to Pat and he came to the conclusion that their "hidden agenda was trying to make Christians out of us." John, who was a big man, said Pat got so angry at the thought that he feared for his own safety. Pat said there were two things inmates didn't do in prison. One was to hug another person, because that was taken as a sign of homosexuality. The second was to be "caught with a Bible on you," because the prisoners most likely to carry them were pedophiles who would hang out at the chapel for protection from other prisoners who despised them. According to Pat, it was "baby rapers" who hung out at the chapel and no one wanted to be thought of as one of them.

But Pat, who had led a Lorton prison uprising, saw himself as both meaner and tougher than anyone else, so how could he show he was afraid to take the Bible back to his cell? He later told me that after throwing it on his cot and storming around, he picked it up and started reading it, and in time, came to believe in Jesus Christ and also led his lieutenants to Him. Pat then asked if I would go to Lorton and lead his friends who were still there, and other men, in Bible study. I could have claimed I was busy, because I was. But I had this battle with God only a couple of weeks earlier and I didn't want to fight Him again, so I said "Okay, I'll do it." That was my beginning, going into prisons.

One of the other fascinating things Pat told me was that he and his lieutenants had planned to kill a deputy warden or deputy superintendent. They had nicknamed him "Gestapo" because he found out everything they were doing and kept thwarting it. So they figured the way to deal with him was to kill him, and just like terrorists, they planned how to do it for a long time. But when it came to actually kill him, they said to each other, "We can't do that, we're Christians now."

Quie is laughing heartily, recalling the incident.

"'Well,' they asked, 'what should we do?' Someone said, 'Maybe we ought to pray for him.' So they prayed for him. Then, after a while, they said, 'We ought to go and talk to him.' So they did and they led him to Christ also and he started meeting with them in their Bible group before I got there."

"Son of a gun," I said.

"Yes. *Amazing*," Quie said.

"I presume they told the guard what their original plan was."

"At least they weren't bashful about telling me what it was. Then I got to know people like Too Smooth, Ace, and Money, names like that." Laughing again, Quie said, "I never had experiences like that before. I've come to learn that God lays people at your gate and you ought to pay attention to them."

———— •◆• ————

Al Quie first met Chuck Colson in September 1973, after Nixon's chief counsel had left the White House and was talking to Tom Philips, the president and CEO of Raytheon Corporation about working for the Massachusetts-based defense contractor. Philips, evidently, had been as hard-driving (some might substitute the word ruthless) as Colson had been in getting ahead, but as Colson later wrote, Philips had changed course, having come to Christ at a Billy Graham Crusade in Boston. As I understand the story, Colson was intrigued by the transformation and Philips gave him a copy of C.S. Lewis' *Mere Christianity*. At the risk of radically collapsing and shortchanging all that happened next, Philips came to believe Colson had come to Christ and he called his friend Doug Coe, asking if there might be a group in the Washington area which might teach and disciple the new convert. This was the same Doug Coe who had come to see Quie in 1959, with the two subsequently working together in prayer groups in Congress. They remain close friends.

It also was about two years after Quie began visiting Lorton, and in that time, he surprised himself by how comfortable he had become—a dairy farmer from homogenized southern Minnesota—in meeting with black convicts in an east coast prison. Nevertheless, he said, "Even though I had come to where I could handle meeting with all African Americans in prison, meeting with Chuck Colson was not something I looked forward to, as he was *too* far out of my comfort zone." As noted this was in September 1973, and while Watergate had not yet fully exploded, and while Colson certainly had not yet been indicted, his reputation as perhaps Nixon's toughest guy—known in D.C. circles as the president's "hatchet man"—preceded and enveloped him.

Coe suggested the group that should work with Colson was one already up and running and made up of Quie, Sen. Harold Hughes, a Democrat from Iowa, and Rep. Graham Purcell, a Democrat from Texas. Coe himself met regularly with the group.

In explaining his problem with Colson, Quie said he had seen him "playing to the 'shadow' of Nixon."

When I was elected to Congress in 1958, I was invited to join the Chowder & Marching Society, a group made up of one Republican from each committee in Congress. We'd meet Thursday afternoons after work so that we could share what was happening in our committees and work better together. Nixon had been a member when he was in the House and continued when he was in the Senate and he kept coming back again when he was vice president. I was just amazed how brilliant he was. For example, he not only knew all about my special election, he knew how well I did in various precincts. He didn't know about all members of Congress in that way, of course, but special elections were important to the party, especially in rural areas because a lot of farmers were not happy with the Eisenhower administration's farm policies. Ezra Taft Benson, the agriculture secretary, was not very popular at the time.

I asked what Quie meant by Nixon's "shadow."

"I'll give you just one example of the dark side of his personality. When Nixon ran against Jerry Voorhis for a House seat, and later against Helen Gahagan Douglas in his Senate race, he never said they were communists as such, but his campaign would send out information about them on pink paper, so it was subliminal. Those things just repulsed me, and frankly I didn't ever want to meet this person Colson who worked for Nixon later on. But as was the case before, I didn't want to fight with God, so I said okay, I'd meet with Colson."

The group had been meeting in a little chapel between the House and Senate, "but we didn't want anyone *ever* to see us with Colson." So even though the other members lived in Virginia, they decided to meet for the first time with him at Quie's home, as his and Gretchen's house in Silver Spring, Maryland, had a "long driveway with heavy maple trees and no street lights. We called the meeting for nine o'clock at night when it was dark in September." This was 1973.

I asked at this point if Robert Redford or Dustin Hoffman might have been hiding nearby.

I tell people I just know what Nicodemus felt like when he came to see Jesus under the cover of darkness, because that's what we were doing. Gretchen served some treats with coffee or whatever it was. With me it would have been tea, because I never liked coffee. I wondered how to get things started, so we got into a conversation with everyone sharing a little bit about what they knew about Jesus. That's when I remember Chuck saying, "Well you know, what really bothers me, having been a Marine, I know what foxhole conversions are. That's what I'm so afraid of. If this is a foxhole conversion, I'm just so concerned what it will do to Jesus Christ."

Harold Hughes was a big and burly guy who originally had used some pretty strong language in telling Doug Coe what he thought of Colson. But right after Chuck said what he did, Harold stood up and said, "Chuck, if you've come to know Christ, and I believe you have, I'm your brother for life," and he wrapped his arms around him, right there in our living room. Oh man! What a moment. They walked as brothers together after that. That was the beginning of it. We started meeting every Tuesday morning for breakfast at Fellowship House, a mansion on Embassy Row that some rich person had given to an organization then called International Christian Leadership (ICL) for purposes just like that. We also did a few weekends together. Chuck had worked with the Teamsters during the 1972 election, so we spent one of those weekends in Bible study, prayer, and fellowship at their retreat center on the eastern shore of Maryland.

"Has Chuck written about this?" I asked.

"Yes, some of it is in *Born Again*. It all comes out a little different, of course, when he writes or talks about it."

————— ·◆· —————

Colson's Watergate problems revved up in 1974 when he was indicted for crimes he didn't commit but nevertheless admitted to another one—having to do with obstruction of justice in the Daniel Ellsberg–Pentagon Papers case—that special prosecutor Leon Jaworski didn't even know about until Colson volunteered the information.

"Chuck was the most amazing person I've ever been with who you could say was being discipled, as he absolutely depended on his friends. He wanted to make certain we all agreed that was what he was supposed to do and he tried to wait until we came to consensus on his pleading guilty. That's how he knew the spirit of God was in those meetings. On this one matter, though, he had to make his own decision and we supported him"

"The popular story," I said to Quie, "is that you volunteered to serve some of his prison time."

He said he'd get to that, but that he first wanted to talk about the day his now-friend was sentenced.

Doug Coe, Graham Purcell, Harold Hughes, and I went to be with him when Judge Gerhard Gesell was going to decide if Chuck went to prison or not. Chuck had said that nobody had ever gone to prison on such a charge before, but I knew he was in trouble when the judge told his attorney, "Don't go barking up that tree." At the end, Gesell made the decision: one to three years. I was devastated.

Chuck then went before all those media microphones outside the courthouse. You can see the pictures in books. There behind him were his brothers—except me. I had said to myself, "I'm not going to let everybody see me with a guy being sent to prison." I was busy, I told myself. So I headed out, but there was a reporter whose name I don't remember who wrote for either *Time* or *Newsweek*, and I saw him heading for me as I was trying to get to my car. I was going to run, but I figured it wasn't dignified for a congressman to run. So he headed me off and the first thing he said was, "I saw you in the courtroom." I said yes, and quickly added the names of the other three, because if I could implicate a couple of Democrats, it might ease people's impression of me.

This was not the only time Quie laughed loudly in remembering the story.

The reporter said he had just one question for me. "Are you going to visit Colson in prison?" Right then, it flashed through my mind and I remembered when my dad was pressing me on my Catechism lesson. He had asked if I enjoyed studying it. I wanted to please him by saying yes, but I had to be honest, so I said no. So I just had to be honest with the reporter and I said, "Yes, I will," and he said of Chuck, "My, he's a lucky man."

Did the story ever show up in the magazine?

"I don't remember ever seeing it; no, I don't think so. But I had said I would visit him before God and now the public; I had said it. Often, maybe especially when you're in politics, having your peers and other people know something puts a little more pressure on you than just God knowing about it."

I suggested that saying no, that he *wouldn't* visit Colson in prison, would have been the much more problematic answer, as it would have betrayed hypocrisy. Saying yes showed compassion.

"But you see," Quie said, "he caught me right at the moment I was running. Inside me, I was running. I was chicken."

Colson started off at Fort Holabird Prison in Maryland where Quie visited him. He was transferred to the Maxwell Correctional Facility in Alabama where Harold Hughes saw him, but when Colson was needed at the Watergate trials, he was moved back to Fort Holabird where Quie met with him again. Gerald Ford (who Quie knew well) was now president and his attorney general was William Saxbe (who Hughes knew well). According to Quie, Colson asked him to seek a pardon on his behalf by Ford and he asked Hughes to do the same with Saxbe.

"Here I am, stuck," Quie said. "How could I show that I was a brother of Chuck in Christ if I didn't try to help him? But how could I also as a brother in Christ with the president ask him to do something that would prevent him from getting reelected? I told Chuck that Ford would never get reelected if he pardoned him, that it was bad enough he had pardoned Nixon, which I had disagreed with."

With the strain of incarceration perhaps dulling Colson's political antennae, Quie remembers him saying, "Oh, no one will ever notice."

It was at this point that Bob Andringa, the lead Republican staff member for the Education and Labor Committee, told Quie about an obscure federal law he coincidentally discovered that allowed a person to serve out someone else's sentence.

> Just then, I said, "Oh, that's what I'm supposed to do." I didn't argue with God; I didn't even tell Gretchen. I just figured I was going to do it. Chuck was testifying at another person's Watergate trial right around then and I assumed he would stop at his lawyer's office before going back to prison. It was similar to how, in deer hunting, I had learned how to figure out where the deer would be so that I'd be there when they got there.

I reminded him that it also was the way he caught up with Gretchen for their first conversation in the late 1940s. He calculated she would be at the art building at St. Olaf College at a certain time . . . and the rest turned out loads prettier than a possible spell in the hoosegow.

"I called the attorney's office. Frankly, it was a little like that proverbial vacuum cleaner salesman who really says to himself, 'I hope nobody's home. I hope nobody's home.' Despite what I was telling myself, I really didn't want to do it. But when I told the receptionist I'd like to speak to Chuck Colson's attorney, she said, 'Oh, Chuck's standing right here by my desk.'"

Quie was too good a tracker.

"So I told Chuck what I wanted to do, and that I wanted his attorney to look up the law. But he just screamed, 'No! No! No!' Just like that. To which I thought, 'Well, if that's the way you feel about it.'"

"He talked you out of it."

"Yes, Chuck talked me out of that one. He later wrote that while he had already accepted Jesus Christ as his Savior, he hadn't accepted Him as Lord of his life until we had that conversation. In all this, I see the hand of God."

And with another big laugh punctuating his stay-away journey from jail, he concluded, "The Lord *stayed* that hand."

Earlier, Quie had told Colson the person whom he should seek a pardon from was the judge himself.

"He'll never do that," Quie recalled Colson saying. But two days after Quie's offer, Judge Gesell did exactly that.

"How come?"

"I don't know. Some people think I talked to the president and the president talked to the judge. Presidents don't do that. But I've got no clue why he was let go when he was. Something, I guess, just touched Gesell. Chuck's father had died and his son had been arrested on a marijuana charge. Maybe that had something to do with it. So unbeknownst to Chuck, all of a sudden some member of the prison staff comes in and says, 'You're leaving,' and he leaves. It was a marvelous time when he came out. We met just about every Tuesday morning from that time on until I ran for governor in 1978."

The story is well-known: As Colson was leaving Fort Holabird, seven months into a sentence that could have lasted much longer, a prisoner yelled to him something like, "Well, Colson, we'll never see you again."

The dismissal—with forever ramifications for Al Quie—would prove to be emphatically false.

———— •◆•————

Chuck Colson started Prison Fellowship Ministries in 1976 and asked Quie to serve on its board of directors. He refused the invitation until 1983, as he had a long-standing policy of declining such assignments in any organization that might have connections with government as long as he remained in elected office. But his involvement in the rapidly growing institution grew rapidly itself after he left the governorship.

> Shortly before I went on the PF national board, the state director in Minnesota stepped down and I was at a screening meeting where candidates were being interviewed for the job. As I sat there, I realized we weren't paying enough to get the kind of leadership we needed, so I leaned over to Bob Clemens—he had been doing Bible studies in prisons—and I whispered, "Why don't you get somebody like me to do it?" He said, "Well, why don't you do it?" I quickly made clear what I meant was someone who was getting retirement income who we wouldn't have to pay too much for. So they started thinking along those lines.

> Gretchen and I were living at our place near Faribault at the time and in my devotions every day the question Bob asked kept haunting me: "Why don't you do it?" This must have been into 1984 now, but after two weeks I said to Gretchen, "What do you think of me being the area director for Prison Fellowship?" She said it would be a great idea, which I've joked about ever since as it was the first time she had said anything like that about any suggestion of mine about what I ought to do.

"I was going to ask before," I said, "when you had Chuck and others secretly showing up at your house in Silver Spring, and when you were visiting prisoners at Lorton, what did Gretchen think of all that?"

"We talked about it, of course, but she didn't have any negative feelings about it. She was open to all of it. It didn't take me away from her—much more, anyway, than I was away already. It was running for office and being in the limelight that bothered her."

Quie was appointed area director for PFM for Minnesota and the Dakotas in 1984. To be closer to the Twin Cities, they sold their hobby farm near Faribault (upwards of an hour's drive south of the metropolitan area) and bought a house in the western suburb of Minnetonka. By 1987, however, he started spending increasing time in Reston, Virginia, PFM's international headquarters, first as senior vice president for Prison Fellowship-USA and then as president. Colson at this stage was chairman of the board. While it was understood that Quie would serve as president only on an interim basis by his own choice, he made it clear to all concerned that there wouldn't be anything tentative about his approach, as he planned to attack the stint as "the full-fledged president." Adding up his time in the national posts, he spent about two and a half years in the late '80s commuting weekly between Virginia and Minnesota. He resigned from the PF board in June 2006 to focus on changing the Minnesota Constitution in regards to the retention of judges, though he remains involved with the national organization and the InnerChange Freedom Initiative in Minnesota. We'll get to his work with judges next chapter and to his work with InnerChange in a moment.

———————•◆•———————

"The first thing I wanted to do when I became area director for Minnesota and the Dakotas," Quie said, "was to see what was actually happening in the prisons here." He also spent a lot of time interviewing men as well as women who had been released and who had managed to keep from returning.

> I went out and found people who had stayed out of prison for five years or more and talked to a number of them. A pattern developed: Everyone who had succeeded in staying out could name the straight person who had walked with them when they came out. Every one of them could do it. In all the years I've done that, only once have I talked to anyone where that wasn't the case, and in that instance, he said a whole church

walked with him. So in that case, it actually was more than one person.

When I spoke to people who were incarcerated again after having been released, perhaps going through the cycle several times, they all said nobody had walked with them. As soon as they got out of prison, they would run into the guys who used to sell them drugs, or they'd be frustrated by not being able to get a job and they'd wind up walking into a bar and getting drunk. All these people broke parole or committed new crimes and were back in again. There was one guy who was in prison originally for writing bad checks and then back again because of burglary. One of the reasons I was interested in him was because he had gone to St. Olaf as I did. But there was no one who had walked with him when he had been out.

So I figured we needed a mentoring program that started in prison and continued when inmates got out and I started thinking through an arrangement where we had one person in Minneapolis, another person in St. Paul, and then one person in each of the four quadrants in the metro area. They would be in charge of pulling mentors together. After about a year I turned the project over to someone else, but that was the beginning of Prison Fellowship's mentoring program nationally. I learned as I went along.

We had pushed for Bible leaders who, in addition to working with prisoners, needed to meet regularly together so they could be in prayer and fellowship with each other. They needed to do that at least once a month. I did the same thing when I became vice president for Prison Ministries–USA with the four national vice presidents around the country who reported to me. They were each in one of four regions, and although they'd occasionally come to Washington, most of their interaction with each other had been by phone, which I didn't like. So we had them all move to the D.C. area. They could arrange their travel schedules to their respective parts of the country the way they liked, but there would be one day we'd all spend time together in Reston in Bible study, prayer, and sharing together about our work—just as I wanted our mentors and Bible leaders around the country to spend time with each other on a routine basis. I believe in what might be called a small group concept of governance, though one of its potential problems is that while people in charge might require the men and women they supervise to take care of business in that way, they don't do it themselves. But you're a phony if you don't do it yourself. You have to practice small group governance all the way up and then keep the system as flat as possible. I did the same when I became president of PF and we really developed good relationships among people when I was there.

After a few organizational exegeses like the above, I told Quie that I was really more interested in his more personal stories. "The only reason I tell you all this," he said, "is that what you do organizationally can't be separated from what you do personally."

Good point.

———•◆•———

While remaining on Prison Fellowship Ministries' national board of directors, Quie returned home in July 1989, ending his weekly trips to Reston, and re-engaged intimately in PFM's work in the Upper Midwest—so much so that in 2002 a wing of a prison was named for him: "The Albert H. Quie Unit of the InnerChange Freedom Initiative" at Lino Lakes Correctional Facility in Minnesota. Chuck Colson, who flew in for the afternoon ceremony after being honored by a college earlier in the day, delivered a legendary salute. I was there when Colson said (I paraphrase):

"Here I am," Colson said, "a convicted felon and I just had a chair named after me at a distinguished university. And here's Al Quie, 'Mr. Education' in Congress and a former governor—who just had a prison named after him."

"Tell me about IFI," I asked Quie. "How did it get started?"

Inner change means you change inside, so that you have freedom from all the things that are causing your evil ways. Some people who were working in Prison Fellowship came up with the idea that we ought to have a unit in prisons where people who were incarcerated could come together, where there would be more intensity and intentionality in teaching Scripture and right living. The aim was that they would have greater continuity of relationships. We started in Texas because the commissioner of corrections was open to it. The governor at the time was George W. Bush and he was open to it, too.

IFI has been pursued in several states, including Minnesota, Texas, Arkansas, Kansas, Missouri, and Iowa, although federal courts hammered corrections and other officials in Des Moines into submission on First Amendment grounds and the Iowa program has ended. Much can be written about the program, whose mission I find compelling, and whose approach, if pursued properly, is perfectly consonant with the Constitution's Establishment Clause. But that's a discussion for another occasion, as more germane here is what Quie describes as its sense of the invisible. He's quick, by the way, to make clear that he was not the person principally responsible for bringing IFI to Minnesota. "I only helped."

"How would you feel," he rhetorically asked at an apt point, "if you were incarcerated and everybody left you?"

How would you feel if you had no visitors, if nobody ever came? That's what more than half the people in prison probably face. People who are totally alone feel totally rejected. Yet then we expect them to turn out better. And when they don't turn out better, we keep them in prison even longer. We also keep putting more and more people behind bars and we keep building more and more prisons.

I think back to that one-cell jail in Nerstrand and wonder how a person can live when he can't see the sunrise and can't hear the wind blow through the trees? Being part of God's creation is such a joy and being a steward of it is such an amazing responsibility. Every human being needs a purpose in life. How do we give it to them in prison? How can they gain it? How can they keep it when they come out? It's just like a plant being nourished by sunshine and rain. People flourish when they know someone loves them unconditionally and they have an opportunity to show love for someone else. They also need respect. Of course, most people have no interest in respecting prisoners who have done terrible things. But just yesterday someone said that when we learn about a person who's 90 percent bad and 10 percent good, we should work on the 10 percent and after a while it will grow. However, if we focus on the 90 percent, only that part of him will grow.

We have to be able to see the infinite worth of every human being. For me, that comes out of my whole faith. It has to come from that. As a person who believes in Jesus Christ, the objective part is what happened to Him on the cross and the fact that He rose again. The subjective part is how the Holy Spirit works in us. It isn't something that's controllable at all.

While governor, Quie served on the Minnesota's Board of Pardons along with the attorney general, Warren Spannaus, and the chief justice of the state's supreme court: first Robert Sheran, who held that post when Quie took office, and later Douglas Amdahl, whom Quie appointed. In one case, the three denied a pardon to a man who many years earlier had killed his father, mother, and sister when he was twenty or twenty-one years old. He didn't win release until many years later, but for about thirteen of those years, Quie visited him frequently at both Stillwater and Lino Lakes.

"Clearly you empathize with these people," I said, "but you don't drink, you don't smoke, you don't do drugs. Is it possible for you to even conceive what they do? Is it possible to conceive of yourself in prison?"

It's particularly disconcerting for Quie to imagine himself locked up because of his claustrophobia. A non-prison version of the problem cropped up several years ago during radiation treatment when he was healed of prostate cancer.

"I tell you, a huge panic hit when the two people who set up the radiation equipment walked out of the room and closed a door that was at least a foot thick. It just came to my mind: 'What if something happened out there so that they were all taken away and I would be left alone?' There was no way I could break down that wall. I tell you, a huge panic hit me. I knew the only thing to do was to pray about it. On another occasion, during an MRI, they asked if I wanted a sedative and I said no."

"I would have said, 'Shoot me up.'"

"Then they said I could have earphones and asked what kind of music I wanted. I said 'classical' . . . and they put on a *dirge*. I told them to get rid of the music; I'd sooner deal with my thoughts."

Hospital stories and jokes aside, I asked if he ever thought about the time he offered to serve out Chuck Colson's sentence and what it would have been like to be actually locked up.

The only way I could handle it would be to yield completely to God and pray and turn it over to Him. I see movies where people are stuck someplace and think about how terrible that would be. The same thing with the people who were trapped in their cars when the 35W bridge came down. But I have confidence that God would help me so that I could live through a crisis like that and be better at the end of it. I just know that would happen. But I'm thankful to God I haven't had to go through anything like that—yet, anyway.

So much for envisioning himself incarcerated. What about whether he can fathom the vicious things some people do to wind up in prison? As he had done in our first conversation, he recalled when, as a child, his father would chastise him, "and I would feel angry and rejected. I didn't even want to take a bite of food because I loved my martyrdom so much."

But Dad would always "welcome me back" and I would eat. What you have to say is that I liked the evil that was in me more than the grace that was offered to me. If that was the case with me, I can understand how it could happen to other people whose circumstances were far worse than mine. This is not to make excuses for them because you can't blame everything on circumstances and the environment. Everybody is free to make choices. People must be responsible and train themselves to be disciplined. But you asked if I can conceive of what they do and the answer is yes.

Even though the man just mentioned who murdered three members of his family was high on drugs at the time, Quie quotes him saying the real reason he did what he did was "because I was evil." He also told Quie he had come to believe that anything a person might do while drugged or drunk was something they could do while straight and sober, too. Whether or not this is true, and I have my doubts, the fact is Quie recalls drugs or alcohol, often both together, having something to do with virtually every single case that came before the pardon board during his four years as governor.

———— •◆• ————

If the frame of reference has more to do with matters of policy than faith, Al Quie's key views about criminal justice might be summarized this way:

- Despite his predisposition to mercy and redemption, he's not naïve about the importance of punishment and retribution.

- While he naturally believes the public must be protected from people who commit crimes of violence, generally speaking he believes we send too many people to prison, especially for drug crimes, and then we keep them there too long.

- In regards to people convicted of murder, he cites evidence that they're much less likely to re-offend than those convicted of less serious crimes.

- He struggled for a long time about capital punishment but has come to oppose it across the board. He believes redemption is possible for everyone, even in capital cases.

- He's confident that Minnesota's correctional system is more competent and more just than most.

- He also sees a direct tie between his continuing efforts to improve early childhood education and assuring an impartial judiciary on the one hand, and his ministry to those who have made terrible, even evil mistakes on the other hand. "If we provide love, safety, and rich language experiences for children as they grow up, and if we increase the likelihood judges will be respectful of all comers," he asserts, "all will benefit."

But in the same way his focus in elementary and secondary education is invariably on the intimately interpersonal, Quie's focus when it comes to criminal justice is invariably identical. He was exquisitely in character, for instance, at a 2007 meeting of Minnesota community leaders when he was the only person to argue that a main reason so many former prisoners re-offend is that they're lonely on the outside. He spoke in a similar human rather than political or bureaucratic vein when, in our conversations, he emphasized how mentors can add immeasurably to the lives of prisoners—but how, if they're not faithful in their visits and friendships, they can just as certainly subtract from those lives as well.

> Prisoners tell me how it's "just amazing" that people visit them, but how it's even more so when they come back again. There's a geometric change that occurs when a mentor comes back again. That's what I tell people who are mentors: When you commit yourself to another person, you must be reliable. The only thing that should stand in your way of a scheduled visit is if your wife dies and there's a conflict with the funeral. Relationships with prisoners can be so tenuous, that any indication of rejection can be very damaging. Just being late can get inmates thinking they're being rejected again. Usually a lot of healing has to happen before an inmate will chalk up a missed visit to simple forgetfulness.

In this regard, Quie cited research that suggested a positive tie between the number of meetings prisoners had with mentors and how they did on the outside. On the other hand, if visits ended abruptly after just one or two sessions, usually because mentors simply stopped coming, inmates tended to do even worse than those in control groups who were never visited by a mentor to begin with. "It's the whole idea of rejection again," he said. "Growth comes from continuity of relations."

———————•◆•———————

"Tell me," I asked, "about your own more recent visits to prisons?"

In the early days of IFI at Lino Lakes (it started in 2002), Quie would meet with inmates and participate in programs weekly. It's now monthly in part because of the substantial amount of his time spent on judicial retention. Nonetheless, his interest in getting to know the men more than superficially hasn't seemed to diminish. As for the men themselves, if they're under 35 or 40, they were either a kid when Quie left office or they hadn't been born yet, so it's fair to say he's known mostly for his prison reputation. Or to put matters a bit more respectfully, as the guy whose name is on the wall. "One of the reasons I go back is so they can see a real person behind the name up there and so they can test me."

To the question if he has ever been threatened in prison, he said never, as no one "would have any reason to do that." Of a less physical sort of intimidation, there was one prisoner, after he was released from Stillwater Correctional Facility, to whom Quie said, "As far as I'm concerned, you're the biggest con man I've ever met in prison, but I never felt you conned me. Did you?" To which the former inmate said no, as there had been "something" about Quie and he hadn't wanted to ruin the relationship they had. "I don't fear these guys at all."

I started to bring the conversation to a close by recalling how I had asked him several weeks earlier about whether he viewed his upwards of 90 minutes of prayer every morning as a joy or a chore. Joy was the answer. The parallel question this time around was how he viewed his prison visits.

I look forward to them. It can be a duty, as I've been very busy working on keeping the judiciary in Minnesota impartial. But then, on the day before I'm going to the class up there, the faces of the people come back to me and I begin thinking and meditating on them. I think, for example, about a guy who might have caused me to give him more attention than the others for one reason or another. I'm thinking right now of a guy who I really hit it off with, but who was removed from the program because he did something hostile to somebody else. I had been alone with him in a room and he didn't do anything hostile to me.

Every time somebody leaves the IFI program before completion, I hurt. It's just like if a child of mine left the family. I figure other people in the group have to hurt, too, and I talk to them about it. There's one person currently up there who every month was less and less with it. But this last time I was there, I engaged with him and he came alive and I really want to see how he is when I go back next Friday. I also think about other individuals, the ones who haven't revealed their past as much, and try to figure out where they are. The men in IFI grow in courage to be transparent; that's what they do in the program.

———— •◆• ————

In January 2008, Chuck Colson presented Al Quie with the William Wilberforce Award, given annually by Prison Fellowship Ministries "in recognition of exemplary witness for Jesus Christ, perseverance, and selflessness in combating social injustice and advancing Christian values in the face of opposition." As celebrated in the 2006 movie *Amazing Grace*, Wilberforce, a Christian and politician, led the way in the eighteenth and nineteenth centuries in ending the British slave trade.

Chapter Eleven

Impartial Justice
"Al Quie is a sinister, elitist muckety-muck"

In the interest of accuracy and full disclosure: As far as I know no one person has ever called Al Quie a "sinister, elitist muckety-muck" all at one time. The slam is admittedly an amalgam. Rather, critics have occasionally used epithets and words like these separately in regards to his efforts to improve the selection and retention of Minnesota judges. For example, Jack Nordby, a Hennepin County District Court judge, described Quie's work and that of a commission he chaired as a "sinister move afoot to steal once and for all the constitutional rights of Minnesotans to elect their judges." Two members of neopopulism.org, Tom Dahlberg and Erick Kaardal, wrote of Quie's "elitist ambitions . . . to take us backwards into the authoritarian appointment of judges by the elite bureaucratic class." And then there was lawyer Greg Wersal, who described the very essence of the Quie Commission as, "You got one group of muckety-mucks giving the rubber stamp to another group of muckety-mucks."

Al Quie an *elitist*? A *high-horse* muckety-muck? And not merely a pedestrian pilferer of constitutional rights, but a *sinister* one? Is this the same Al Quie who has more faith in the common sense and decency of average folks than perhaps anyone I've ever known? What in heaven (but also down here on earth) did he do?

———— •◆•————

As he said in his farewell address in December 1982, Quie considered his two largest achievements as governor to be the indexing of personal income taxes and the merit selection of judges. I would add to the mix his sacrificial leadership in fixing one mammoth budget shortfall after another, but for present purposes, that endeavor was of a different genus. Indexing continues, and it's so totally ingrained in Minnesota's tax landscape that it's hardly ever cited other than by the most inside of insiders. In other words, its ongoing contribution, while important and measurable, is essentially invisible. The situation is fundamentally different when it comes to Quie's method of appointing judges, as it has become not only implicitly embedded in the state's legal landscape but also explicitly. It's increasingly recognized in key quarters as a pivotal reform warranting expansion. Its heightened salience is a direct result of Quie's current leadership on behalf of further ensuring a talented, impartial, and accountable judiciary for Minnesota. In fact, if improving educational opportunities for American young people during his 21 years in Congress remains his national signature achievement, improving the way Minnesota appoints and retains judges—starting in 1979 and resumed in recent years—is becoming ever more so his statewide mark.

We will get to how Al Quie came to chair, in 2006-07, the Citizens Commission for the Preservation of an Impartial Judiciary and subsequently how he came to chair — and still chairs — a follow-up group called Minnesotans for Impartial Courts. But first, let's return to yesteryear, when Minnesota governors might have been just as apt to appoint well-connected friends (known sometimes, fairly or not, as "cronies") as they were to name carefully vetted, first-tier men and women to the bench.

———— •◆• ————

On taking office in January 1979, Quie's experience with courtrooms in general and judges in particular was limited. There was the time as a high school student when a corn bin on the family farm blew over during Minnesota's famous Armistice Day storm of 1941. His father didn't think it had been anchored down properly by the people who installed it, and he sued. For a spell, teenager Quie thought he might have to testify, a prospect he found "kind of awesome" insofar as the only thing he knew about courts was what he had read in books. *Perry Mason* was still years away and *Law & Order* was even further in the future. As it turned out, he didn't have to testify, though he recalls his father talking at length about the judge and the proceedings. He lost, by the way.

Quie's first time in court didn't come until years later when he was in Congress and testified about a gun accident involving two other people with whom he had been hunting. Let's just say Vice President Cheney wasn't the first person ever to accidentally shoot a pal in the face with buckshot. That was largely the extent of his dealings with the justice system until he began visiting inmates at Lorton Prison in Virginia in the early 1970s where, he said, he never heard them talk about the judges who sentenced them. He also doesn't remember them ever complaining about their lawyers. I found all this hard to believe, but Quie recalled them being preoccupied instead with their guards and overall prison life. Mostly, he said, they were interested in "understanding how a person could never have had a brush with the law," as it was a possibility they found hard to conceive.

"I would say," Quie reported, "'How can I be talking to you since I have no experience in the situations or reasons why you wound up in prison.' And they would say, 'We've got all kinds of people here who've got experience in crime. We'd like to find out from a person who has stayed away from crime.'"

"Were they amazed," I asked, "that someone could live a life on the right side of the law?"

Quie said yes, adding that even though the men he met with were all African American, he never heard them talk about the hugely disproportionate number of blacks at Lorton. As for personally sitting through a trial, that didn't come about until 1974 when Chuck Colson was in the dock. Perhaps not incidentally, one of his lasting memories of that event was what he viewed as Judge Gerhard Gesell's disrespect for the defendant when he sternly told Colson's lawyer not to go "barking" up some tree.

In rounded-off measure, these episodes constituted the bulk of Quie's hands-on exposure to judges and courtrooms before coming to realize quickly and fully, shortly after taking office, just how many judges he would be obliged to appoint. Article VI, Section 7 of the Minnesota Constitution states that judges "shall be elected by the voters from the area they are to serve," making it possible for lawyers to run for judgeships in much the same way men and women run for any other office. But as a practical matter, governors in the state wind up appointing upwards of 93 percent of all new judges, as will be explained later.

I asked myself, how am I going to do this? I mean, I didn't know that many attorneys, to say nothing about people who had those kinds of capabilities. Frankly, I was not confident regarding my ability to gauge the capabilities of potential judges and to choose the right ones to handle the job. Then Robert Sheran, the chief justice of the Minnesota Supreme Court, came to talk about how judges were appointed. I viewed his visit as fortuitous at the time, but I now say, "God sent Bob Sheran to me." He was very helpful.

The one principle I was determined to pursue was that I wanted judges to follow the rule of law; I wasn't going to get into any discussions about social or political issues with them. I wasn't going to appoint anyone for political reasons. But how was I to find the best people? The chief justice and I talked about it, and we included Buzz Cummins, an attorney on my staff, in the conversations. It started to form in my mind that a just and equitable way of doing it would be to bring good citizens together in merit selection panels in each judicial district or county, as I hadn't liked some of the appointments of both my Republican and DFL predecessors. I would appoint half of the members to these nominating committees, but I had to decide who would appoint the others. I figured, well, the people who best knew the qualities judges should have were people who already were on the bench, so I had judges pick a quarter of all the nominating committee members in each judicial district. I also decided that lawyers should be involved, so I asked the bar associations in each judicial district also to pick a quarter of the committee members. People on my staff wanted me to appoint at least one more person than half in each instance, but how would people respect us and the process if we insisted on that?

When a seat opened up, I would be sent the names of three candidates, and they were the ones I interviewed and chose from. I did this by executive order. Rudy Perpich, when he returned as governor in 1983, didn't like what we had set up and revoked my executive order. In the final year of his last term, however, the legislature enacted legislation providing for a Judicial Selection Commission, and subsequent governors have used it as well. I still like my principle that half of its members should be appointed by the governor—no more, no less—but the present system with the governor appointing seven of the nine permanent members of the commission and the supreme court appointing the other two has worked well.

I jumped in at this point to note that 1979 was only half a dozen years after *Roe v. Wade*, and any number of people assuredly had been pushing him hard to appoint only pro-life judges. He concurred that was the case, and I asked what his response had been.

I didn't want either judicial activism or legislating from the bench. As you know, I had a 100-percent pro-life voting record in Congress, and I felt very strongly about abortion. For example, I had introduced legislation in the House, similar to a bill introduced by Senators Harold Hughes and Mark Hatfield, which would have given states the right to make decisions on abortion with only one caveat: If doctors and families were faced with a true question of having to choose between saving a mother's life or a child's life, the mother's life would be the one protected.

I had established my pro-life position, in other words. But I was always uncomfortable when people came to see me, both in Washington and St. Paul, and urged me to take stands on that or any other issue based on emotion. In the case of Justice Harry Blackmun, when he wrote the Supreme Court's decision in *Roe*, he relied on what he understood from medical science. We had dinner once afterwards, and we talked about it. But in the same way I didn't want to make decisions based on emotion, I didn't want to make them based on what was supposedly scientific evidence either. Instead, I wanted to focus strictly on legal and theological arguments and their sources. And because I didn't want judges to be activists or legislators, it simply followed that despite my personal opposition to abortion, I wasn't going to use it as a litmus test. A litmus test I did use was determining which candidates would most likely follow and respect the rule of law, the Constitution, and precedents. But as the appointing authority, I needed to probe further. A question I asked all applicants was how they defined the difference between justice and love. Judges should make decisions about proper punishments for people who commit crimes in accord with the law; that's the justice part. But as a human being they should also operate out of love. They need to be concerned about victims. They need to understand how crime affects communities. And if possible, they also need to give offenders hope that someday they'll be rehabilitated and able to live successfully as citizens in society. I was interested in that kind of balance, and I asked everyone to think it through. I realize now, they were intense interviews, as I asked tough questions that usually don't get asked in situations like that—though word did get around pretty quickly that those were the kind of questions I was interested in. The candidates didn't have to agree with me exactly, of course. I just wanted to know how they thought, and I picked the person I thought was the best of the nominees.

There are ten judicial districts in the state, currently composed of 288 authorized judgeships. Add seven supreme court seats and nineteen on the court of appeals, and that's a lot of appointing.

The just-mentioned Carl ("Buzz") Cummins III has noted that when Quie issued his executive order, "there was substantial skepticism among members of the bench and bar about how objective the commissions and Quie's appointments would really be. The answer came quickly enough when he announced his first judicial appointment: Thomas Howe, the former DFL chairman in Carver

County to the Carver County bench." As one might expect, Cummins added, Quie's move "attracted substantial criticism from Republican partisans, but he gained instant credibility with lawyers, judges, and those who cared about maintaining a fair, impartial judiciary."

———·◆·———

Al Quie is chairman of the board of Minnesotans for Impartial Courts. It's a post that evolved directly and immediately out of his chairmanship of the Citizens Commission for the Preservation of an Impartial Judiciary, commonly known as the "Quie Commission," which considered the "nature and scope of the threats to an impartial court system in the aftermath of *Republican Party v. White*" and assessed "options for preserving and promoting an impartial court system." The "Republican Party" in question was Minnesota's very own.

The case had been initiated by Greg Wersal, a Twin Cities lawyer and an unsuccessful candidate for associate justice on the state supreme court who, on First Amendment grounds, challenged a Minnesota Canon of the Code of Judicial Conduct that prohibited a "candidate for a judicial office" from "announcing his or her views in disputed legal or political issues." In a 5-4 decision in 2002, the U.S. Supreme Court had ruled states could not restrict speech in that way, with Justice Antonin Scalia writing the majority opinion, joined by Justices Rehnquist, O'Connor, Kennedy, and Thomas. "There is an obvious tension," Scalia acknowledged, "between the article of Minnesota's popularly approved constitution which provides that judges shall be elected and the Minnesota Supreme Court's [so-called] announce clause which places most subjects of interest to the voters off limits." But while a state has the right to name and retain judges by means other than elections, if elections *are* in fact held, the majority argued that candidates cannot be muzzled. Or, more formally, Scalia wrote, "The greater power to dispense with elections altogether does not include the lesser power to conduct elections under conditions of state-imposed voter ignorance."

In a concurring opinion, Justice Sandra Day O'Connor took matters a step further.

I join the opinion of the Court but write separately to express my concerns about judicial elections generally . . . I am concerned that, even aside from what judicial candidates may say while campaigning, the very practice of electing judges undermines this interest. We of course want judges to be impartial, in the sense of being free from any personal stake in the outcome of the cases to which they are assigned. But if judges are subject to regular elections, they are likely to feel that they have at least some personal stake in the outcome of every publicized case. Elected judges cannot help being aware that if the public is not satisfied with the outcome of a particular case, it could hurt their re-election prospects.

More than simply arguing that if a state opts to hold judicial elections it has to allow those who run to speak freely, O'Connor took the occasion to question elections as a wise way of filling judgeships to begin with. "If the State," she wrote, "has a problem with judicial impartiality, it is largely one the State brought upon itself by continuing the practice of popularly electing judges." A practice that was pursued, she noted, by 38 states in addition to Minnesota.

In writing for the minority, Justice Ruth Bader Ginsburg rooted her argument in the fact that judges "are not political actors."

I do not agree with this unilocular, "an election is an election," approach. Instead I would differentiate elections for political offices, in which the First Amendment holds full sway, from elections designed to select those whose office it is to administer justice without respect to persons. Minnesota's choice to elect its judges, I am persuaded, does not preclude the State from installing an election process geared to the judicial office.

On remand to the U.S. Court of Appeals, the Eighth Circuit in 2005, loosened the reins and restraints on expression even more by holding that states also were forbidden from preventing judicial candidates from engaging in clear-cut partisan activities such as identifying themselves as members of political parties, seeking and accepting partisan endorsements, personally seeking or accepting campaign contributions, and the like. What was constitutionally allowed now ran even more markedly counter to Minnesota rules and traditions. And while the majority led by Justice Scalia represented the court's conservative wing, and while Minnesota's Republican Party was the official victor, suffice it to say that not all Republicans in the state, starting with Quie, welcomed where the ruling might lead.

One of those more-than-skeptical Republicans—or more accurately, non-active Republicans, given his current line of work— was G. Barry Anderson, a former Minnesota Court of Appeals judge who had been appointed to the state supreme court by Governor Tim Pawlenty in 2004. Despite having served earlier in his career as counsel to the very same state Republican Party that had prevailed, he feared the *White* decision would lead inevitably to Minnesota having to contend with the same kind of expensive, vitriolic, and credibility-sapping judicial politics that afflicts states such as Texas, Alabama, Illinois, Ohio, and increasingly Wisconsin. For example, the day after Wisconsin Circuit Judge Michael Gableman defeated sitting Supreme Court Justice Louis Butler in April 2008, a reporter for the *Wisconsin State Journal* wrote that although the race theoretically had been nonpartisan and the "state's ethics code for judges cautions judicial candidates from aligning themselves with any political party," Wisconsin's Republican Party and the Democratic Judicial Campaign Committee "made hundreds of thousands of phone calls on behalf of their favored candidates in the days before the election." The price tag for television ads alone was estimated to be at least $4 million. This followed a 2007 race for a Wisconsin Supreme Court seat that was even more expensive, with the bulk of spending again coming from out-of-state political action committees.

Figuring that it would be wise to create a nonpartisan group to investigate ways of mitigating potential excesses of *White* in Minnesota—heading problems off at the pass, in cowboy parlance— Anderson and a few others had been putting such a panel together, but they needed a respected and ecumenical figure to serve as its principal face. After considering a number of major players for the job and being turned down by one, Anderson met with Quie in January 2006 at the same Perkins restaurant in Minneapolis where Quie and I later agreed to do this book, hoping to persuade him to serve as a co-chair. Quie, who came loaded to bear the burden with three pages of questions, agreed on the spot to take on the effort, although he made it clear that he had no intention of being a figurehead, esteemed or otherwise — and he didn't "do co-chairs" either.

I asked why not.

"Who's responsible? 'Oh, you're responsible.' 'No, you're responsible.' You keep changing. My idea of leadership is that a person ought to lead, lay out where he stands, and then encourage people to take shots at it and challenge the leader's positions from different directions, so the group can really hone in on the right ideas. I don't think Barry ever thought I'd take hold of the project, grab it, and lead it the way I have."

As a sign of seriousness, Quie resigned from the board of directors of Prison Fellowship Ministries after 23 years of service and put aside several other civic chores, including the chairmanship of the worship board and the council of Minnetonka Lutheran Church, in order to free sufficient time for the new assignment.

The Citizens Commission for the Preservation of an Impartial Judiciary wound up with 30 bipartisan members from "diverse backgrounds in law, politics, business, labor, and academics." The commission's final report was released in March 2007, thirteen months after the body began meeting, and recommended (1) that the "initial selection of judges occur through a merit-based selection process and gubernatorial appointment"; (2) that there be comprehensive performance evaluations of all judges in order to promote their "self-improvement" and to "provide voters with information so that they can make informed decisions at the polls"; and (3) that "judges be subject to periodic retention elections so that they can be held accountable for their performance in office." A "retention election" is one in which there are no challengers on the ballot; rather, voters simply get to vote up or down on incumbents. A few commission members wrote minority reports, one of which recommended that Minnesota eliminate judicial elections altogether, with a commission instead deciding whether judges should be retained in office.

In its pivotal paragraph, the commission's report argued:

The *White* decisions have fundamentally altered the rules of conduct for judicial campaigns in Minnesota. Under *White*, judicial candidates may now choose (without fear of later sanction from the disciplinary authorities) to announce their view on legal and political issues, directly solicit campaign contributions, seek political party endorsements, identify themselves as political party members, attend political party gatherings, and commit themselves to political party platforms. Judicial candidates also may seek endorsements from special interest groups. The commission's concern is that as campaigns for state judicial office begin to look and operate like campaigns for legislative or constitutional office, the potential increases that special or moneyed interests will influence how cases are later decided. Moreover, even if Minnesota could somehow operate state judicial elections so that contributions to judicial campaigns did not in fact influence the results in specific cases, the appearance that campaign contributions had such an effect would in itself justify change to our system. As shown by recent studies, a majority of the public—and judges themselves—believe that contributions to judicial campaigns influence later substantive results for litigants in decided cases. This is intolerable.

As blue-ribbon-style commissions go, this one had no money, had no staff other than a volunteer "reporter," was never incorporated, and was chartered or charged by no one other than its members. But when I asked both Quie and Anderson if anyone had ever questioned the group's legitimacy by asking who were these guys and what gave them the right to promulgate anything, their fast answer was no, never.

———— •◆• ————

"You've been nervous, upset, frightened—pick a word," I said one morning, "that races for judgeships could become too politicized. But a common and powerful theme through many of our conversations over the last several months is that people must have a voice. There must be transparency and accountability in what government does."

Yes was all he needed to say.

"So before getting into some of the details of the commission's recommendations," I said, "talk, if you would, about the tension between keeping judges above political frays while still respecting and celebrating the right of people to choose their leaders." In response to this, he was off and running, as one might expect when the subject is a passion.

Well, we didn't come to a conclusion about finding a balance right away. It took us about ten or eleven months of discussions and, in particular, three public hearings around the state, in Brainerd, Mankato, and St. Paul. I was preparing for a commission meeting at which Ray Waldron, president of the Minnesota AFL-CIO, was going to speak, when a person sent me information that someone had emailed him about how OutFront Minnesota, a gay-rights group, had endorsed several people running for judgeships in Minnesota. I already knew, of course, that the AFL-CIO had been endorsing judicial candidates, and all of a sudden it hit me. When you get right down to it, what's so wrong about the Republican Party or any other party—or any other group of people, for that matter—endorsing men and women running for judgeships? And really for the first time, I guess, I realized that the Supreme Court, especially Sandra Day O'Connor in her separate opinion, had gotten it right after all. If a state was going to elect its judges, be they partisan elections or not, people ought to be able to express themselves completely, because that's guaranteed by the First Amendment of the United States Constitution. The trick, obviously, is for the electorate to make retention decisions without those elections turning into excessively partisan affairs where far too much money is spent, thereby destroying judicial impartiality. Watching the race for a seat on the Wisconsin Supreme Court in April 2007—boy, were they going after each other, with the Republican and Democratic campaigns plus all those outside groups spending just millions of dollars. I really didn't want that to happen in Minnesota.

The newspapers in Milwaukee and Madison wrote about all the activities of the two parties: Where the candidates—Linda Clifford the Democrat and Ann Ziegler the Republican—stood on social issues, how much money individuals and groups had contributed to their campaigns, the whole nine yards. Then I read where the candidate who wound up losing, Clifford, had been asked in a debate if she would follow the rule of law. Her answer was something like, "Yes, I would—up to a point." I just thought to myself right then and there, whatever the polls or trends might have been saying at the time, she had just lost the election, because there's a *natural* expectation and a moral standard deep within people when it comes to following the rule of law. We're a government of laws here. It's drilled into us.

The other thing that became apparent to us was that most people, no matter who they are, don't know nearly enough about all the judicial candidates appearing on ballots. This was the case all the time. And if an incumbent judge was running without opposition, everybody on the commission recognized that voters had no voice in the matter whatsoever, as such a judicial candidate theoretically would need only one vote to keep his or her job. Even though it was clear we couldn't find a perfect system for the retention of judges, we needed to find a way of making certain that they would remain impartial as well as independent while also being accountable to the people. Adding it all up, all of us on the Citizens Commission reached the conviction that the merit selection approach I initiated by executive order in 1979 would be our recommendation and that it should apply not only to district judges but also to members of the supreme court and court of appeals. We were unified on the recommendation that the public evaluation of judges' performance is essential for both voters and judges themselves.

On another occasion, Quie spoke of how he had originally supported Minnesota rules that "put zippers on the mouths" of judicial candidates while simultaneously being bothered by those very same constraints. "I didn't know who to vote for. I tried doing what I could to learn about candidates for judgeships, but I was pretty much limited to newspaper stories right before elections. I had come to know so well the qualities of the lawyers I had interviewed for judgeships when I was governor. If only, as a private citizen, I could find out more about them, how much better that would be. So I was torn."

The merit selection system Quie put in place in 1979 covered only district and county courts, not the supreme court. The court of appeals hadn't been created yet, as it wasn't launched until later in his term by constitutional amendment. "We tried to figure out how to make merit selection work for the supreme court, but putting together an effective statewide group, rather than just district-wide or county-wide groups was too complicated at the time. So we said back then, 'Hey, we'll just set up the local ones but use the same principles of merit in selecting appellate judges.'"

Quie actually wound up appointing a majority of the seven-member supreme court during his four years: Glen Kelley, John Simonett, Jeanne Coyne (the second woman ever appointed to the state's highest court), and Douglas Amdahl, whom he later elevated to chief justice. The fact that Amdahl sported a butch cut was probably irrelevant. More pertinent and interesting was that he was a wonderfully modest son of a cobbler — humility personified. Quie, in fact, still uses a pair of saddlebags made by Amdahl's father, having first done so when he made his first Continental Divide ride in 1983. "Great workmanship and excellent leather that has always stayed soft, though I've taken good care of them all this time. Talk about saddlebags that have been used."

A further reason, Quie argued, for changing the way Minnesota picks, keeps, and, every once in a while, dismisses judges is the disjunction between what the state constitution says about the method and the way things really work on the ground. More specifically, the constitution says that all judges are to be elected. But as a practical matter when Minnesota judges retire or otherwise resign, they almost always do so before their terms are over, giving the governor the right to fill the vacancy. Those 93 percent or so of state judges who come to their jobs that way are later obliged to run for "re-election," though the advantage they've enjoyed since 1956 of having the word "incumbent" on the ballot after their names is usually powerful to the point of electoral omnipotence.

> So we say one thing in the constitution, but we then do things differently. I've said this many times: "When you say and believe one thing but do something else, it will corrupt your soul."

> But when you say one thing yet you do and *believe* something else, you ought to change both what you say and what you do. That's why I've come to believe we should change the constitution and just appoint judges without the pretense of claiming that the *regular* or *normal* way of putting people on the bench in Minnesota is by electing them. That's just not even close to being true, and we get more reliably competent and impartial judges with merit selection.

> A lot of this, obviously, depends on governors intensely interrogating every candidate. They can't delegate it to their staffs. I'm not going to cast aspersions at other governors before me, but you can see I have some feeling on this. Appointing judges is one of the most important responsibilities any governor has, because they stay on beyond his or her term in office. I don't put anything higher than making those decisions. A judge has even greater responsibilities than a governor, because judges are dealing with individuals all the time.

Quie's reference above to changing the constitution in regards to appointing judges can be confusing at first glance given his strong interest in giving citizens a voice. He draws a critical distinction, though, between how a person becomes a judge as opposed to how he or she stays one. He favors governors doing the original naming but wants voters doing the retaining (or not).

The very first question I asked Quie the morning of our main conversation about the judiciary was, "Why is this issue just so powerful for you?" After talking about the integral role of judges in Old Testament Israel, he spoke of how small societies (using Iceland when it was "starting out" as an example) might not need an executive branch, but they absolutely need a judicial one. On another occasion he spoke of how "we know from experience, literature, and Scripture that an unjust judge is harmful to people without power and who are oppressed."

———— • ◆ • ————

Quie Commission recommendations are perhaps most clearly understood as a series of four main components (not the three consolidated ones cited above): Judicial candidates are vetted by a merit selection panel; the governor then appoints one of the finalists to the open seat in question; in time the new judge is evaluated by a performance panel, which rates him or her either "qualified" or "unqualified"; this is then followed by a retention election at which citizens get to vote up or down on whether the judge remains on the bench for another term. The term "retention" election, as noted, is used in contrast to "contested" election insofar as judges would not face challengers as they now sometimes do; rather, they would occupy ballot lines by themselves and would "win" if they garnered more "yes" than "no" votes. Quie expands on these steps below, starting with the third: performance evaluation. Although, as you read on, please keep in mind that the word "commission" can refer to four different groups: (1) the Quie Commission itself, formally known as the Citizens Commission for the Preservation of an Impartial Judiciary; (2) the current Minnesota Commission on Judicial Selection; (3) a proposed Appellate Court Merit Selection Commission; and (4) a proposed Performance Evaluation Review Commission. Yes, someone should have planned ahead better, but detail and context should keep everything clear.

What do we do about people who don't currently know anything about the judges they're asked to vote on? It's important to know how they've performed, and that's how the idea of a performance evaluation commission came up. It's not a unique idea, as seven other states have them, including Arizona, Colorado, and most recently Kansas.

But public performance evaluation like this is useful not just because it provides voters with information. It also can provide judges themselves with information about how they're doing so that they can become better judges. And even though it's not in the legislation being considered by the legislature, I've come to the conclusion that what judges need is a very good, long-term training program, lasting maybe two or three years. A person really doesn't know how to be a judge before they are one, just like I didn't know how to be a governor before I became one. There's a learning experience; you've got to get up to speed. But when it comes to the evaluation part, the Performance Evaluation Review Commission will look at whether judges have followed the rule of law. Do they have integrity? Are they punctual and follow right procedures? Here's a really key one: Do they respect the litigants? The commission will then let voters know what it has found.

I asked about the non-trivial matters of the makeup of the Performance Evaluation Review Commission and the method it would use in making its hugely consequential recommendations. Half the body, he said, would be appointed by the governor, with the other half named by the chief justice of the state supreme court.

Nobody [on the Quie Commission] could come up with a way of non-governmental officials making the appointments. The idea of the Bar Association doing it, for example, went over like a lead balloon, and I didn't like the legislature doing it because it's so political. So we came to that conclusion because we wanted to hold two people responsible, the governor and chief justice. Ten people would be appointed statewide, and two each from the ten judicial districts, making for 30 in all, with a majority having to be non-lawyers. That was a bone of contention, too, because some members of the [Quie] commission thought that only judges and lawyers can understand the issue. Nonsense!

In the more technical language of the Quie Commission report: "Midway through the judge's full term and again no less than nine months before his or her election, anonymous survey forms eliciting performance evaluations shall be distributed to attorneys, litigants, other judges, and other persons who have been in direct contact with each judge surveyed and who have firsthand knowledge of his or her judicial performance during the evaluation period."

The Quie Commission also recommended that a judge's initial term, following gubernatorial appointment, be four years, with subsequent terms following voter retention doubling to eight years. This would lengthen both first terms and follow-up terms by approximately two years each and would provide a "larger overall record of performance from which to make renewal decisions and evaluate performance."

———— ◆ ————

Let's return to the emphasis Quie puts on judicial impartiality and independence, both in fact and perception.

> I never personally solicited funds all the time I was in elective office because it offended me so to do that. Instead, I had others do it, people who had been gifted to do it, and I made certain that everything was made public. We never followed any rule that only contributions over a certain level had to be disclosed; we revealed every contribution so people would know the names of everybody who contributed to my campaigns. I believe in total transparency in that way. But the federal system continues to bother me. Ronald Reagan's nomination of Robert Bork for a Supreme Court seat turned into a fiasco; I thought it was very bad. Bork's son, by the way, worked for me in Congress, and I've always had high regard for both of them.

Turning state courts into similarly nasty, money-drenched arenas where controversial rulings or verdicts might unleash big-money campaigns against excellent district or appellate judges is precisely what Quie seeks to avoid. Judges can't do their jobs properly, he argues, if they're constantly looking over their shoulders concerned about some group coming after them at a future election with deep-pocketed partisan or ideological retribution in mind. He frequently cites numbers like these: For the years 1999 to 2006, $155 million was raised for state supreme court races in the 22 states with contested elections. The figure was $1.6 million in the twenty states with retention elections.

Breaking the numbers down further (as Quie is apt to do), the twenty states with retention elections can be divided into two unbalanced groups: seventeen in which judges are first appointed by governors, and three in which they actually first come aboard in contested elections. Spending in the seventeen strictly retention states between 1999 and 2006 was about $300,000. It was about $1.3 in the three mixed states.

Even under the best of circumstances, Quie argues, office holders in general who hope to keep their jobs are incapable of being completely oblivious to how those prospects might be damaged if they consistently act in complete accordance with their deepest beliefs. "I hadn't fully realized that until I announced in January 1982 that I wouldn't run again for governor. There were anxieties in my subconscious that left me, and I could then make better judgments with a clearer head than I ever could before."

"Such as?"

"Matters," he said, "having to do with raising taxes, labor disputes, environmental issues, and educational questions."

"How did not worrying about staying in office change your approach to education?"

To great laughter, both his and mine, he said: "I didn't give a hoot what the Minnesota Education Association thought anymore. You know, I had a pretty good education reputation in Congress, and after a while you realize that teachers respect you even though their union doesn't like you."

Survival causes people to do things they never thought they would do. Not survival in terms of staying alive, but surviving in a prestigious position or a kind of lifestyle. I remember in

Congress, when members' districts became more liberal or conservative after redistricting. Their voting patterns would frequently move in those ways. It wasn't just Machiavellian schemes that caused it. It's the way humans are made up. So with judges, you want them to have impartial independence. But at the same time, they can't operate contrary to the law and the Constitution, and people have to hold them accountable.

------------•◆•------------

Minnesotans for Impartial Courts was publicly launched at a press conference in February 2008, with the most-quoted line offered by Associate Supreme Court Justice Alan Page (who actually had won his first term in a contested election). "This country would go crazy," the former Minnesota Viking and NFL Hall of Famer said, if Super Bowl referees "had an interest in the outcome." Page had been one of 30 members of the Citizens Commission for the Preservation of an Impartial Judiciary (the "Quie Commission"), which spawned Minnesotans for Impartial Courts.

Several bills to accomplish what the commission had recommended were introduced at the 2008 Minnesota Legislature but they failed to gain sufficient "traction," a term that was used often throughout the session. Interpretations for the lack of out-of-the-gate progress centered on the fact that the crisis the commission warned about hadn't arrived in the state yet, or as some legislators said, "If it ain't broke, don't fix it." Beyond the fact that some players, including Greg Wersal, the lawyer who had provoked the original litigation that led to the *White* decision, were adamantly opposed to what Quie and his colleagues sought to do, the legislature's hesitation seemed to be based on a lack of consensus among lawyers and judges about the right solution to the problem. In addition, a number of district court judges expressed concern that the proposed changes would leave them vulnerable to well-financed, last-minute campaigns by unfriendly groups to unseat them. Quie's principal response, and that of other advocates to such fears, was that there was little precedent for problems of the sort in states already employing retention

Al Quie with retired Supreme Court Justice Sandra Day O'Connor at the Humphrey Institute of Public Affairs, May 2, 2008. Justice O'Connor argued against partisan judicial elections. Courtesy of Paula Keller.

elections. But even if a judge were ousted in ways that some might view as unfair and less-than-judicious, Quie argued his or her seat would be filled by someone selected by the governor based on merit, not power politics. In a follow-up exchange, he referred to how the re-election defeat of California Supreme Court Chief Justice Rose Bird in 1986, along with two of her colleagues, lingers in some minds, particularly liberals. "The issue," he said,

> had to do primarily with capital punishment. She voted overwhelmingly for defendants, angering victims and others. Yet while I, too, have come to oppose capital punishment, it's not the end of the world when a judge comes to the end of his or her term and isn't retained. Judges do get removed from office, but fact of the matter is it's much more likely to

happen in contested elections rather than retention elections. The danger for democracy and people without power is not the defeat of judges but the retention of incompetent or biased ones.

The legislature will return to the issue in 2009, and if it then enacts what Quie and colleagues have in mind, Minnesotans will get to vote up or down on a constitutional amendment in 2010. While the list of organized opponents and skeptics was and remains short, the list of supporters is substantial and eclectic. Sponsors, for example, of a Minneapolis luncheon in May 2008 at which former U.S. Supreme Court Justice Sandra Day O'Connor spoke on behalf of Minnesotans for Impartial Courts included the likes of the Minnesota State Bar Association, the Minnesota AFL-CIO, the Minnesota Chamber of Commerce, the League of Women Voters of Minnesota, and the Hubert H. Humphrey Institute at the University of Minnesota, as well as assorted think tanks and policy organizations, left, right, and middle. Quie didn't speak at that event, but it was about the only instance of his not doing so during that stretch, as he was averaging several speeches and other appearances around the state on the topic every week.

Writing a year earlier on the same subject, and apparently unpersuaded that Quie was secretly a sinister, elitist, or muckety-mucking old man, the Minneapolis *Star Tribune* editorialized how the former governor and congressman was still speaking out for "the common good" and how he remained "as eager as ever to translate noble theory into practice."

———— • ◆ • ————

Towards the very end of our last recorded conversation, I said something to Quie about how seeking to assure fair and first-rate judges was the strongest of his current policy passions. No, he said, it still was young children, making sure they had good starts in life. It's a fervency to which we now turn, with a focus on early childhood education.

Chapter Twelve

Early Childhood Education
"Enhancing the Invisible"

"The worst crime we commit," Al Quie frequently says, "is raising our kids in ways that will cause them to suffer." It's a claim, he acknowledges, not without hyperbole, albeit accurate enough to continue fueling his life's devotion to children, a preoccupation that increasingly has come to pivot on improving educational access and quality for one- to four-year-olds. It's an absorption, in fact, that encapsulates virtually every passion and theme associated with his more than half a century of public life, starting, for the best example, with his accent on parents.

———•◆•———

I had just asked Quie about his involvement with Ready 4 K, one of the two highest profile organizations in Minnesota seeking to expand and institutionalize early childhood education in the state (with "early childhood education" understood as a much more substantial and didactic endeavor than simple "child care"). I had mentioned that it had been Don Fraser, a Democrat with whom he had served in both the state senate in the 1950s and later in Congress, who had recruited him to the Ready 4 K board of directors.

Don and a couple of other people came to speak to me about half a dozen years ago about an organization they were putting together that turned out to be Ready 4 K. As you know I engage in those kinds of discussions frequently. At the end of it, I told one of the people in the room, Todd Otis, who was going to be the president of the group, not to ask me to be on

251

Al Quie speaking at a meeting sponsored by the Council on Basic Education in Williamsburg, Virginia, in 1996. He was chairman of a panel critiquing what he called "ridiculous" standards for the teaching of history proposed by faculty at UCLA. Steve Muller, a former president of Johns Hopkins University, is on his far left. Chris Cross, head of CBE, is in the middle.

the board because I was too busy with too many other things at the time. I was already on a number of boards. But then that *thing* happened to me again, the same little pain I get in my heart when something is wrong and I'm not being entirely truthful with myself. The same feeling I had when I kept saying I would run for re-election as governor, but something was telling me I shouldn't. So that had gone on for a couple of years when Don came back, in 2004, and asked if I'd go on that board. I wanted to get rid of this pain in my heart, so I said yes right off the bat. "You don't have to argue with me. I'll join."

After we agreed that his heart pain was a pretty good Geiger counter, Quie continued with what he told Fraser, who, following sixteen years in Congress, served another fourteen years as mayor of Minneapolis. "I've been watching Ready 4 K," Quie had said, "and you're ignoring parents."

I then qualified my acceptance by saying I'd be happy to come on board, but only if they were all right with my unabashedly promoting parents having more say about what kind of education their children ought to get. Don said sure but when I got there I found there was only one other person on the board who seemed to really agree with me, a woman named Ada Alden, someone who had done a lot of work in this area in the western suburbs, a person with a good head on her shoulders.

I started going to meetings and it was clear that the people with the dominant voice were the early childhood providers and others who had been involved in the public schools. But slowly, in the language we used and in other ways, we started elevating the parents' role. My drive, as always, was to try and figure out a good balance involving government, business, nonprofit organizations, and, of course, families.

If there's a difference in Quie's views about the intimate importance of parents when talking about early childhood education as compared to what he sees as their all-defining role in other situations, it has to do with his repeated comments about how the world has changed. He still unhesitatingly argues that nothing could ever supersede or substitute for the singular connection forged between mother and child. And possibly more than any Minnesota politician theoretically retired or otherwise, he talks about the importance of fathers in raising healthy children. His old-school credentials, in these ways, are solid. But it's precisely his recognition of the huge toll taken by rampant family disintegration that has led him to sing from a slightly revised hymnal and embrace new educational and other developmental opportunities for pre-kindergarteners.

"We tend to live in the past," he said one morning. "I try not to assume that the way it was when I was a child is the way it's going to be or the way it's got to be now. We're not returning any time soon to when children had two parents almost all of the time unless one of them died. So who will teach them about faith, the life of their communities, and their moral responsibilities towards other people?"

In similar vein, he also acknowledges how individuals "increasingly have many means of getting away from each other," eroding bonds and attachments even further. Updates like these are on target, but ignored is why the demise of marriage is far more severe in some communities rather than others. Given Quie's take on how children learn and fare, this is much more than an academic or sidebar question.

The drive for measurably expanded early childhood programs both in Minnesota and nationally is directly prompted by huge achievement gaps between white and black (and other minority) children and a growing determination to close them. While the near evaporation of marriage in many neighborhoods is not the sole cause of such gulfs, it's undeniably a central one. Especially germane here is Quie's keen and ceaseless interest in understanding exactly why some people succeed educationally and in other aspects of life while others don't. As he's fond of asking: "What's the causality?" Or completing the circle at hand, if far too many young people are foundering, at least in part because of an epidemic of out-of-wedlock births and divorce, what's causing the epidemic in the first place? This is another area where Quie's views on race and racism, his harsh evaluation of our nation's history on the subject, and what he sees as the "dominant culture's" heavy and ongoing "obligations" because of that history are not the grist of ordinary conversations. Speaking specifically and at length about non-marital birth rates among African Americans— which are upward of 70 percent across the country and over 85 percent in Minneapolis—he stressed the point: "They didn't do it all by themselves."

At the risk of leaving an impression of finger-pointing and blaming, it's critical, obviously, for African Americans to come to grips with the problems they're causing themselves. They have to do what's necessary to help themselves better when it comes to education, raising children, and other things. But we also have to ask what it is about the dominant culture that has helped put them in the state they're now in. We have to look at ourselves, because unless we can see we're also a cause of the problems and then repent, they're not going to be solved. It absolutely isn't going to work if you just say, "You guys straighten it out and then come see me when you do." As human beings, we interact in ways with each other that can be both harmful and helpful. We are so unaware of our harmfulness.

A few minutes later Quie made reference to anti-Semitism, and how "memories of pogroms" caused Jews to "protect each other and pull together" as the best means of remaining safe as a community, at least fragilely. He also spoke of "Jewish parents' insistence on education."

Now, why didn't something more like that happen in the black community? Well, we intentionally broke black families apart during slavery. The plantations were big and far apart, and that alone made it difficult for blacks to connect with each other, though there were many other critical and cruel reasons, of course. The only place they could come together was in church, as there was enough belief in God among the plantation holders to allow that. Then there were decades of sharecropping, followed by the start of their migration from the south to the north during World War II and all the problems that always come when large numbers of rural people move to cities. Unsurprisingly, a lot of blacks wound up on welfare. But rather than giving welfare to families where there was a husband and wife, the government in essence said, "No, only women and children can have it." So the men would leave. And then whites would say, "Isn't that terrible?" and they'd criticize the "low morals" of black people and wonder how they could they do such things. But whites who said things like that were wrong, because survival drives people to do things they otherwise wouldn't do, and many blacks were just trying to survive.

White culture did all these terrible things and then we somehow claim there's no blame on our part? Well, I'll tell you, we've got a lot of blame. As recently as the 1960s when the major civil rights bills were passed, black men with college degrees were shining shoes in Minneapolis. Blacks who came to work in the stockyards in South St. Paul weren't allowed to live there; it was a terribly segregated city. I remember that from when I campaigned there. That's why I say those of us who are white and members of the dominant culture can't shirk our responsibilities.

As for what those responsibilities might include when it comes to young children, beyond espousing conventional policies such as making quality early education programs more available and pursuing what might be described as a moderate conception of affirmative action, Quie's core answer (as in other circumstances) is for blacks and whites to "walk together." In this specific instance, he urges men of all races who are blessed to be in loving two-parent families to reach out and work closely with other men who have little if any experience with what scholars call "equal-regard marriages." Very much alert to the possibility that recommendations of this sort can be interpreted as patronizing—yet also acutely of the mind that straight talk is essential—Quie argues, for example, that we need to "bring people in from the African American community and just plain teach them and then walk with them so we learn from them. Relationships, relationships, relationships: That's what we have to focus on, and with real intentionality."

We need to spend a few minutes on where things stand with efforts to expand early childhood education in Minnesota—the policy landscape. But before we do, it's intriguing to see how Quie's analysis of the continuing effects of slavery, segregation, and discrimination is nearly identical with what the distinguished political scientist James Q. Wilson wrote in 2002 in *The Marriage Problem: How Our Culture Has Weakened Families*:

It's hard to believe that two or three centuries of slave life followed by a century or so of Jim Crow left no lasting impression on African Americans, but of course proving such a connection is virtually impossible. But let us for a moment conduct a mental experiment. Given what slaves endured, what would we imagine would be the legacy that their children and grandchildren inherited? We would probably suppose that boys would grow up with little close identification with their fathers and some interest in repeating the youthful sexual exploits that transient work and long absences from home made possible. Few would recall many happy experiences associated with a two-parent family. Girls, on the other hand, would grow up thinking that men were irresponsible and that women would have to make their own careers out of whatever opportunities presented themselves. Children would expect to be raised by their mothers and grandmothers and possibly by other women, perhaps distant ones, and would not be surprised if there were no fathers present.

There are multi-millions of exceptions to such patterns of behavior, Wilson is quick to correctly acknowledge. But what is striking, he contends, is the extent to which they also "accord with reality for a large (albeit a minority) of African Americans today."

———— • ◆ • ————

Save for the not inconsequential fact that public dollars have been hard to find, the stars are aligned for a significant expansion of early childhood education in Minnesota. And inarguably the rock star among mere every-night ones in the unstoppable drive has been Art Rolnick, an economist with the Federal Reserve Bank of Minneapolis who in March 2003 published a paper with Rob Grunewald entitled "Early Childhood Development: Economic Development with a High Public Relations Return," in *fedgazzete* (a publication of the Federal Reserve Bank of Minneapolis). He argued that governments could assure larger, long-term returns by underwriting quality early childhood education programs than by allocating tax revenues for virtually anything else— most notably enticing businesses to relocate with tax holidays and other unproductive breaks. He also is anything but a fan of publicly financed ballparks and stadia as economic development tools. Educators, politicians, and others who were already convinced of the educational and social virtues of early education programs were naturally thrilled by his muscular fiscal justifications. But what really revved the movement was the way in which senior business leaders were stirred by Rolnick's findings as well as by his continuing evangelism and hands-on involvement in the matter. Nearly 200 business officials in 2005, for example, attended a Minnesota Business Forum on School Readiness. At about the same time, the head of a major statewide business association said, "Our members recognize this as a critical issue. We're at the point where anything we can do to ensure that kids stay in school and get on a career path is worth doing." Not incidentally, Rolnick says he was compelled to investigate the economic advantages of early childhood education by what he saw as the excessive appeal by advocates such as Quie and Don Fraser to its moral rather than harder-headed benefits.

Rolnick, who is senior vice president and director of research for the Minneapolis Fed and an early board member of Ready 4 K, argued at an American Experiment luncheon in 2006 how the rate of return on the well-known (at least in some circles) Perry preschool program in Ypsilanti, Michigan, in the 1960s had averaged sixteen percent annually on the original two-year, annual expenditure of $10,000 per child (in inflation-adjusted dollars). "And most of that return," he said, "was a public return because costs for special education, remedial training, and crime dropped significantly." He also cited long-term studies of larger programs in North Carolina, Chicago, and Syracuse, all of which, he said, pointed in the same direction, featuring rates of return ranging between seven and seventeen percent. "The research is clear," he said, "with high-quality early childhood education interventions, we get high public returns." He also talked about how emerging brain research "shows that the earliest years—zero to five— are critical years for brain development," making educational programs for very young children more important still.

Growing directly out of Rolnick's research and Otis' activism, along with the work of business leaders such as Rob Johnson of Cargill and Chuck Slocum, was the founding in 2005 of the Minnesota Early Learning Foundation. Its charge was to "recommend cost-effective strategies for preparing children to succeed in school," doing so by pulling together evidence about "what works best and most cost-effectively in promoting learning readiness among children of low-income families" as well as families facing "other challenges." With more than $8 million of mostly private assets at the end of 2007,

MELF is currently conducting pilot studies in four communities in the Twin Cities metropolitan area and southern Minnesota.

In addition to Rolnick, members of the MELF board include chairmen, presidents, and CEOs of the likes of Best Buy, Cargill, Ecolab, United Health Care, Blue Cross and Blue Shield of Minnesota, and the University of Minnesota. With such a lineup, its leaders unsurprisingly (and to Quie's full approval) talk of the eventual emergence of a decentralized, market-based system in which parents—in essence, via vouchers—hold largest sway. Their envisioned organizational chart is radically different from any found in the nation's public school systems, especially big-city ones where children of color tend to do their worst.

Support for expanded early childhood programs also would seem to be grounded in the grassroots, as witness a 2006 survey funded in part by Ready 4 K and conducted by two respected public opinion firms, one frequently identified with the right and the other with the left. According to the survey (which a Minneapolis *Star Tribune* editorial took great pleasure in celebrating), 71 percent of respondents said that "making sure that all children in Minnesota start kindergarten with the knowledge and skills they need to do their best in school" ought to be state government's highest policy priority. This made it the highest rated of all possible answers, beating out not only improving health care access for low-income families but also reducing tax burdens on all families. This was the same survey alluded to in Chapter Three that led to Quie's reconciliation with a pollster and former state Republican Party chairman who had disparaged his Republican bona fides in 1982. Fueling activists further has been their contention that Minnesota has been falling increasingly behind the rest of the country in public support for early education programs, in sizable measure because of deep cuts made during a severe state budget crisis in the 2003-04 biennium.

It's fair to say that Minnesota media have been near-ceaseless cheerleaders for expanded early childhood initiatives in general and for what Rolnick and MELF have in mind in particular, paying only slim attention to possible trapdoors, including potentially profound difficulties in reproducing exceptional programs in mass ways— "bringing them to scale," to use the jargon. It's an obstacle that Rolnick, to his great credit, acknowledges fully, but one that he sees alleviated by rigorous programmatic evaluation and market competition.

In sum, he envisions a system that (1) funds children most at-risk; (2) focuses on parents; (3) is serious about assessments; and (4) starts as early as possible in children's lives. "As brain development research suggests," he has said, "if you start at three, you're starting too late." In regards to this last point, while only three- and four-year-olds would be in early childhood "classes" as such, nurses and other mentors would work with low-income mothers starting before they gave birth. He hopes to fund all of this with an endowment, funded both privately and publicly, that would grow before long to $1.5 billion or more. This would enable eligible parents to enroll their children in "high-quality" programs costing in the range of $11,000 to $13,000 per child annually, a figure that presumably would increase with inflation. Nothing about what Rolnick has in mind runs counter to anything Quie has in mind, although the former governor is intellectually and otherwise encoded to doubly emphasize the familial and spiritual side of almost all ledgers.

This is the early childhood environment to which Quie has been contributing. Beyond what we've already discussed, what distinctive views and voice does he bring to the debate?

————————•◆•————————

As long ago as the early 1980s, when I first worked for him, I recall Quie proposing that if children had to attend preschool or day care, it should be in close proximity to where at least one parent worked so that they could drive or ride back and forth together as well as eat lunch together every day. He would talk regularly back then about how something important was lost when, for an assortment of reasons including an explosion of women in the paid workforce, relatively few boys and girls any longer walked home for lunch and then walked back to school afterwards, as I did, for instance, in New York in the 1950s right through sixth grade.

Jump ahead to 2006 and a column by Lori Sturdevant in the Minneapolis *Star Tribune* in which she wrote of Quie's "vision" in the matter. According to the governor (by way of Sturdevant's framing),

"Small schools serving grades pre-K through 3 should be located at every retail center, every industrial park, every major corporate headquarters, every place where groups of adults regularly spend their daytime hours." Sturdevant, who has written books about former governor Elmer Andersen, talked about how Quie believes that parents, to the extent possible, "should take their children with them to work, spend breaks with them, be on hand for school events, and have daily contact with teachers." She wrote of how Quie favors parents being "at least as near to their children as were his farming mother and father 75 years ago, when he went to a rural schoolhouse that served a school district two miles long and four miles wide." In the same column, Sturdevant cited Duane Benson, the executive director of MELF, as describing Quie as "ahead of his time." Not incidentally, Minnesota may have the highest proportion in the nation of mothers who work outside of their homes.

Sturdevant's use of the term "vision" above was well chosen, as it speaks to one of the two most interesting things I've learned about Quie since he left office. I've already noted that one of the products of working on this book is that I discovered just how ambitious he always has been, politically and in other ways. Somehow his un-agitated manner suggests a less-driven temperament. The other surprising item is something I learned half a dozen years ago, when along with former colleagues from his administration, we sought to decipher a handful of main themes of his professional life that, as one might expect, were hard to separate from his personal life. It was reasonably easy to settle on education, families, and faith as the big three, but in doing so, I came to realize that his career had been punctuated by an unadvertised gift of what I've also described as "vision"—although a sourpuss might describe it as a talent for embracing commonsensical ideas and then having the patience for the rest of the country to catch up. Whatever the interpretation, be the issue educational freedom, smaller schools, the fatherhood movement, the marriage movement, or faith-based initiatives, Quie has believed deeply in variations of all of them and has pushed for each for a long time and with ardor—and continues to do so.

Quie's focus on families, joined with his distaste for bureaucracy, further joined with the habitual failure of low-income children to succeed in even small ways in large public school systems, explain why it's unsurprising that he agrees with Art Rolnick and other MELF leaders that early childhood dollars must attach to parents and their children and not be controlled by school systems or other government agencies. He also agrees, once again naturally, that both public and private institutions and early childhood programs, including religious ones, should be eligible to participate as long as they meet high quality standards as gauged, most basically, by whether they adequately prepare their students academically.

All this is longhand for the fact that Quie likes vouchers, though he prefers talking about "portability," which he views in more encompassing (and less politically problematic) terms. Softened language notwithstanding,

> Some people on the Ready 4 K board think I want to take all authority away from the actual providers, the educators, and I'm not interested in doing that at all. Portability is something that a lot of people in public education just hate, so we have this battle going on. My job is trying to get everyone to see the big picture and talk with one another. One way or another we're going to bring this together. One way or another we're going to get a system out of this thing. But I very much agree with Art that it's essential for parents to make the biggest decisions about what early childhood programs work best for their very young children.

I asked where Don Fraser, the man who recruited Quie to the Ready 4 K board of directors and a DFL hero in Minnesota, stood on vouchers and portability. "He's very quiet about it," Quie said, "and hasn't said anything directly. But he has expressed absolutely no opposition to it. He's a quiet person who doesn't show his hand fast." Fraser also remains, like Quie, a superlatively active older gentleman (although five months the governor's junior). The fact that the two of them are leading players in advancing educational opportunities for infants and toddlers is . . . I'm still looking for the right word. Otis is less at a loss when he writes that their collaboration is "testament to how thoughtful and farsighted they are."

Quie's support of educational vouchers, it should be noted, is not at all new, as one of his Governor's Forums in 1982 (as discussed in Chapter Eight) spotlighted the subject, much to the apoplexy of at least one DFL heavyweight. And of course everyone loves the GI Bill, which is a prototypical voucher program.

On several occasions I pushed Quie on whether his exceptionally strong interest in early childhood education would be less vigorous if fewer kids were forced to grow up in single-parent households. He resisted going this route, preferring to cite, as noted earlier, the growing centrifugal pressures on all families. Still, as woven throughout the book, no advocate for early childhood education in Minnesota puts more stock in the importance of intact, two-parent families when it comes to the well-being of children than he does. Likewise, I know of no early childhood supporter in town who talks as explicitly about the "invisible" when imagining what constitutes "quality" programs.

Without dismissing the contributions of teachers, nurses, social workers, and other "professionals," Quie nonetheless asked one day, "Who has been mainly responsible for raising children through the eons of time since God created us?" Answering his own question, it's been parents, he said—mothers and fathers, not systems or programs.

But if we're to talk about early childhood "systems" and "programs," as we're obliged to when seeking to serve tens of thousands of children, what makes for excellent ones? Identical with his approach regarding "older grades," the key again, he stresses, lies in relationships: Relationships that entwine teachers, parents, and children in common purpose—and which by their very nature are the stuff of spirit. "I don't know if I'm coming through on this," Quie said, "but we have to find ways of enhancing the invisible that exists in relationships."

Also invisible but critical, he argues, are comfort zones, and just as horses need them if they're to learn, children and their parents require them, too. (Not a scent of disrespect intended here, as Quie uses analogies like these in sacred celebration of both species.) "The only time you can train a horse is when he's in his comfort zone."

Just yesterday, we were in a small enclosure and I could sense that my horse was out of his comfort zone. I wanted him to do something, but he just reared straight in the air because he felt encroached. So I let him quiet down and took him to where he could have his comfort and he got over it. He was then obedient in every way possible.

We also force kids into places—like preschools—where they may not be in their comfort zones and then expect them to thrive. It doesn't work that way. Comfort zones are where children feel safe. Watch good parents. I watch them when I drive in the morning. They're out there with their kindergarten and first-grade children waiting for the bus to pick them up. What a sense of security and love those children have. But I also think about how plain upset they can be when they're dropped off at a preschool program or day care center. I mentioned this at Ready 4 K one day and a woman had a wonderful insight. "One of the things parents should do," she said, "is make an extra set of house keys or car keys and give them to your son or daughter when you drop them off." By having the keys, the woman said, kids will have greater confidence that their parents really will be coming back and they'll be picked up again. By just by holding the keys, they'll have a greater sense of security. When she told me this, it was one of those "ah-ha" moments. I never thought of that before.

Using almost the same phrasing as he did when I worked for him more than 25 years ago, he said, "Right up there with the three things all people need—food, water, and air—is the need to love another person, to know that another person loves you, and to do something of consequence for someone else." And it all starts "with mothers when they're with child."

————— • ◆ • —————

Al Quie is a preschool optimist, which caused me to say at the end of our main conversation on the topic, "You know I haven't disagreed with you too many times. I just hope you're right and I'm wrong, but I just don't see things working out as well as you, Art Rolnick, Don Fraser, Todd Otis, and the others believe they will."

It's impossible to disagree with Quie, obviously, when he says it would be an enormous step forward if all children who were intellectually and physically capable of reading well were, in fact, able to do so by fourth grade, spurred by expanded early childhood programs. "If we succeed on this," he has said, "it would be known not only all over this country but all over the world. It would be that dramatic." Although also obvious, I'm afraid, is the question of whether the benign effects of even the most solid preschool programs can be made to routinely last long enough for enough children, as more than four decades of Head Start evidence is not encouraging. Reading well by the fourth grade, by the way, has become a touchstone for Quie, who has gone so far as to argue with more seriousness than glibness that the entire testing superstructure of No Child Left Behind should be ditched in favor of simply finding out if ten-year-old kids (or thereabouts) can read proficiently.

"There are two competing goals or directions in early childhood education that can't be reconciled with each other," he elaborated several months after our main conversation on the subject. "One goal has children ages three through eight transported to public school settings as we know them, employing professionals with college degrees who teach and care for them. This is currently the case for boys and girls ages five to eight.

The other goal, as I've discussed, is to have programs located wherever parents of children ages eight and younger are located in the daytime. Parents would bring their boys and girls with them and they all would be expected to have noon meals together. Mothers and fathers would have relationships with other mothers and fathers as well as with staff members. As for those teachers and other professionals, they would share with parents what they come to learn about their children, and parents, in turn, would teach the professionals how to love and understand the uniqueness of their kids.

If the first approach is further pursued and established, it will fail because families must be partners in their children's development and learning.

But if the second approach is pursued and established, it will succeed because it will lead to at least one parent playing a more integral role in their child's progress.

To most people, the first direction looks easier to accomplish because it would not change what we already do in K-3.

The second direction looks virtually impossible to most people because such programs would seldom be located in school buildings and they would dramatically change how K-3 is currently organized.

But, the first way of helping children is producing fourth graders where only about 37 percent of them in Minnesota read proficiently. The figure nationally is even worse, at about only 30 percent.

On the other hand, fourth graders in programs across the country that resemble the approach I favor tend to read proficiently at more than twice the national rate.

Both routes, he readily acknowledges, would "require more public dollars." They would be expensive, "but failure in child rearing is already expensive to the state and its economy."

Still the state cannot organize and regulate our way out of the problem. We should trust civil society, where parents can play a more collaborative role in growing solid citizens for the future than they usually can in state or governmental organizations. A woman by the name of Sandra Christenson was correct when she wrote that, "schools and teachers alone seldom help students achieve their full academic potential. This is not an indictment of schools and teachers. Rather, this is a fact of child development."

Christenson, a University Fellow at the University of Minnesota, wrote for the Children, Youth, and Family Consortium in the Spring 2008 issue of *Consortium Connections*.

By my overcast lights, Quie is right on a number of additional pivotal issues.

Leaders of the public school establishment, he contends, starting with those who run teacher's unions, can be just as rigidly fundamentalist in their line of work as absolutist politicians can be in theirs. In expanding preschool opportunities, Quie believes such educational dogmatists can be sidestepped by taking concerted advantage of private and religious schools and free markets. I very much hope he's right. But if I were to warn of one more danger, it's that he and Rolnick and the captains of industry currently and earnestly in the fray are destined to be so for only a limited time; those who differ vividly with them on undergirding principles will be immersed in the battle, practically speaking, forever. Of a piece, Quie believes that adequately fixing giant and clumsy systems of public education is impossible. He doesn't see it happening in his lifetime anyway.

He further recognizes that huge achievement gaps between white and minority students in Minnesota predate substantial cutbacks in early childhood spending that were prompted by an immense budget crisis in Tim Pawlenty's first year as governor in 2003. In other words, he recognizes that increased spending alone, no matter how generous, will do little to close one of the largest, racially contoured chasms in the country. And Quie emphatically appreciates that for all the necessary talk about taking promising programs to "scale," doing so will be very hard—and not just because the most vital things about early childhood education need to be kept intimate.

"I do believe," he has said, "every child can develop to their full potential and live in grace with other human beings. I also believe all would be hopeless if it weren't for the hand of God. But I'm optimistic we're not going to continue killing each other off forever, particularly large segments of our population whose kids aren't developing properly."

I asked what he meant by the last statement; how literally should it be taken? "Are you saying that if we don't get early childhood education right and K-12 right, we'll continue having lots of poor, angry, vulnerable people? I don't want to use the word 'war,' but are you talking about even more serious tensions and problems than currently exist?"

"Oh, yes, sure."

"Between haves and have-nots, with increasingly ugly and dangerous racial implications; is that what you're saying?"

He answered yes again, this time returning to what he sees as the shameful fact that the United States, proportionately, may incarcerate more people than any other nation in the world, with African Americans comprising a hugely disproportionate share of that number.

"There are projections," he said, "that say by 2030, at the rate we're going, more than twice as many African Americans will be in Minnesota prisons than are there today. So I ask myself how are we going to solve that problem and it's clear we have to go all the way back to the little kids in families where the whole thing starts. What's my passion for the issue? We're really going to suffer if we continue this way, but if I can do *something* while I'm still here . . . if I can only get through to people so that they understand."

"One last question," I said, "though I've been teasing it for a while and you've been suggesting your answer for a while. How confident are you that early childhood programs will accomplish what enthusiasts like you say they will?"

"I believe," Quie said, "it behooves us to try as best we can to make this work because I have *no* confidence whatsoever things will turn out okay if we don't do anything. That's just not going to happen."

Chapter Thirteen

Riding into the Sunset
"Awestruck"

In what I thought would be our final full session (I was wrong), right before Christmas in 2007, I opened by noting that the first question I had asked at our very first conversation for the book, five months earlier, had to do with his earliest memories growing up on a farm in southern Minnesota. He had mentioned two, both having to do with horses, one at age two and the other at three. "What I would like to do today," I now said, "is talk about your whole life with horses, everything about them, the whole gamut. It seems to me, without getting too metaphorical, horses have meant something very spiritual to you, if I'm using that term in a way you find attractive. Yet at the same time," I added, "you've had a fun old time just riding around. Talk to me, if you would, about the range of experiences and emotions you have had with horses in your life."

Never was less giddyup needed.

———— ◆ ·————

"I told parts of this story before, but back when I was governor, I was asked by some friends with whom I met regularly to think and meditate on a spot I would go where I was really at peace, really in my comfort zone. What came to my mind? What did I envision? I envisioned a hill in the pasture on the farm where I would go as soon as my parents trusted me to walk that far by myself. I would find excuses to do that. Just to sit there on the hill looking over the stream and the vistas beyond that. It's the same feeling I have when I get out in the mountains."

"Let me interrupt for a second. How old were you when your parents allowed you to do this?"

"I don't remember how old I was, but I do remember I did it sometimes even before they allowed me."

"Just like unhitching a team of horses at age three," I reminded him.

"There was another story similar to the one about the hill," he went on.

My bedroom had a door that led out to a flat roof. We called it the sunroom below and the sun porch above. My folks didn't want me to do this, but when everybody was asleep I would shinny down the drain pipe and spend the night outdoors. To get back upstairs in the morning before anyone in the house got up, I figured out I could grab hold of the pipe, pull myself up, hook a foot on the windowsill, grab the drain trough, and then pull myself over a railing and get back in. I got by with that for a long time. I just loved to sleep outdoors.

The citified part of me asked, "Without a sleeping bag or blanket?"
"No. It would be summertime. I'd just go out there and sleep."
"No pillow?"
"No, nothing out there," he repeated.

One night when I was sleeping outside, a bee or a wasp or something landed on my eyelid and I must have felt it and flickered it, because I got stung and came to breakfast with a puffed up eye. My mother said, "Now Albert, how did you get that?" I said, "Well, a bee stung me." And she asked, "Was there a bee in your room?" For some reason she couldn't imagine that. I guess my folks taught me to be honest because I said, "No, it was outside." She asked how I got outside, I told her, and that was the end of that.

Interrupting his laughter, I asked how old might he have been at the time.

"Oh, I guess I was ten or twelve, someplace in there. I moved out of that room to another one after that."

After a brief digression, Quie began tying his love for the outdoors with his love of horses.

Al Quie high in the Rockies during one of his nine summer rides along the Continental Divide during the 1980s and '90s, covering 261 days.

Where does the awesomeness of the whole universe come to you? For me, it's frequently at night. I remember being in New Mexico when I was studying Native American education needs. There was no smog whatsoever and the stars were huge, just huge. I was driving one night, I wasn't even on horseback, when I had to stop the car and say to the guy who was with me, "Let's get out here and look at this." We just stood and looked at the whole sky, and then we saw a star plummeting across the heavens before fading out. For some reason, I have the same admiration for horses and their beauty. I told you earlier about when my dad put me on that horse, on that beautiful bay Morgan mare. I can still see her there. But it's not just their beauty, it's the learning and living relationships I have with them, too. There's just something awesome about them.

Quie said the only way to make all this clear was to tell stories, starting with Spanish Lace, sister of Spanish Bull, the horse he rode during all nine of his summer trips along the Continental Divide from 1983 to 1991.

I remember when I got Spanish Lace in 1979. She was just a young filly. Some way or another I had learned how to relate well with a horse. When I would come to the gate—this was out at Marine on St. Croix when I was governor—if she were in the far distance, she would hear my voice or see me and come galloping over. When a horse is feeling great, her whole body just shows that joy. It's as if she's saying, "I get to see this guy again, and I'm feeling so good about that." Spanish Bull, though, was taking some time getting there, like he was saying, "I know what this means, it means work." At some point, Spanish Lace began doing the same thing; instead of running to me, she'd run to the other end of the pasture instead. I don't know exactly why, but maybe it's like a father and child. They start off running to you, "Oh, Daddy." But then you reprimand them and they go the other way.

Spanish Bull was so interesting. Several years later, when I kept him near Victoria, Minnesota, I went out there one day to ride one of my other horses. I still have my horse Nugget out there, but everything is different now. I drove in, and Bull was over in the pasture paddock not paying any attention to me. I hooked up the trailer and went over to another horse, but he was still ignoring me. I brought out the other horse, groomed him, and sent him into the trailer. All my gear was already in there; I would saddle at my destination. Bull still wasn't paying any attention to me. But when I started driving out the driveway, he realized I really was going and he barreled right down to the fence, racing and whinnying all the way. It was like he was saying, "You forgot me." So I stopped without caring if there was traffic coming or not and said, "Bull, we're going. You take off by yourself." He couldn't understand that, but he turned and walked over to the other horses. After that, I noticed that whenever I came in and parked my pickup truck, he was the only horse who perked up his ears and looked at the truck. He actually was the only horse who did this when I first turned into the driveway—but then he would ignore me again.

In addition to Beverly Hermes' notation in the transcript at this point of "hearty laughter," I wrote after going over it for the first time, "I'm smiling as I read this."

Quie began talking about another horse "who was very difficult to catch."

> I worked with him so we could catch him, and then he'd want to come up to me. But I hadn't worked out his comfort zone sufficiently. So nonchalantly one day, I just reached out and touched him on the rear end. But I had invaded his space and he didn't like it, and just as it dawned on me what I had done, he kicked me with both hoofs right in the chest, but I never felt it.

"Why?" I asked.

> The hoof marks showed on my chest, but I never felt it. He was so good. He did that to me to say, "You invaded my space. Stay away." He kicked me just like a colt kicks its mother or the mother kicks the colt with both hoofs. He had touched me, but I didn't feel it. When I was younger I wouldn't have understood what he had done and how he had done it, and I would have tried to straighten him out. But now I just stood there so thankful he had not hurt me. After that I worked on him, so now I can put my hand on his rear or anything like that. We call it desensitizing.

On a couple of occasions, Quie likened his training philosophy to the sympathetic and patient method brought to public attention in Robert Redford's 1998 movie *The Horse Whisperer.*

———•◆•———

"Let me interrupt for a second," I said. "Has anyone ever said, 'Albert, you're over-interpreting? You're attributing human emotions to animals?'"

"I talk about horses this way," he said, "because that's the only way I can explain what they are and what they do, through my own emotions."

I recognize, obviously, it's altogether different with them. They have a different way of understanding. They're not humans. Rather, we're predators and they're prey, so I try to put myself in the mode of a prey animal. But I also make sure they look at me as the alpha horse. And when it comes to talking to them, I use words not because they understand them, but because they hear the tone of my voice.

Take Nugget. We were in an indoor arena that had a mounting stool, three steps up, which stored grooming tools. I had worked him for about an hour and a half, and he was perspiring some. He needed to cool off, so we walked around for a while before I unsaddled him, carried the saddle and bridle to the tack room, cleaned up the manure he had dropped, and cleaned up the place more generally. When I came back Nugget was walking away from the stool and looking at me like a guilty child. I mean he just looked at me with his head cocked. When colts, for example, do something wrong with another horse, they look at their mother and cock their head a little bit, as if to say, "I guess I was wrong," especially if she's coming to straighten him out.

That mounting stool was totally upside down so I said to him, "Nugget, that's wrong. You go right back there and turn it back up." He looked back and walked over there, and with his nose, he turned it right side up. But in the force of doing that, the lid flew open and hung down the back. He came towards me and I said, "Nugget, you haven't finished your job. You go back there and close that lid." And he turned, and with his nose again, he flipped that lid closed and came back to me. Now, he doesn't understand English, but there was something about the tone of my voice and the movement of my body—it was something in horse language—that caused him to do what he did.

Here's another Spanish Bull story from Quie's nine-year Continental Divide adventure, which we'll get to shortly.

I remember some people were watching me when we were near Chama, New Mexico, one year. There was a steam train at the station that goes up into Colorado and back again. I wanted Bull to see it so he would understand that even a big train wouldn't hurt him. After I unsaddled him and let him graze, and after the train had left, he ambled over to where it had been, maybe because he thought the grass was better there. There also were some people camping there. So I called and said, "Bull," and he stopped and he looked back at me. I beckoned with one of my hands and said, "Come on back here, Bull. Come on back. You can't go down there." He looked over to where he wanted to go, looked back at me, and he turned around and walked back to where I was. A couple of the campers also came over, and one of them said, "I didn't know you could train a horse like a dog." I had never done that with him before, but he understood in some way. Horses love company with human beings. Or I should say, they love company with humans if the relationship is right.

How does a mare let her colt know that he's straying too far and bring him back? I've heard her nicker softly. But I've also seen colts run back when I heard no sound at all, but the mare only did something with her body. So it might have been that the tone of my voice was like a nicker to Bull. Or maybe it was the movement of my hand. Who knows?

Talking about Spanish Bull on another occasion, Quie spoke of opening a gate and ushering him into an area where he "saw the other horses, his buddies he loved to be with. You could just see his whole body lurch towards them, but after he went a little ways, he stopped. He just stopped and after looking back at me and then back at them, he came back and stood by me with his head right up to my shoulder, as if saying, 'I'd sooner be with you.' The feeling of a horse saying 'I'd sooner be with you' is practically like a woman who you love saying, 'I love you, too.'"

"Let me tell you one more story," Quie said, "that's a phenomenon to me. I used to keep my horses with a man by the name of Burdette

Stief down by Jordan, and he had a whole bunch of purebred Arabs and American Show Horses, about 85 of them in a pasture."

There was one American Show Horse out there. "Black Tie" was his name, light gray with a black mane and tail. He was just gorgeous, and I figured that was the horse I wanted to work with. I asked if I could hone my ability with him, and Burdette agreed. So I walked out, and that horse knew I was after him. He was sort of in the middle of the herd when I arrived; they were all spread out grazing. When I came to the edge of the herd, he walked to the opposite edge. So I walked over there and he continued walking. Have you ever played "Fox and Geese?" You try to catch someone by running around the perimeter of a circle and then cut across the middle to head them off. I did all of this, and it was just like that kind of game. He wasn't excited or anything, but he was just making sure I didn't get him by keeping the herd between him and me. After a while, I quit and went home and thought about it.

The next day I went out there, and this time I decided to concentrate on another horse, and Black Tie totally ignored me. I walked over to pet the other horse but Black Tie didn't move, though I stayed aware of where he was. I then purposely backed into him, just lightly before I quickly stepped away. But I also turned towards him as if to say, "I'm sorry." I went on to ignore him again, but a short time later I rubbed him a little bit with my shoulder, quickly stepping away once more in case there was any tenseness on his part. A short time later I rubbed his withers, which is like saying, "I like you." Then he quit his grazing and lifted his head up. If I were to interpret it in human terms, it was if to say, "If you like me, I'm going to like you." So he looked for a place to rub his muzzle on me. I gave him my hand because I don't have any withers to rub.

I put the halter on him, and he followed me, although reluctantly. He got even more reluctant when we got out of the herd. He was halter-broke, and I put him in the box stall. Then I got acquainted by rubbing every part of his body until I got to where I could put my fingers in his ears and his mouth and there was no tension. I took him out into the arena with a lunge line and taught him to walk, trot, and canter. The speed at which he was learning was just amazing, but I was really concentrating on teaching him and on our relationship.

Well, I figured, maybe I'll teach him how I put a saddle on. So I got my saddle and blanket and set them down so he could get acquainted with them. After I rubbed the blanket on him and put both things on him, I walked him around and tightened the cinch another notch. Then I thought to myself, you know, he's doing so well, maybe I could even get on him. He was a tall horse, so I got a stool to mount without putting much weight on one stirrup. After mounting, I let him stand for a while. Then the question was how to get him going, because he didn't know any of the cues. After sitting on his back for a while, I just leaned my weight a little bit to the side, and he stepped and caught his balance. Then I waited a little bit more and moved my weight to the other side. Then pretty soon we were walking. I had taught him oral commands on the lunge line as well as my body commands as we were walking around. He then took each of his gaits—walk, trot, canter—and I took two figure eights on him [Quie is whispering at this point], and I then put him away. No horse had ever learned so fast with me. That horse was really attached to me when we were finished and it was easy for Burdette to sell him, because when he showed him, Black Tie came right over and looked the potential buyers in the eye, who then said, "That horse tells me I should buy him."

"I'm telling you all of this," Quie said, "so people understand what's behind my love for horses: their phenomenal uniqueness. No two horses are alike. I talk about their mental and physical abilities and the whole relationship we have, and you can tell I'm awestruck." At another point in our conversations, Quie described horses as being

Dinner somewhere along the Continental Divide. Quie said he knew it was dinner, since if it had been lunch, there wouldn't have been a kettle in the picture, only a sandwich, apple, and granola bar. If it had been breakfast, there would have been a griddle for pancakes, eggs, and bacon.

relational and totally honest, as well as having self-interest and near perfect memory.

———— •◆• ————

"Riding the Continental Divide," Quie said in what really did turn out to be our final full session "was not my purpose in life. Neither was my political life. My purpose in life is to accomplish something, in some way or another, to make things better for others. And I'm pursuing it." His work on behalf of early childhood education and ensuring an impartial judiciary, currently top the list here. Nevertheless, a few moments earlier he had no hesitation in describing his nine-year ride through the Rockies as the "greatest challenge" he'd ever faced and the source of the "greatest sense of satisfaction" he'd ever had.

"One of the reasons," he said, "is that I was 24/7 with my horses out in the mountains, and that was a dream I had since I was a little kid."

I had won elections and all, but tremendously talented people enabled me to do that. But with the ride, I put it together and organized it myself. I did the logistics and studied the maps, and we never had an outfitter or guide. The trail hadn't been laid out yet, so there was that sense of discovery and accomplishment. You're on your own, you can't get to a safety zone at all, and if something happens, you could die—not that anyone did. It's stimulating when you're out there, no human civilization anyplace around. Either you find your way back to humanity, or you're dead. It puts all my senses together. You flow with nature and the stresses of modern life evaporate.

But it was magnificent also because the men who rode with me have said it was the most important thing that ever happened to them. People generally didn't know each other before, but after three days they'd come together in teamwork and start flowing in the rhythm of nature. They'd be part of the basic moorings of human interaction, the hopeful side. On layover days we didn't ride but gave horses and mules a rest. We'd meet together, and I'd share spiritually with them. We'd hold hands and pray with each other, standing on a mountain top, like Moses when he spoke to God—just without the burning bush. That's an awesome experience.

I recall Quie talking in 1982, his final year in office, about how one of the reasons he decided not to seek re-election was he wanted to make the ride down the Divide while he was still reasonably young and healthy enough.

The Continental Divide runs along the crest of the Rocky Mountains from Canada to New Mexico, where it continues along the crest of the Sierra Madre Mountains. Rivers, streams, and precipitation falling on the east side of these mountain ranges drain towards the Atlantic or Arctic Oceans; water on the west side drains to the Pacific. Quie rode the U.S. section of the Divide during nine consecutive summers from 1983 through 1991, with the first trek lasting two months, the next seven taking six weeks each, and a final one taking two or three weeks. A grand total of 39 men and two women rode with him, generally in two-week shifts, with eight of them riding more than once over the years. When I asked if there was a quick way of describing who they were, he said they were people who, like himself, had always dreamed of the experience or who accompanied those folks. One or two, he said, rode to overcome fears.

Quie figures they traveled, on average, about 450 miles each summer, up and down and around and through some of the most beautiful geography on earth. Part of the substantial extra distance resulted from an absence of straight lines high in the mountains; birds flying between the Canadian and Mexican borders enjoy a route less than half as long. But the parties also did a fair amount of backtracking—sometimes even on purpose. For example, they twice rode a portion south of Glacier National Park in Montana since Glacier itself had too much snow in 1983 when Quie began. Sometimes they had to backtrack because it was the only way to get off a mountain. And on another occasion they lost three days riding in a big, unintended circle in Montana when Quie's compass broke and no one else had one. That might have been the time Al Severson, one of his oldest cowpoke friends, asked with a wink and a jab: "Two more circles, and can we go home?" As the one living and breathing constant on all nine rides other than Quie himself, it's hard to tell what Spanish Bull might have thought of the possibility.

"There was another horse along one summer, in New Mexico, by the name of 'Hutch' who I had trained for my friend Burdette Stief," Quie began a story.

"Today," I said, "I'm going to ride Hutch and pack Bull." We were entering the Gila Wilderness from the north. I had taught Bull how to be packed, but I had always ridden him, and he had been the leader, so I figured he might be unhappy with the change. I packed him up, being very careful with the lash rope, with everything tied down tight in case he didn't like it. I started to lead him to Hutch, but he was totally upset. He bucked and kicked his hind legs higher in the air than I'd ever see him do before. I was hanging onto a twelve-foot rope, but the interesting thing is he never tightened the rope. He made all this commotion around me but he never tightened the rope. Finally, he knew he wasn't going to get that stuff off and he stopped. I then led him to Hutch, but he did it in short steps and with a hump in his back all the way. He was not a happy camper. He was insulted.

I got on Hutch and told the other guys, even though Bull wasn't too happy yet, "Come on. We're going to go." I was leading him, and then he just lurched forward to get ahead. So I put my hand out, and he went back. Then he lurched forward on the other side of me, and Hutch tried to stay ahead again. When we came to the trail, I said, "Bull, I'm going to let you lead." So I ushered him ahead, and you could see in his body language that he now was feeling proud. We had gone probably two or three miles that way when we came to a "Y" in the trail and I didn't know which way to go. I stopped and began reading my map, trying to figure it out. Bull had already picked the left branch of the "Y" and waited for me to follow. But I decided we needed to go right, so I started moving in that direction and said, "Come on, Bull. You can follow me now. We're going to the right." He looked at me like to say, "You've made this mistake so many times before. Let's go this way." I practically believed him, but I kept on riding my way, and he kept on walking his way. It was only when he saw that nobody else was following him, they were following me, that he hustled over. I started riding faster so that he'd fall behind us, but as I did that, Bull hustled even faster and went in front of me and Hutch. He led from then on.

Here are two stories from among a hefty handful Quie recounted about coming exceedingly close to buying another farm, so to speak. In addition to epiphanies of faith and beauty, marking much of what he condensed from the nine rides, were near-mortal disasters, life-and-death events and themes we'll return to in several pages when he ponders rides into coming sunsets. As for now, Spanish Bull stars again.

"One day in Colorado," Quie recalled, "Bull and I rode into quicksand and he sank in."

Hoofs don't have much surface to hold a horse up with all that weight, and he sank right down. I had read about the possibility and knew right away what had happened, so I threw myself off and rolled onto the roots of a tree that was right next to us. For a human to stay alive, he has to stay horizontal. Bull, though, was sinking, but when he saw me stand up, he was able to rear up, turn his front end, hook his hoofs onto the roots, and pull himself out. How deep was he? He was so deep that the saddle pads on the blanket had sand and water on them. When he had turned, his rear end went in so far that the saddle, from the middle of it back, was underneath as well. But he pulled all that body out of there and stood on those roots trembling right beside me.

Another time, just to tell you about this horse, we were going across Rollins Pass, again in Colorado. It was July, but the lake above us was still frozen, and all that melting water was rushing downstream, deeper than it normally would be. I could see by the movement of the water that there was a rock there, though I figured it was no problem. But Bull, in coming up to it, stepped on a submerged boulder. It was big enough for him to stand on but no bigger. He stood there for a while, and I assumed he could figure out what to do, as I didn't think the water was any deeper on the far side of the boulder than on the near side. But when he stepped off, his front end just disappeared under water. He reared back, and in all that force, I flew off to the right of him. Think of the power that would enable a horse with his front end under water and his back end still on the boulder to get back completely on the boulder, yet that's what he was able to do. But now I'm lying in the water and see Bull in that second losing his balance. He didn't want to come down on me, but if he did, I'd probably drown before he could get his feet up or he'd probably kill me in his struggle. I threw my feet up against the boulder, the stream swept me around it, but I got to my feet and got to shore, in part swimming. Bull jumped off and made it to shore as well. I had extra clothes on the pack horse and changed in the cold wind. It was an amazing learning experience, though the group commented that my hair wasn't the only part of me that was gray.

Beyond noting that he "could just keep going and going and going" in serving up stories, what lesson did Quie take from all this? "I just can't tell you," he stressed to me again, "how uncanny horses are."

———— •◆• ————

"Let me ask," I said, "what does your family think about your fascination? Do Gretchen and your kids say, 'Well, that's my husband's,' or 'That's my dad's quirky life with horses. It's lovely, we indulge him, but we really don't understand it.' Or do they recognize how intrinsic it is to you?"

"Maybe this is partly facetious, but it's also partly true," he said, "for Gretchen, the horses are the other woman."

"I was thinking about that. I was thinking *exactly* that," I pounced. "Is she jealous of them?"

"Yes, that I've spent so much time with them," was his unhesitating reply. But he also said it was interesting how Gretchen is now likely to say "good" when he goes out to ride, as she recognizes that "with all this work on judges and other activities, I'm tense. I'm working harder and for longer hours than I have in a while, and she knows that going out on horseback is the most refreshing thing for me."

"Does Gretchen ride?"

"No, she doesn't anymore."

"But she did?"

She did because I pressured her into it. She's fearful of horses and never resonated to riding and being outdoors like I do. She's been bucked off and broke her wrist, and when we lived in Maryland, our horses occasionally got out and she'd have to get them back, which she didn't enjoy. In one of those situations, an alpha horse's son was being protective of his mother, as well as aspiring to the alpha position himself, and he put his ears back and rushed at Gretchen. To have a horse bearing down on you with his ears back is a pretty frightening situation. Gretchen swung the halter at him, showing that she wasn't going to run, and that was enough for him to turn and bolt away, although he kicked at her as he did. That was an unsettling experience for her. But for years she was such a good sport and did a lot with me and the kids, camping in the mountains and elsewhere. We kid her that she turned in her sleeping bag on our 25th anniversary [which would be 35 years ago]. She likes sleeping between sheets.

That preference was reconfirmed in what proved to be her last overnight in the mountains in about 1979. At the urging of Quie's brother Paul, he and his wife Betty, plus their two youngest children, along with Quie and Gretchen and their son Ben, rode and camped in Scapegoat Wilderness in Montana. "I get such a kick out of this story," the former governor said with less than ideal chivalry.

Gretchen was cold one night and said "Al, can you get up and put something on me? My sleeping bag isn't keeping me warm." So I took one of the canvasses that you pack horses with—what you put over the loads to shed rain from the packs—and put it on her. When she woke up in the morning she looked at the canvas and asked, "What are these spots?" I said, "That's elk blood." To which Gretchen wanted to know, "What other person would put a canvas with elk blood on top of his wife to keep her warm?"

"She was *indignant*," Quie recalled in one of his bigger laughs of the morning. "But I figured any guy who shinnies down a drain pipe so he can sleep outdoors with bugs and all is too thoughtless to figure that out."

One of my favorite Quie answers was to a question about whether his relationship with any of his children had changed because of all the riding they had done together, either along the Continental Divide or someplace else. I anticipated a predictable yes, but he gave a simple and telling no. "We already had been in tune with each other," he said. "We interact with each other without having to speak. I'll give you an example from a long time ago."

In 1968, he recounted, "Gretchen and I were in Holden Village, a Lutheran Camp in Washington State with four of our children. Fred was already at college and working that summer with a trail crew in Montana. An older man who worked at the camp guided us on a camping trip, backpacking up higher for an overnight. He said he had never seen anything like us before. 'As soon as we got to the camping area, and without anyone saying anything, your children put down their packs and started picking up firewood, putting up the tent, and getting things ready. You were a team. My confidence in the future of mankind just improved.'"

Two of Quie's children, Fred and Ben, rode portions of the Continental Divide with him. But all five, he said, are "absolutely better with horses and outdoor skills than anyone else I ever rode with in the mountains." Other people were good, he acknowledged, but perhaps with a touch more immodesty than he intended, he noted how he had taught his kids; he hadn't taught those other people. "I trained them, and they emulated the way I did things. I didn't have to tell them what to do because things became so natural for them. We were a team with little coaching necessary."

This has been the case even though Fred, Joel, and Ben have never been as excited about horses as Jennie and Dan are. As noted earlier, Fred and Joel were enamored with baseball growing up and Ben loved to do aerial tricks on his bike. In contrast, Jennie and Dan very much share their father's interest, and "Whenever we talk, I love telling them about some new experience I've just had with a horse or something I've just learned about them."

———————◆•———————

So far in this chapter Quie has almost drowned in quicksand and then more conventionally in water. Unmentioned from his nine rides down the length of the country were dicey moments with a grizzly bear and a hair-raising nanosecond with a lightning strike. Also not cited was the time his four-horse trailer almost rolled off a cliff. From other periods in his life, we haven't said anything about two boating accidents, one on a northern Minnesota lake and the other on Long Island Sound where he got good and wet. Once, in 1981, he and I were flying back to the Twin Cities from western Minnesota in a four-seat plane, and the pilot couldn't get the landing gear down in the regular way, so Quie had to crank it down manually. I remember the incident reasonably well, but he had forgotten it until I reminded him; as close calls go, evidently it just wasn't interesting enough to make his personal cut. For good measure, encephalitis almost did him in as a young man—it should have done him in, his doctors said.

"It seems to me," I said, "you've cheated death many times."

Quie laughed.

"I was going to say," I added, "this hasn't been in any reckless way. But maybe you have been reckless. Have you ever given any thought to the number of times you could have died?"

"No, although Gretchen has said I've had more lives than a cat. I must have a tremendous guardian angel up there." But then correcting himself to a degree, he allowed how he had, in fact, occasionally looked back to his escapes. "But they're all in the past and nothing to worry about anymore."

"I'm not saying you should worry about them. But do you view them in some macho or fatalistic way?"

"No, neither. They just happened. That's what I say. I can't think of them in the way you say. There are other things that can happen to you. You could be just driving down the highway and somebody could just plow into you." At which point he broke into another story, this time about how he hit a patch of ice around Little Falls and lost control of his car, almost doing in Gretchen and himself, along with other people unlucky to be on the winter road at the time.

A few minutes earlier, I started asking what he loved so much about riding the Continental Divide—but then quickly caught myself and said, "Oh, I know what you loved so much about it. But did you also love the danger, the precariousness, the cheating of death?"

Much more as a matter of fact than bravado, he again said no. Danger was just something a person had to "handle" if he wanted to go to the "mountaintop." Mountaintop experiences, he said, were "full of *awe*, they're just *fantastic*." If you want safety, you can "stay down in the valley and watch."

"A couple of metaphors in that," I observed. "Do you want to wax poetic for a moment?"

"Well, it takes nerve to step out of your comfort zone. And when I look back, there were times when I learned an awful lot by stepping out of mine. I'm thinking, for example, of the time I hung out with a street gang in New York and the time I walked the streets of Watts after the riots. Those were mountaintop experiences, and I love mountaintops." This was not the first or even second time he referred to those two seminal events in our conversations.

Like a futile Grinch, I invited him back to sea level by pointing out how a person could love heights a bit too much, getting himself killed in the process. He interpreted this as an invitation to tell another scary Continental Divide story, co-starring Doug Coe this time, about how a "huge wind caused trees to bend at 90-degree angles before toppling over."

So what does Al Quie admit to fearing? (He's sorry, by the way, that he frequently worried Gretchen by telling her about all the times he "was so absolutely close to death.")

"I couldn't sleep the night before we left every summer," he conceded, "but that was because I never wrote down all the food, clothing, camping equipment, and horse gear I needed to take along. I had everything in my head and would run through it again and again. If it had been Gretchen, she would have had everything charted and organized. I solved the problem by leaving in the evening and driving all night, running things over in my mind. I'd get to my destination the next day and was able to pick up things there if I'd forgotten anything."

"I'm assuming," I asked, "that you don't fear death in any exorbitant way?"

"No, no, no. Dying may prove to be difficult because of the amount of cancer in my family, but I don't fear what happens hereafter." And with a smile ending in a laugh: "I try not to think of eternity because it seems like such a long time."

"That's all you want to say about that?"

"I used to fear death."

"When, how, why?"

I think it was because I didn't understand who I was. I thought of myself as what you could see, the physical. But when I was a junior in high school and my dad lost his arm, he was still the same person. I came to the realization that who we are is not our physical bodies. Reading a book by Watchman Nee, *The Latent Power of the Soul*, in about 1960, was very helpful. I had thought of the soul and spirit as the same thing, but he helped me understand that wasn't the case. Between that and the realization that everybody is going to die, I had to face reality and see death for what it was. And with Jesus becoming more and more real to me, the idea of seeing Him face to face, to be in His amazing presence, I started looking forward to it.

When Dad was on his death bed two weeks before the election in 1978, I stopped and saw him. He said he was so glad that I had told him some time before, "Dad, I'm no longer afraid to die." That made so much difference for him; that his son was not afraid to die. He told me not to worry about him, and he gave a note to my brother Paul, "Jesus has redeemed me. I've got nothing to worry about."

"Did he die of cancer?"

"No. He was 93 and they just put down 'old age.' He just died. Close to the end he asked Paul, his physician son whom he was tremendously proud of, 'How much longer will it take?' Paul said, 'I think about 48 hours.' When my brother came back 48 hours later, Dad was still alive, so he looked at Paul and said: 'We sent you to medical school and that's all you know?'"

"How many hours or days did your father die after that?"

"Twenty-four. Paul missed by twenty-four hours."

After telling him I personally didn't fear death in any dreadful way, although I certainly did fear my wife dying first, I asked how he might react if Gretchen preceded him.

Following a two-part sigh, he said, "My selfish hope is that I would go first. But my family is the opposite of normal when it comes to dying, with men frequently living longer than women. Mother, for instance, died in 1960 but Dad didn't die until 1978. So I face that. But my reaction might be, 'Well, I'd go out and ride the Continental Divide one more time all by myself. I'd do it all by myself."

"With the idea," I asked, "of getting lost and fading away?"

"No, no. *Just to do it again*! A guy—maybe I'd be 93—riding the Continental Divide. Oh, man. I'd love to do that. But that isn't going to happen. My arthritis. Oh, man, how that would kick up at night in that cold air."

Wherever you think laughs, macabre or otherwise, might conceivably fit in these last few minutes of conversation, feel free to insert them because chances are Quie beat you to it.

———— •◆• ————

Right after Quie read a first draft of this chapter he informed me that I didn't know as much about horses as I did about some other things. My wife, who grew up with horses, was in the room at the time and overheard at least my half of the phone conversation. Let's just say she enjoyed inferring the governor's critique, perhaps a tad too much. Fixing my technical errors would be easy enough, but Quie was also of the mind that something larger—in some ways, much larger—was missing. So he wrote what I might respectfully describe as a riff. Here are portions.

Love, anger, nobility, congruency, deceit, and integrity are all observable but also invisible. There are others: rejection, hope, anxiety, and faith—or the lack of it. . . . The integrity and total recall of horses can be depended on. Theirs is like the language of God. We can sense the nature and character of God by what He has created. The very idea of beauty, goodness, and power in a horse is just a little taste of the infinite to me. For a horse to want to please me is an awesome realization. The wilderness is the same. It has its own ecosystem. There are still places where nothing of mankind is seen except for one's own party. Those times when I've gone alone, completely vulnerable to nature, have been rich experiences. . . . I read history. In the wilderness, I am before history, but I can never be before time and back in eternity. All of us, however, will leave time and move into eternity. We will be in the total reality of the invisible.

———— • ◆ • ————

"We were talking last week," I said, "about Ronald Reagan and how the people around him finally felt compelled to tell him he wasn't healthy enough to ride any longer. How much do you fear that your family someday will say the same thing to you?"

"When the time comes, I want people to have courage enough to tell me that that's the end. I don't think I'll wind up getting lost out there. I think my brain will stay with me, but you shouldn't be up on a horse anymore if your balance isn't good enough or something of that nature. That time may come, and I expect to see it for myself, but I want people to tell me if I don't."

"How close to that do you think you are?"

"Oh, my hope is I can still ride when I'm 90. I'd be happy. Though I know I once said I'd be happy if I could ride until I was 80."

"That means you have a little under a half a dozen years left."

"The way I am now, there's no indication I can't do it," Quie answered, first saying he was very careful but then quickly amending himself.

"Sometimes," he admitted, "I get on my horse bareback, without a bridle, just to see how our communication is with each other. It puts me to the test that I'm dependent on Nugget sensing my energy, my body, and my intuitions. It's a wonderful sense of togetherness when he walks trots, canters, stops, side passes, and even opens just by what he feels in me. I've practiced vaulting off, so if something were to happen I could move quickly enough not to hurt myself, though I know it's foolish."

"If someone in the family does someday say, 'Dad, you really shouldn't be riding anymore,' you say you'd take it in reasonably good cheer. But it presumably would be very, very difficult."

"Presumably," Quie agreed. "I knew that when I hit maturity, from then on, it was downhill slowly, because eventually we're going to die. What I'd like to be able to do is to be as cheerful as Dad was when he could no longer take his walks. When it comes to my driving, what I say to my children is, 'When it's time to take my car and truck keys away from me, have the courage to do so and I will remember this conversation and not be grumpy about it.'"

"How old was your father when he couldn't take his walks anymore?"

"He was probably 91. I look with envy at people for whom it just snaps. They're just over with. Pfftt! They close their eyes and they're gone. But I don't expect that to happen, because for most people, it doesn't happen that way. I probably told you this [he hadn't], Medtronic was making low-cost defibrillators available to churches, but I told the council at Minnetonka Lutheran Church they should put a sign on it that said, 'If Al Quie passes out, don't use this.' What a neat way to go. You pass out, and that's the end. No trouble whatsoever. But then when it came to a vote, everybody voted for it except me. I said, 'Nooo.'"

———·◆·———

"So," Quie asked, "what have we left out? I've told you what I think is the very essence of life, that somebody cares about you unconditionally and that you care about somebody unconditionally. When a person can't think of another human being who cares about them in that way, how poverty stricken and alone they are."

And then he wondered: "How can people who are too selfish to care about other people know how to forgive them?"

"Are you the kind of person," I asked, "whose glass is half full or half empty?"

"I always have the expectation that my glass will be full."

"Not just half full, but full?"

"Yes, full. And when it's only half full, I say it's on the way to fullness because I see the reality of God's hand."

Index